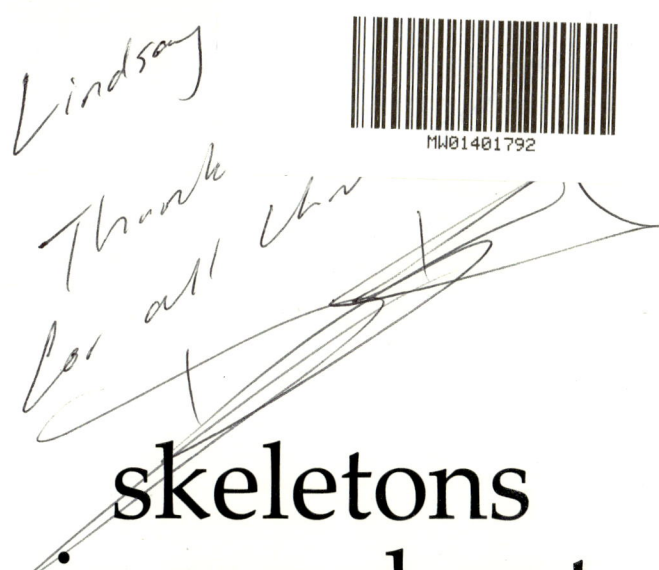

skeletons in my closet

101 life lessons from a homicide detective

Second Edition

DAVE SWEET
WITH SARAH KADES

skeletons in my closet

101 life lessons from a homicide detective

Second Edition

DAVE SWEET
WITH SARAH KADES

Copyright © 2023 Dave Sweet and Sarah Graham
Original butterfly art © 2023 Coral Simpson
Cover design by Juan Padron
Dave Sweet author photographer Leah Hennel

All rights reserved. No part of this publication may be reproduced, distributed, or transmitted in any form or by any means without the prior written permission of the publisher, except in the case of brief quotations embodied in critical reviews and certain other noncommercial uses permitted by copyright law.

The opinions, views, perspectives, and philosophies reflected in this book are those of the authors and may not represent those of the publisher. Every effort has been made by the authors to respect the privacy of citizens and the delicacy of the situations described in the book. Identifying descriptors, such as names, dates, and specific details, have, in many cases, been altered for the sake of that privacy.

Stark Publishing
Waterloo, Ontario, Canada
starkpublishing.ca

First printing December 2023

Hardcover ISBN: 978-1-7390474-9-8
Paperback ISBN: 978-1-7390474-8-1
eBook ISBN: 978-1-7390474-7-4

ATTENTION SCHOOLS, BUSINESSES AND BOOK CLUBS:

This book may be provided at quantity discounts for educational, business, or book club purchases. The authors are also available to speak to groups both virtually and in person.

For inquiries, please contact Stark Publishing: info@starkpublishing.ca

To all who serve and the family members who stand with them.

Contents

FOREWORD 13
ACKNOWLEDGMENTS 15
INTRODUCTION 17
A LIFE OF SERVICE 22
    REKINDLED 22
    THE JOB 26
    SERVICE 33
    SACRIFICE 42
OWNING YOUR PATH 49
    SCRIPTS 60
    SUCCESS 65
GRAY MATTER 84
    DISCRETION 84
    ABSOLUTES 102
WHITE PICKET FENCES 109
    FIRST IMPRESSIONS 116
    RESPECT 120
    SUPPORT SYSTEMS 123
    ADAPTABILITY, BOUNDARIES, AND CHASING THE SHINY
    OBJECT 125
    LOYALTY VERSUS SECRETS 128
    DARK PLACES 133
THINKING FROM A DIFFERENT BOX 140
    AVERSION TO ACCLIMATIZATION 142
    COMPARTMENTALIZATION AND REFRAMING 149
    CATASTROPHIZING 156
    UNDERSTANDING WHY 160

MENTAL MATURITY 166
OUR PATH TO THRIVING 170

UNLEASHING YOUR INNER JEDI 172

RECIPROCITY AND COMMITMENT 173
LIKABILITY AND AUTHORITY 185
CONFORMITY OR GROUPTHINK 193
SCARCITY 198
FEAR 201

RIPPLES 208

THE LAW OF CAUSE AND EFFECT 209
MEDIA 219
GAME OF CHESS 223
JURIES 227
LIVING THE LESSONS OF CAUSE AND EFFECT 232

NINE PRINCIPLES 239

THE COMMAND TRIANGLE 245
COMMUNICATION AND ACCOUNTABILITY MECHANISMS 253
INVESTIGATIVE OR CRIME-SOLVING STRATEGIES 259
PARTNERSHIPS 262
LEADERSHIP AND TEAM BUILDING 263
MANAGEMENT, LEGAL, AND ETHICAL CONSIDERATIONS 270

WHEN THE DEVIL'S ADVOCATE WEARS A HALO 274

RISK MANAGEMENT 279
SIMPLE SOLUTIONS 291
FOLLOWING EVIDENCE 295

HOW TO SELL A LIFE SENTENCE 305

THE PRESENTER (INTERVIEWER) 310
RAPPORT BUILDING 314
THE PITCH (PRESENTING THE EVIDENCE) 321
CLOSING THE DEAL 324

CONCLUSION: GAVEL DROP 329

101 LESSONS 332
PEEL'S PRINCIPALS 338
FOOTNOTES 351
REFLECTIONS FROM THE CLOSET: BEHIND THE SCENES 353
    OUR EVOLUTION TO SUCCESS 357
    LEAVE PEOPLE BETTER THAN YOU FOUND THEM ... 360
    PERSPECTIVE IS AN ANTIDOTE TO WORRY 361
    LISTENING TO THE SILENCES 361
    JUST BECAUSE YOU CAN DOESN'T MEAN YOU SHOULD 362
    B.B.D.S (BIG BOY DEBRIEFS) 363
    WRITING REAL LIFE 365
    WORKING WITH A HOMICIDE DETECTIVE 366
    LIVING THE LESSONS 369
    INVESTIGATOR'S COMMENTS 373
AUTHOR DAVE SWEET 378
AUTHOR SARAH KADES 379
UNCONVENTIONAL CLASSROOM SERIES 380
    FORTHCOMING 380

Foreword

Each of us decides which lessons we choose to learn and which we allow to sink deep enough to become part of our own wisdom. I've walked alongside this path with Dave as he has shared his stories, tracing with words the roads he took and the wisdom learned and earned. Some lessons are calloused with good use, a few still shiny and new, and some are buried under a scar or two. We hope this book resonates and that there is wisdom within its pages to help you navigate your own path.

Not everyone has a warm fuzzy when they think of law enforcement. I knew that before I started writing with Dave. What I didn't realize was just how much of a gap there can be between police and the public. As I worked on this project, friends shared previously undisclosed reservations and comments (some rather explicit) about police officers but also expressed their interest in reading it. They trusted me and knew that if this was a project I would undertake, they would want to listen to what the book had to say. That support still humbles me, but really, it speaks to its relevance and timeliness.

If I knew people who, even given their cautious opinion of police officers, genuinely wanted to read his story to understand a perspective different from their own, there likely would be others.

Dave's résumé reads like a wish list for any author wanting to collaborate with someone in law enforcement. His drive is complemented by compassion, his bite tempered by wisdom. His experience is painfully real. I can't tell you how often I stumbled against troubling realities while writing this book, but that was the point.

He wanted to write this book for his children, explain where he'd been when he'd missed special days as they were growing up, and explain the job. I wanted to write it for everyone else. We're all someone's kid, and most of us have picked up baggage of some sort along the way. By unpacking Dave, I hope readers can unpack what they needed to within themselves, find the space to understand another's perspective, and maybe unpack the world around them a bit more. Sometimes, we simply need a place to start the conversation.

Since day one of this project, Dave has been a complete and total pain in the ass—and an incredibly caring individual I am honored to call a friend and co-author. Five years after our first edition was published, I still believe in this project and our friendship. What surprised me was my own vault. I hadn't realized I had created one as we wrote the first edition—and that I had shut damn tight—until Dave wanted to add several thousand words to this edition. Reading and writing projects are like that. We learn as much about ourselves as we do about the content.

Thank you for coming on this ride-along with us.

Sarah Kades (Sarah Graham)
October 2023

Acknowledgments

Sarah and I would like to acknowledge *Skeletons in My Closet: 101 Life Lessons from a Homicide Detective* was written on the traditional territories of the peoples of the Treaty 7 region in Southern Alberta. This includes the Siksika, the Piikani, the Kainai collectively known as the Blackfoot Confederacy; the Îethka Nakoda Wîcastabi First Nations comprised of the Chiniki, Bearspaw, and Wesley; and the Tsuut'ina First Nation. The city of Calgary is also the homeland to the historic Northwest Metis and to the Metis Nation of Alberta, Region 3. We would like to acknowledge all Indigenous urban Calgarians, First Nations, Inuit, and Métis who have made Calgary their home.

Writing this book—and the subsequent five years since its original release in 2018—has been more rewarding than we ever could have imagined and would not have been possible without the support of my organization, peers, and colleagues.

To those who helped us in all the myriad ways—it truly takes a village to give a book wings—our heartfelt thank you. Special thanks to Mischievous Books, who believed in us in 2018 and continue their support as we move the project to Stark Publishing. Our warmest gratitude to *Stark* for picking up the torch with this five-year anniversary edition. Special thanks also goes out to ML, AK, TT, NM, MS, SG, CW, BT, BF, and SOS.

Thank you to Sarah—I couldn't have picked a better partner in crime. You have weathered my storms gracefully and always stayed true to yourself. Your commitment to this project has meant so much, and I truly appreciate you. I would be remiss if I did not also acknowledge your family, who have no doubt shown so much patience and understanding as you poured your time into this book—now as a second edition.

I would also like to acknowledge my children, family, and friends. Your support and backing for this project has been immense from the start and truly appreciated.

Lastly, I would like to acknowledge all the families I have met along my journey. I hope you know how many of you have moved me as I have borne witness to your grief and watched your transformation over time. You are truly inspirational and have taught me so much. Thank you.

Introduction

"Have you learned the lessons only of those who admired you, and were tender with you, and stood aside for you? Have you not learned great lessons from those who braced themselves against you, and disputed passage with you?"
- Walt Whitman

More than a decade ago, I was sitting around a pool in Palm Springs, California, watching my kids play while I stretched out on my lounger, cold drink in hand. I had just finished an investigation where a young mother had been murdered, her half-naked body dumped in a drainage ditch, not to be found for months. Her little boy was left to be raised by strangers; the father had been sentenced to life and now sat in a jail cell for the senseless crime.

This case was no more horrific than others. It was the culmination of them that had me reflecting on my own mortality, my family, and my career. We get good at handling the darker sides of human behavior. Sometimes, cases float (or catapult) into our awareness long after the reports are filed and verdicts are in. This career has allowed me to reflect on my success and family and realize how lucky I am. So many go through tragedy, strife, and unfortunate circumstances.

My kids live in a world where they are provided the things they need and many of the things they want. As I watched them play with such carefree happiness, I wished to share with them an understanding of what others go through and the lessons many of these situations have taught me. I wanted to write a book that talked about these things, lessons from Dad that they could turn to as they grew older. My father, from whom I learned so much, passed away during the writing of the original manuscript. Everything hit home even harder.

I began outlining ideas:

*Staying out of dark places
keeps you safe,*

*Just because you can do something
doesn't mean you should,*

Not everyone lives behind white picket fences,

*Always leave people in a better place
than you found them.*

These became the building blocks for *Skeletons in My Closet*. I recognized early on that writing about real life would require a tempered soul if I wanted the lessons and philosophies to come out in a meaningful way. Frankly, the work I do conditions a person to the job. Writing a book to be read by an audience wider than those in law enforcement meant there was a significant chance some of those messages might be lost in either police-speak or with a modified social filter, neither serving the reader.

In 2016, I pitched the concept to Sarah Graham (Kades), an author I knew from the local writing scene, who I trusted could help deliver my stories authentically and responsibly—and my polar opposite. Back then, I was more conservative after twenty years of service dealing with the darker aspects of humanity. Sarah's a free spirit and had over fifteen years in environmental fields and was more liberal and nimble in her thinking. Her Yin balanced my sometimes-overbearing Yang. In my view, the collaboration worked, perhaps because of how different we were and what we each brought to the table.

From the beginning, Sarah shared my vision for the book. We both saw that one of the things that comes from a career in policing is a myriad of life lessons which so many of us, regardless of our careers, backgrounds, or specific challenges, could resonate with. We intended to share some of the wisdom from my career in law enforcement, from street cop to undercover police officer to homicide investigator. We hoped readers could take some of these stories, lessons, philosophies, and strategies to enhance their own lives. The lessons in this book are framed and shared with a strong sense of social responsibility and a desire to inspire positive change.

I am humbled and awed by the extraordinary community support for this book. It is not a book about blood, guts, or gore. It is not a book full of war stories nor musings on the scrutiny and judgments twenty-first-century policing has attracted from its critics. It is not a "rah-rah" book for cops everywhere, either. This book is introspective, the stories sincere, and the lessons practical. They are good reminders to all of us about what really matters.

I believe our work encompasses the many facets and lessons a career in policing can teach. I hope we have written a book that captures a different side of what people may think of cops, and one that our peers, our families, and my service can be proud of.

My career has been an unconventional classroom with unexpected teachers, surprising lessons, and challenging homework—like writing this book.

Why the butterflies? For Sarah and me, the butterfly represents the transformation of complex or horrific truths—witnessed in chaos—and flipped on their heads to find the positive commentary. It represents the lessons that come through this process and my fifty years of collected wisdom. The intention of the butterfly is to highlight our key messages throughout this book.

Dave Sweet
October 2023

A Life of Service

"Police, at all times, should maintain a relationship with the public that gives reality to the historic tradition that the police are the public and the public are the police; the police being only members of the public who are paid to give full-time attention to duties which are incumbent on every citizen in the interests of community welfare and existence."

- Sir Robert Peel's Principles of Law Enforcement, 1829

Rekindled

I never met my grandfather, but he profoundly impacted my life's path. He was a New York City police officer. Thirty years my grandmother's senior, I only knew him from family stories, a small collection of memorabilia, and a handful of newspaper clippings. Those articles, chronicling his distinguished New York Police Department career between 1905–

1912, included rooftop chases, dramatic arrests, and saving the life of a drowning man. Heady stuff for a kid. How my grandfather came to be a justice of the peace in Alberta, Canada, only added to his mystery and intrigue.

> **LED "COP" AN EXCITING CHASE OVER HOUSETOPS.**
>
> Thomas Shinners, 22 years old, of 32 Hamilton avenue, held on a charge of robbing a men's furnishing store at 1 President street, was to-day held for the Grand Jury by Magistrate O'Reilly in the Butler street court.
>
> Shinners was arrested by Policeman Young, of the Hamilton avenue station, after an exciting chase over roofs. He was photographed at headquarters this morning.

Imagine as a young boy, the images that came to mind while reading a headline like this. I pictured New York City in 1905. The buildings only a couple of stories tall. I imagined steam and factory smoke hanging under dimly lit streetlamps and my grandfather in a long caped policeman's uniform jumping from rooftop to rooftop in hot pursuit of his suspect, just like a superhero would.

For my mom and her younger sister, he was simply their dad, a strict disciplinarian of a different generation. For me, he was a larger-than-life figure and part of our family's history. I grew up captivated and inspired by his choices to serve others.

 *Our history does not define who we are, but it can influence who we become in unpredictable ways.*

This was the case with me. My grandfather's life intrigued me. I also wanted a career that made a positive difference for people. As cool as chasing bad guys on rooftops sounded when I was twelve, at nineteen, teaching high school physical education seemed a more compelling choice. In my experience, coaches and gym teachers were healthy, happy, and carefree. It helped that I had great teachers who made a significant, positive impact on me. Their dedication and service inspired me, and I started college focused on a degree in education.

I was taking core education classes, doing my thing my way, but in the back of my mind was the echo of my mom's voice, "You're a lot like your grandfather." Her sentiments influenced my choice of electives, and I sat in one criminology course, then another. Those courses rekindled the spark that had been smoldering since I was a kid. It wouldn't be the only time I thought I had life figured out, only to find myself firmly on a very different path.

I changed my major to criminology and was now steering myself toward a career in law enforcement. I believed this choice could lead to the best of both worlds; policing has different career streams, including working in schools or with youth in the community. The road would be tough, the process arduous. Besides the explicit hurdles, it was also the mid-1990s, and police services across Canada focused on applicants from diverse cultural backgrounds. As a result, there had been an extraordinary number of applicants, many of whom would not normally have applied. Well-meaning individuals who felt it was too competitive, my chances too slim, cautioned me against pursuing this path—but my parents taught me:

 *It is up to each of us to choose to believe in ourselves.*

Maybe there could be a place for me.

In the spring of 1996, I walked into the large lecture hall full of 2,400 recruit hopefuls to take the aptitude exam, the first step toward vying for one of twenty-four spots in the upcoming class. I still remember how nervous I felt that day. With several deep breaths, I settled my mind enough to pass the exam requirements. I proceeded through the remaining phases of the process: fitness testing, three separate interviews, a polygraph examination, psychological testing, and finally, health and background checks.

I was hired a year and a half later.

On a brisk November morning, I stepped into the front lobby of the downtown police headquarters and started the 125th recruit class. Finally, I knew where I was going and what direction I was headed. That switch in college majors had positioned me for a career that could merge law enforcement and teaching.

Years of undercover drug work, let alone the Homicide Unit, were not anywhere in the plan.

The Job

The American radio broadcaster Paul Harvey spoke the now-famous *What is a Policeman* in 1970. He said,

> *"A policeman is a composite of what all men are, mingling of a saint and sinner, dust and deity. What that really means is that they are exceptional, they are unusual, they are not commonplace."*

My first years as a rookie police officer were difficult, but not how many would imagine. I was trying to find my way, carve out my twenty-something identity (whoever that was), but also deciding what career path in the service I wanted to pursue. Those recruit classes provided the opportunity to hear from different senior officers who shared what career directions they had taken and what they looked like. I leaned forward and listened more intently to the guys that were more weathered from the field, the ones who were a little more broken, exposing sharp edges, than to those uniformed officers whose buttons were more polished and boots spit-shined.

There are so many choices in law enforcement: K9, tactical units, surveillance teams, traffic section, community liaison, and investigator, to name a few. As I sat in recruit classes listening, the career paths that appealed to me were dynamic and diverse. I knew that, generally, uniformed members would spend their first five to ten years working out of a patrol car before being given opportunities in the service's specialized areas. Where did I fit? That question kept pace as I went out, day after day, call after call.

As a uniformed patrol person, you are the first responder to everything, and I mean *everything*: injury accidents, domestic disputes, noise complaints, parties, prowlers, assaults, mental health events, and all things bizarre.

Some calls were tame...

Like the time my partner and I attended an elderly woman's home to check on her well-being after her family's growing concerns that she was losing her mental faculties. The woman loved her birds and had misplaced a beloved parakeet, causing her considerable anguish. As we sat on her couch discussing the possibility the bird had flown out the patio door, my partner couldn't sit still. Finally, he leaned forward, and the parakeet's head emerged from under the couch cushion, unbelievably no worse for wear.

Some calls were more feral...

Like when a Rottweiler chased me onto the hood of my police cruiser. My quick-thinking partner sacrificed his brown bag lunch to the angry animal, giving me time to slide over the hood and into the car, leaving the snapping animal with his sandwich instead of my lead.

Some calls still bring back strong feelings of fear and exhilaration...

On a cold winter night, my partner and I were

responding to a domestic assault when he lost control of our police cruiser on the ice. Time slowed as we spun in multiple circles before nearly wrapping around a lamppost and parking in a snowdrift.

Or the time I was one of the first responding officers to a man who had barricaded himself in his home with a rifle. From an outside corner of the house, I crouched in the early morning light and watched through the window while this highly agitated older man, with a little potbelly that hung over the waistband of his checkered pajamas, paced in his front room, gun cradled in his arms. The only thing separating us was an exterior wall, enough to slow but not necessarily stop a bullet. Exacerbating my stress was the reality that on that morning, my breath hitting the cold air could have betrayed me and revealed my position.

Or the time my partner and I responded to a suicide complaint where the victim had barricaded his door with a couch. As I shouldered my way in, the suicidal man took advantage of the still partially blocked door to swing his knife at me. The knife glanced past my cheek, and the blade caught the fabric of the couch, slicing the material enough for a corner to slump to the floor. That was before he changed tactics and brought the knife to his own neck. His gaze locked on mine, he pushed the blade deep into his throat and drew it across.

Or my closest call that happened while conducting a "routine" traffic stop. I had stopped a driver I suspected was impaired. After positioning my police car behind the suspect's, I approached his door, and he sprang from the driver's seat, catching me off guard and knocking me to the road. Taking a beating and fighting for my life, I struggled to keep the attacker from releasing my sidearm, which he had gotten a good handle on. I remember the sensation of him yanking on the gun, tugging my belt up with each violent pull. I tucked one arm in, like a chicken wing, and over his hand to keep the gun holstered. Each time I went to reach for my radio with my free hand, another barrage of blows rained on my head. As they did, my thoughts harkened back to my newborn son at home. A Good Samaritan stopped and pulled the crazed person off me seconds before he would have defeated the last mechanism, keeping my gun in its holster.

Then there were the calls you can trace back and know that was when you began to harden, the ones that stay with you, the ones that still sting, years later…

Like the many times we were called to a home in the middle of the night to wake the occupants inside and notify them of their loved one's passing. In one instance, a grief-stricken mom, after being told of her husband's death, asked if we could tell her child. We sat on the living room couch with her nine-year-old son. He was wearing thick glasses and leg braces he needed to walk. We were trying to comfort him as he repeated over and over through his sobs, "Sir, who will get groceries for my mom and take me to the hospital again?" Then he added, "Officer, you have to catch the person who did this to my dad." There was no one to catch, yet how could I tell this little guy, "Your dad did this to himself. He took his own life earlier today. No one took it from him."

About twenty years ago, I responded to a property damage complaint called in by a single mom of a young son. Her ex-lover had left her with a broken front window following a final farewell fight and a bill she could not pay. While I was at the house taking the information for my report, the four-year-old boy caught in the middle of this mess clung to my leg and, over the next forty-five minutes, hung on as I moved between the kitchen and living room. As I gathered my things to leave, he cried out for me to stay and be his "dad." I can still hear his sniffles and feel his fingertips grip the inside of my pant leg.

Or one Christmas Eve when a five-year-old was turned into social services after shocking claims of abuse at the hands of his stepfather. The seagull-patterned welts and bruises all over the boy's body matched the abuser's belt. I remembered the jumble of emotions that ran through me every time the little guy stopped mid-sentence in his interview to remind us he needed to get home and into bed so Santa Claus wouldn't miss him.

Some calls were embarrassing...

Like when my partner and I were called to a known drug house in the district (an assigned geographical and administrative zone). When we arrived, I recognized a young gal with outstanding warrants in the corner of the living room. As we approached her to make the arrest, we noticed an older fellow on the couch not doing so well. His skin had a gray pallor and felt cool to the touch. I called for an ambulance, and my partner used my handcuffs to restrain the female and asked her to take a seat. When the ambulance arrived, the paramedics immediately recognized the older guy was overdosing and administered a drug to combat the effects of the morphine he had taken. Once stabilized, he became combative with the medics, drawing both my partner's and my attention. That gave the female an opportunity to quietly escape. According to the neighbors, her last known direction of travel was west toward the transit station. She wore blue jeans, a white T-shirt, and was accessorized with my handcuffs.

There were also the cases that solved themselves ...

On a hot summer day, a bank was robbed. My partner and I happened to be in the area and saw a shirtless male walking down an alley a short distance away. Looping around, we caught up to him, and I said, "Excuse me, sir, city police. We are investigating a robbery that occurred at the bank down the way." He replied, "Well, sir, I am the one you are looking for. The money is in my left boot." Sure enough, inside his left boot was a rolled-up bundle of cash stained from the dye pack that had exploded as he left the bank.

Then there were the truly bizarre incidents ...

Like the time I was dispatched to a call at a laundromat. It read as a lost-and-found complaint, though the item lost was an organ (*not* the musical type) and was apparently found in the bathroom. My brain had tripped over that. Not sure what we would find. We entered the bathroom, and on the floor was a large, pink, vascular object about the size of a fist. There was nothing else unusual in the washroom, just the misplaced organ lying on the floor. It kind of looked like a kidney, but neither my partner nor I knew what it was. As the junior guy, I was the lucky one who got to pick it up and put it into a clear plastic evidence bag. I vividly remember its squishy feel and foul odor. Our plan was to ask an expert what it was, so we took it to a nearby grocery store to see if the butcher could at least recognize what it was.

The butcher wasn't in.

Okay, how about we try a hospital? Someone there must know what it is. Once there, we caught the attention of the nurse with the unfortunate timing of being at the triage desk at that moment. She called for a doctor to have a look. When the doctor arrived, he explained he wasn't sure what it could be but speculated that perhaps it was a "product of conception."

Vomit rolled up into the back of my throat.

While calling for the medical examiner, another doctor walked by and asked to have a look. Know what prairie oysters are? I did, but I had never seen them before. Turns out I had been walking around with bull's testicles.

These calls and thousands of others helped shape me.

It is not the years of service but the volume of decisions, experiences, and mistakes made that build a person's expertise.

Early in the job, I made the conscious decision to develop a well-rounded career. I wanted a universal experience that allowed me to understand the many facets of policing. I didn't realize it at the time, but making that decision led me to a fortunate place. I have learned so many things about not only my career but also life. Valuable takeaways, even more so now as I enter the twilight of my career and launch myself into my next chapter. The release of this anniversary edition is in tandem with my retirement from law enforcement. As I navigate what's next, I know I will draw heavily on these experiences. Gaining that experience took time, mentors, and patience.

Service

When I was still a young officer, full of way too much piss and vinegar, I got saddled with an old-school veteran cop. I figured a younger officer would be more run and gun, more action, more fun. The old guy with his white hair and bifocals was cramping my inexperienced, thrill-seeking style.

We attended a break-and-enter complaint together. I hate to say it, but these can be routine. I wanted to get a real call, something with action or a chase. Instead, I was going through the house with the traumatized homeowner, my notebook in hand. I did everything by the book. I noted what was taken, looked for evidence that could be collected, identified the points of entry and exit, called for the Crime Scene Unit to come and dust for prints, knocked on the standard two doors to the east and west and checked off the boxes required for my report. Clearly, we must be ready to head out now, right?

Not even close.

My partner spent the next ten minutes talking to the victim about the people in the pictures hanging on her walls and grouped nicely on her fireplace. They talked about her children, her grandchildren, and her family. As I stood there tapping my foot to go, a new call came in. Other police were following a stolen car as my partner continued to politely ask the woman more questions about the people in her photos. There was a bad guy to catch, maybe a foot chase to be had.

I silently lamented how much more fun I could be having in this new, exciting scene. At first, I subtly nudged my partner to go, thinking he must have missed the initial transmissions over the radio. Why else would he stall? He ignored me and continued his conversation with the homeowner, who was now smiling, caught up in her own happy memories. As they continued to talk, I packed up my gear and headed for the door.

Maybe now is a good time to mention I don't do subtle particularly well. I quickly said goodbye and made my way out the front door, thinking he would follow. At the car, I waited for my partner and listened as things on the other call ratcheted higher. Units involved in the stolen car were just drawing up their tactics over the radio on how best to safely stop the vehicle and bring the offender into custody. I had unkind thoughts about my partner while listening intently. Units behind the stolen car activated their lights, but the vehicle did not stop. Units backed off while the police helicopter pursued. I was a million miles away from the action, and my partner was still inside the house. The radio squawked again. The helicopter spotter called the driver out of the vehicle; he ran for it, and units swooped into the area.

Minutes later, I heard, "One in custody."

Ugh. I had missed the best call of the shift. As I sat feeling sorry for myself, my partner finally emerged from the house. He got into the car and drove away. It was the first of many times as an officer I was firmly put in my place. Without taking his eyes off the road, he delivered one of the greatest lessons of my career.

With a snap in his tone, he said, "When we go to calls, we leave people in a better place than we found them. Got it? We take the time, we talk to people, and we allow them to reflect on the things in their lives to be thankful for, like family or friends. We do what we can to remove them from the trauma of whatever experience brought us to them in the first place."

He might have also added, "dumb ass."

A life of service is:

 *Leaving people in a better place than you found them.*

It has been my mantra ever since, and something I make sure I share with those who will listen.

Two men, my grandfather, and that veteran partner, both better known for being surly than poetic, influenced my life and career—for the better.

 Mentors can be as unexpected as their lessons are wise.

It won't always be a full lecture or reprimand; sometimes, it's a single offhand remark tossed out, almost like verbal gunfire, that keeps ringing, making circles in your head. I still hear their words.

 "Why jump over fences when you can look for gates?"

 *"Books never resolved a barroom brawl unless they were used as a weapon or shield."*

 *"Under the provisions of the Ways and Means Act, there is always a way and always a means to solve problems and dilemmas."*

Not all of a cop's lessons are learned in life-and-death situations. Most arise out of innocuous events, routine follow-ups, and meticulous record-keeping. Once, while out on a neighborhood canvass, my partner and I saw a leashed white and orange cat walking around a parking lot. Miss Marmalade was clearly somebody's pet. I turned to my partner.

"We can't leave that cat to just wander."

He agreed, so we hatched a plan to retrieve the animal, which had positioned itself under another parked car in the lot, no doubt wary of our interest in it. On our hands and knees, we both reached under the car. I got a hold of the leash and pulled the cat into the safety of my arms. Now tucked against me, I returned to our car and slid inside. Perhaps it was the confined space—or something offensive about me in particular—but as soon as I shut the driver's side door, the claws came out, and fur began to fly. It clambered off my lap and up my chest, shredding my suit before scrambling to the back seat, where it immediately calmed, giving me time to snap a picture of the little monster.

Now bleeding through my shirt and picking fur from my suit, I waited with my partner for animal services to arrive when an elderly man slowly walked through the parking lot. He looked like he was searching for something. I rolled down the window and asked him what he was looking for.

"A cat," he replied anxiously.

The original Miss Marmalade perched and ready from the driver's seat of our police vehicle.

In the tearful reunion that followed, the man said, "Thank you. My wife died last week. This was her cat and one of my last connections to her."

A common refrain among officers and people in general is that they do not see the difference they are making in their community. I wonder if they mean that society and civility are in decline. It's understandable, the news is full of disheartening stories, but surely it's easy to see the difference a kind word or act of generosity can make. When you think the world is getting worse, that is the time to realize:

Opportunities to make a positive difference are all around.

It is as simple and as profound as leaving someone better than you found them.

Every day, by our actions and words, we affect the quality of life for others and for ourselves.

How we treat people matters, regardless of what we do for a living. Whether you're a cop or an accountant, treating people with kindness creates happiness. Doing something for others fills our karma bank, and it nourishes us as much as those we help. This is where the passion for my career comes from.

By helping others, we create a life of meaning for ourselves.

I agree with the wisdom of the Dalai Lama. No one is too small to make a difference. Have you ever been trapped in a tent with a mosquito while you are trying to fall asleep? Mosquitos are tiny and spectacularly fragile, but their hunger and tenacity provide a good reminder for all of us.

You are never too small to make a difference.

One Christmas Eve about five years ago, a heartbreaking discovery was made by a bottle picker who was searching for cans in a dumpster. As he reached for the next bag in the bin, he felt something different, and as he opened the bag to look inside, he found the frozen body of an infant that had been discarded like trash. The tragedy of this incident became the precipice behind a joint venture between a local organization and a fire hall to build a baby cradle program where mothers who, for any number of their own personal reasons, do not wish to keep their newborns and are concerned with revealing their identity if they were to deliver their baby in a hospital or surrender the infant into child and family services.

Now in existence, *Hopes Cradle* gives new mothers another option of anonymous surrender where none was before. As the cradle program continues to build momentum in communities across the country, one hopes the women who make the complex and difficult decision to surrender their babies can now do so at a safe surrender site in communities that have embraced the program. This is the legacy Baby Eve left us. She was small, and her life on Earth was tragically brief, but the ripples from her hours-long journey may well last a lifetime for another infant born into a similar situation.

Emergency teams work incredibly hard to keep our communities safe and healthy. I remember a case where we were called to a double shooting. When we arrived on the scene, one victim was already dead on the road in front of the bar he had just exited. The second victim was on the sidewalk and looked as good as dead when they put him in the ambulance. The medical examiner who attended had identified brain material on the pavement where the second victim had fallen. Today, this same person walks, talks, and lives a reasonably uncompromised life despite the events of that day. First responders save countless lives and significantly reduce annual homicide rates. I heard someone say once that murder is a game of inches: an inch to the left, you may live, and an inch to the right, you may die. From my experience, if you can make it to a hospital, you will probably survive, which speaks to the talent of our emergency physicians, nurses, and those who got them to the hospital in the first place, our paramedics.

The communities we police rarely see this commitment and passion to be of service. Maybe that's why it matters when they do. On a Thanksgiving weekend over a decade ago, an unhappy man shot up a community with an excess of twenty rounds. For over ten minutes, he fired aimless rounds at police and homeowners in the posh neighborhood. The disturbed man eventually shot and killed himself in the middle of a playground.

In the investigation that followed, which focused on the police response, I was tasked with knocking on doors and making inquiries with witnesses. I heard the same thing over and over; neighbors applauded the bravery of the officers who had kept them safe. When they heard gunshots, they knew where the gunman was because they had seen the police running toward the gunfire, toward the gunman. One young constable, pinned down behind a bear-proof, green garbage bin, was taking fire when a woman came out of her house. He told her to go back inside and into her basement for safety. That officer, probably in the most dangerous situation of his life, thought of the safety of someone else before his own.

Another neighbor shared that he had been making Thanksgiving dinner, and when he put down the pepper shaker, it exploded. A bullet went through his kitchen window and hit the shaker he had just been holding.

The danger that day was very real and highlighted a valuable lesson.

Courage is placing ourselves in vulnerable situations, including opening ourselves to being hurt or judged, but trusting the outcome is worth it.

The community response to this incident was phenomenal and made me proud to be a member of our service that day. The courage of those officers responding to the call and the sacrifice each of them was willing to make, stopped this incident from becoming more tragic.

Sacrifice

By December 2020, I had been in homicide for almost thirteen years and had seen almost every example of murder—cases of intimate partner violence, files involving children, drug-motivated and gang-related murders, mass homicides, and the most common "flash in the pan" type murders which we label *deadly confrontations*. At this point, I knew I had seen it all—mostly. There was one type of case I had never been involved in or, thankfully, had to investigate: the murder of a police officer, a colleague, or a friend. I remained blessedly distanced from this reality until New Year's Eve, 2020.

In our city, New Year's Eve or New Year's Day has traditionally been a busy time for the homicide unit. For those of us on call, New Year's Eve meant keeping a quiet night in because we all knew it wouldn't stay that way.

New Year's 2020 kept with this statistic.

It was just before midnight when I received a dreaded message over the call-out team "group chat."

"An officer is in life-threatening condition after being dragged by a vehicle and is being transported to hospital, be prepared to come into the office if he succumbs." For the next few minutes, I held out hope that all would be well. Surely, if he was being transported to the hospital, all would be okay. My naivety was shattered about five minutes later when the boss sent a second message. *"The member taken to hospital has died. Please make your way to the office."*

Scrambling to get ready for what I knew would be a difficult investigation and new territory for our team, my mind raced. Who was the member? What about their family and friends—it would be excruciating. His colleagues would go through their own hell. Finally, who were the members present at the scene?

In record time, I arrived at the office and was assigned as file coordinator—a position supporting the lead investigator, who was an experienced and methodical detective with about ten years of homicide experience. As his file coordinator, it was my responsibility to ensure that all the information coming into the investigation was recorded, reviewed, and disclosed—if and when charges were laid.

In this case, those charges were imminent. The evidence left behind at the scene, coupled with the efforts made by our fallen officer prior to his death, ensured that we would have little difficulty identifying the persons responsible for his death.

On the night he was killed, Sergeant Andrew Harnett was working alone and had just pulled over the suspects in a gas station parking lot for a traffic violation. Broadcasting his location, the plate number, and the description of the suspect car to the dispatcher was the first procedural task that would help us as investigators later. The second, turning on his body-worn camera so all his interactions with the occupants were recorded. Knowing the officer was working alone, a backup unit arrived to assist, not knowing they would bear witness to the tragic circumstances that would follow.

Sergeant Harnett had checked both the driver's and passengers' identification through police databases. He discovered the driver was a "young person" (under the age of eighteen) and the front passenger was an adult with an outstanding warrant. After he completed writing a summons for the driver, Sergeant Harnett exited his vehicle and approached the open driver's side window to issue the young man the ticket while the backup officers approached the passenger side door to deal with the wanted man. Through the open driver's window, the adult passenger could be heard saying to the seventeen-year-old driver, *"Go, go go."* With that direction and without hesitation, the young driver moved his foot from the brake, slammed the automatic transmission into drive, and hit the gas, causing the vehicle to peel away with Sgt. Harnett attached to the car's "B" pillar. Traveling away from the scene in excess of ninety km/h. The young sergeant did his best to hang on to the outer door frame as the speeding vehicle barreled down a residential street. The young sergeant held on for several blocks until finally, unable to hang on any longer, he was dislodged from the car and fell into the lanes of oncoming traffic, where he was struck and killed by a second vehicle coming from the other direction.

For any investigator who has had to deal with the death of a colleague, there is no doubt something like that will haunt them forever. For me, it was particular footage taken from the body-worn cameras of the backup officers who were first to come across Sgt. Harnett after he had been struck—the horizontal red stripe. The body camera footage showed the red stripe on Sgt. Harnett's trousers laid out horizontally on the pavement. That red stripe is worn by municipal police officers across our country and, to me, has always represented the order of our office. It represents strength, courage, and trusted authority. It is always seen vertically along the outside seam of the pants, from the heel of the boot to the waistband. To see the stripe lying horizontally was unnatural and revealed a vulnerability I had never seen before in the uniform.

The murder of Sgt. Harnett also invoked a public outcry in our community and a rallying of public support, something I hope his family and friends could find some comfort in. This type of demonstrated support is not unique to our city. It can be seen on bridge decks and roads lined with people every time an officer dies in the line of duty. In the two and a half years since Sgt. Harnett's death, Canadians have seen this type of community mourning fourteen more times in small towns and large cities across our nation. This support is a visible reminder to the officers still serving that although it may not always feel like it, there are more that have your back than those that don't. They are the silent majority, not the vocal minority.

Policing can be messy and is sometimes dangerous. It certainly is also disruptive to our loved ones. I had been working in homicide for a couple of years when my seven-year-old son, at the time, met my boss. He extended his hand and introduced himself. "I've been meaning to meet you for a long time, sir. You're the guy that has ruined a lot of good times with my dad."

Our careers impact our families. The highs and lows of the day can wreak havoc in an officer's personal life.

Divorce and suicide rates among police are statistically high. I have known several officers who have left the service on stress-related issues and a few who have taken their own lives. Other emergency teams, such as Emergency Medical Services (EMS), fire, hospital emergency staff, and the military, as well as their families, experience similar challenges. The emotional toll from these careers is a real concern to workers and their families.

Our families have front-row seats as we, often at personal risk, serve our communities at a cost that can't easily be quantified. They recognize the sense of duty and responsibility most of us carry. Our families get it; they live it and support and accept that part of us.

What seems now like another lifetime ago, at least in part because of my career, I became a single dad. Thrust into this unwelcome but no less real situation, my children and I began the process of working together to find our new normal. My beautiful daughter became more inquisitive about the functioning of our home and expressed a real desire to help where she could, learning to use the washing machine, the dishwasher, the microwave, and the stove. She even made my bed in the morning. These were all kind, welcome gestures, but I was feeling a sense of guilt about it all, I remember asking her about her acts of service. Although I was thankful for all she was doing, I suggested that she not worry so much about taking on more than just being a kid. To this, she replied with the sweetest smile on her face, "Daddy, everyone in this world needs someone to take care of them. I'm your someone." Her selfless acts of kindness also illustrate the contagious effect service can have on others around us.

The gruesome realities of real-life tragedy are heavy, yet it is helping people live through those tragedies that helps me define the importance of what service truly is. It is our choice to be in these professions, but just as there is a cost to a life of service, there are also rewards that go deeper than any paycheck.

There is a direct correlation between serving others and our own internal happiness. If you are having a bad day or struggling, my advice is to do something for someone else, be it shoveling a neighbor's walk, cooking dinner for a friend, or volunteering somewhere. Simple, seemingly small acts can have such a large, profound impact on people.

A life of service is so much more than an occupation or calling, it is a philosophy of living.

Understanding this is one of the sweetest *ah-ha* moments my career in law enforcement taught me.

Owning Your Path

*"If you find a path with no obstacles,
it probably doesn't lead anywhere."*

- Frank A. Clark

We choose which direction we will take. Each of us has our own motivations, what keeps us on course, and how we choose to adapt or leave. We decide how we will navigate our way to happiness, but also what we turn to when life gets uncomfortably dark. The saying, *life isn't always fair, but it still is good*, rings true.

As homicide detectives, supporting victims' families is an important role. I have gone to many funerals and heard many eulogies and tributes. A victim's life path—clean-cut or with jagged edges—in no way speaks to their ability for real human connections. I see the wake of their grieving family and friends, the loss clearly deep, and often hear those surviving speak of regret, not only that their loved one was taken too soon, but *I wish* and *I feel guilty that* are the first words some speak when they reflect on the passing.

Grief inspires us to reflect on how we are living our

lives, where we are in our own journey, and where we want to be. Funerals and memorials spotlight that concept of the dash—the unassuming character etched between the birth and death dates on a headstone or printed on a memorial card—and how important the little line is because it marks the actual life lived. Figuring out how you live your dash is choosing how you will own your path.

> *Owning your path is taking responsibility for not only the direction of your life but also for the choices and people you include in it every day.*

In policing, you are your own business unit, and there is latitude on how each officer chooses to run his or her franchise. Just like in life, we have options. Big picture, what are you going to choose? Day to day, when you are on the job, in the car, and no one else is there, what do you do? What decisions are you making, and do they align with your core values? I once was part of a retreat where a facilitator was leading a discussion on values and illustrating the difference between a value system and core values.

The facilitator asked one of the participants, "Do you like beer?"

"Yes."

"Do you love your grandmother?"

"Yes."

"Do you like beer more than your grandmother?"

"No, of course not."

The facilitator then inquired, "Did you spend more money on beer or your grandmother last year?"

A long pause followed. He had spent more on beer.

The facilitator then asked, "If your grandmother was sick, I imagine you would go to her and not the bar, right?" *Of course.*

This is the difference between the things we place value in versus what we value in our core. Core values are the cornerstones we go back to when we are seeking a firmer footing along our path, especially when the terrain is breaking under us.

I believe knowing the answers to these questions:

What choices do you make day by day?

What do you value?

Why are you here?

Aligns our personal north arrow to owning our path.

Our best compass comes from trusting our instincts, following our hearts, and staying true to our core values.

When I started my career, I made a commitment that my actions would never destroy the hard work of generations of officers before me. My path would be something that I could be proud of; the lessons I learned would be sharable with my children and my community. I wanted my career to be well-rounded and to have as many experiences as I could, but I also wanted to be trusted and relied upon by my supervisors, my peers, and the people I helped. I believe that what one officer chooses reflects on the whole. To me, policing is a calling, not just a career, and I can recognize those who feel the same.

It is a different world from when my grandfather was a police officer—or when I joined twenty-five years ago. In my career, technologies have changed drastically. We have gone from handwritten notes to electronic ones, from basic computer and database systems to more state-of-the-art. We replaced reading maps with GPS systems, which tell us where to turn. Advancements in DNA have become so good that a lab can now create a composite sketch of what the offender may look like. We have replaced the testimony of police officers with body-worn cameras. Demands for disclosure have increased a hundred-fold. The profession went from being a noble one to not so much. Marijuana was replaced by cocaine, and cocaine has been replaced by methamphetamines and opioids, leading many communities into absolute crisis. Our profession has become polarized, leading to further erosion of our institution and movements that led to defunding. As crime has spiraled out of control, municipalities that have defunded police services and departments are now considering the possibility they could have been wrong—they actually do need the police in their communities as they grapple with epic drug crises and crime waves the likes of which they have never seen before.

Over the past twenty-five years, police procedures have also changed. Most agencies now have strict rules on vehicle pursuits, and across the country, most jurisdictions have created "watchdog" groups—civilian oversight bodies to investigate use-of-force complaints. Training has continued to improve, as has equipment, to name just a few. Yet, despite the changes, the fundamentals of what a police officer should be remain the same as they did a hundred years ago. In 1910, the Calgary Police Service wrote *Rules and Regulations* for members, speaking to what a detective is. It still applies:

> *"Members of the department must remember that certain qualities are essential to the making of a good detective. They must be honest, cool-headed, sober and of steady habits. They must be active and energetic. They must be able to keep their eyes open and their mouth shut. They must be slow to adopt theories positively, but having made certain of a fact, they should follow it up cautiously, diligently and perseveringly. They must bear in mind that not only the success of their work, but sometimes the reputation of an innocent person may depend upon their discretion."*

A hundred years later, these competencies remain constant. Technology, DNA, phones, computers, and advancing forensics have all transformed the world of law enforcement, but the core essence and expectation that defines the role of an investigator remains the same. Just as police procedures have changed drastically, so has visibility and awareness. With the advent of social media and technology, cameras everywhere record and share information about people who have wandered off the lit path, people making poor decisions. If the person making a poor decision is a police officer, it widens the mistrust between the public and the police—everyone pays.

I remember a few years ago, we all watched a local media outlet air video of one of our police officers physically "taking down" a female prisoner in the booking area who was still handcuffed. With no way of protecting herself, her head struck the edge of the counter before being slammed to the ground. Actions like these—besides the obvious abhorrence of it— dissolve public trust, something we critically need.

Thankfully, in my experience, there is a stronger army of officers who want to do good, who recognize their role as servant and guardian, and who work hard to protect their communities with this chosen path.

It is true that front-line officers are the heartbeat and backbone of a police service, and the reputation with the public can be made or broken by the positive actions or the misconduct of these members.

Sir Robert Peel, considered by many to be the father of modern British policing, wrote "Sir Robert Peel's Principles of Law Enforcement" in 1829. One of these principles hammers down this point:

> "Police must secure the willing cooperation of the public in voluntary observance of the law to be able to secure and maintain the respect of the public; and the degree of cooperation of the public that can be secured diminishes proportionately to the necessity of the use of physical force."

Peel was right. We have all seen videos and news clips or experienced first-hand when cities riot and burn after officers have breached the public's confidence through inappropriate and illegal actions. Through this chaos, the positive stories of authentic service and true guardianship, what the other ninety-nine percent of officers are doing every day, are often dismissed or overlooked.

I am reminded of stories like that of Officer Norman of Little Rock, Arkansas, who patrols the streets of a poverty-stricken neighborhood, spreading and receiving love from the welcoming community as captured on his Instagram account. Or Officer Jeremy Henwood from San Diego, California, who, minutes before he was shot and killed, was seen on a restaurant surveillance camera buying a young boy a cookie.

I think about the officers who have parked their patrol cars to throw a football with a group of kids or join in a game of street hockey; or those who have comforted a child who has just borne witness to tragedy. I think about the officers closer to home: those who, after working a homicide case for a week and running on fumes, finally crash on an office couch or a yoga mat borrowed from the station's gym; or the officer who, on his day off, purchased the materials and offered his own time to fix an elderly homeowner's fence that had been damaged by a hit-and-run driver. Or the officer who recognized the importance of Truth and Reconciliation with our indigenous community and created a sacred space inside our investigative services area where families dealing with crisis could be brought, where smudging and cultural practices could occur, and where healing can begin. Or the different areas and units of our service who pool their own personal resources and money to bring Christmas to a needy family—turkey, trees, gifts, and all. For me, all of these officers demonstrate what a path of service looks like and have chosen to walk that path brilliantly.

At times, individuals who the police have kept safe in the past make choices that put themselves right back in harm's way. This can cause dismay and even disillusionment for police officers struggling to make sense of a seemingly senseless situation.

We often see this play out in return calls back to the same home. To deal with the same abuser hurting the same victim who decided to try to give the relationship one more chance. Or the addict returning to the bottle or the pipe that is slowly killing them. In scenarios like these, the choice seems so obvious to us. But it's not obvious. The people we are trying to help have their reasons for the decisions they are making, and they are often more complex and layered than officers can, in a snap judgment, understand. Instead of being critical, perhaps it is more productive for us to recognize and take inspiration from family members trying to support their loved one in crisis or addiction. Family members of individuals who have adopted this approach have, against all odds, literally saved their loved ones' lives because they refused to give up on their sons and daughters, brothers and sisters.

Over the course of my career, I have met many women who have made the difficult decision to leave an abusive relationship. In almost all cases, those who did so knew they had a supportive family—even though their families had been pushed to the shadows. Abusers isolate their victims, making escape more challenging.

I heard the story of one woman who succinctly demonstrates this. She grew up in a wonderful and loving family. Her father was a successful doctor, her mother a supportive stay-at-home mom, and her older brother a talented lawyer. She went to university and received a master's in psychology. Life was good, and she met the love of her life. They married shortly thereafter, and on their first night, retreating to their room after a perfect wedding day, he ended the night not with a kiss but with a first punch instead. For years, she endured many, many more. Throughout it all, even though she wasn't able to see them much, she knew her family always had her back and were only a phone call away. Meanwhile, quiet and hopeful, they waited for the day the call would come. It did. After arriving home five minutes late one day, the woman entered her front door to find three rifles lined up at the entryway, the gun stocks placed purposefully into the shoes of her and her children's. Message sent. That day, she knew it was finally time to call for help, and she did, never looking back. She and her children escaped a terrible situation with the help of her family.

Their support was what got her through. Not unlike the next case.

A few years back, I worked on a case involving a barely twenty-something kid. At fourteen, she had left her family and a life of security and spent the next few years making a series of poor choices that led her to a savage moment: witnessing the man she had been getting high with for a week being shot and killed inside the vehicle she was sitting in. Choking on gun smoke, scared and in shock, she called for help.

In the investigation that followed, I was tasked with interviewing her and was immediately struck by her complete lack of value for herself. The path she had chosen was not unlike others I had encountered. Some people are running from something, prompting high-risk choices, while others are running to something, with the perception of something better, shinier, something more, whatever they need more to be.

This woman wasn't running away from something. She had the security of a loving family. She was running toward the perception of something better. During the interview, she shared that she had started by experimenting with street drugs. For years she found herself between using and in and out of treatment facilities. She confided that this placed her in a new social group of like-minded druggies. As the next few years unfolded, she became addicted to opiates. While she was talking to me, detailing her descent, she was sweating, shaking, and sick, but the saddest part was that she believed this was the only version of herself. Her choices had broken her.

To me, she seemed different from the others in this story of guns, drugs, and death. You could tell she had been loved by a family, had a good foundation, and had a support system. By failing to choose a path that accepted that love and value or the help that had been present through her rehab stints, she had allowed her addiction to choose a rougher path. She forfeited her life for the addiction. She was trying to run to something that could never deliver.

Over the next several years, I remained in contact with her and her family as she spiraled further and further down. Her body, not to mention her spirit, suffered the continued abuse, and she couldn't have been ninety pounds soaking wet. Her hair had turned to straw, like it does, and her face was the hollow ghost of the once-vibrant kid she had been.

Now arrested and in jail, her mother worked hard to secure treatment for her and diligently visited her while in custody. There was a plan in place. She was going to get help. On the day of her release from jail, this pleasant, now sober (from her incarceration) female left the detention center and walked straight back into her life of drugs. Again.

Another six months went by, and this young woman's mother grew desperate. She feared for her daughter's life. She had good reason to be scared; there was a dangerous new drug on the street, fentanyl, and her daughter was a textbook example of one who, based on previous choices, would hit that direction hard.

For those suffering from drug addictions, over time, the need for more drugs (chasing the first high) almost always leads to more crime to fund the increased craving. With the insatiable nature of addictions, a person's luck runs out. The bigger the addiction's appetite, the quicker they will find themselves back on the police radar. This is exactly what happened. This young woman did another stint in jail. But she had a family who loved her. Not everyone who chooses this path has an advocate, someone in their corner who doesn't give up on them. With an army of support backed by a well-meaning defense attorney, a sympathetic court, a well-intentioned prosecutor, and a loving mother, she has now chosen a path focused on sobriety.

By owning our path, we are better able to help someone else own theirs.

Scripts

Real life doesn't have a template.

Sometimes, we want to label our experiences that way anyway, to find the appropriate box to tick. Putting someone else's concept of how your life should play out ahead of your own is not owning your path. During my recruit training, I heard about four predictable phases every cop goes through.

The first one is the Fascination Stage (one to four years). Basically, everything is new, fascinating, and cool. You're learning so much and in there, getting it done, on this new path that feels pretty *wow* and *bad-ass* at the same time. People look at you differently, and you don't understand that not all looks are good ones. It doesn't matter because the siren and chase is pretty fun.

Then you smack into the Hostility Stage (four to six years), which is when you now know you can't help everyone—hell, you can't really control a goddamn thing. People are horrible to each other, and your job is cleaning up the mess—too late to stop it from happening—and knowing there are many more deviants in the queue waiting to pounce. You've been spit at too many times, sworn at in unexpected places, and had your integrity questioned for helping. Everything sucks.

Then, you mature enough to shake it off and step into the Superiority Stage (seven to fifteen years). This is when you know life can really suck for people, but you know you can make a difference, and you do every time you can. You accept the limitations of yourself and the job but also work on your strengths so you can be effective. You know how to navigate the support systems, minefields, and bureaucratic red tape. You know the job, and you're still here, so you must be doing something right.

Then there is the Acceptance Stage (fifteen years

and beyond), when you look back at your career, at the cases that will always haunt you, and the happy outcomes that get you through the bleakness of the bad ones. The cost of this view was high, but you know the only direction to move is forward. You want to leave a legacy because, otherwise, what was the point of the cost? You see how you can take what you learned and leave something, anything, better than you found it. For some reason, against serious odds, you still give a damn.

When I think back on my own career, I must admit that although the timing of those phases may have been a little off, certainly the concept behind each resonates now. I am also reminded about how supportive my whole family has been, my parents specifically. My mother was particularly in tune with each phase I was going through. In those early years when everything was "badass and wow," she would always remind me to be mindful of the stories I would tell and the little ears of the grandkids who may overhear a detail they shouldn't. As time went on and the luster of the job had worn off, story time was over. Some jagged edges had begun to form, and she would remind me to be kind and gentle. Moving into the peak of my career, where the experiences I had previously were allowing me to enjoy success and fulfillment on my path into homicide, she would remind me to be healthy. Now, as I enter this final chapter of my career, she is astutely aware of my future aspirations, and to that, her message most recently has been—*Dream*.

Even though my career had parallels with the predicted format, it deviated in other necessary ways. When we simply resign ourselves to follow a template others have decided, we are not owning our path. There is a danger that these stages can be a self-fulfilling prophecy. This can be a problem if the script you're following is not your own. Many live life with certain expectations: that they will grow up, finish kindergarten through grade twelve, have a date for grad, go to university, meet the love of their life, marry, have three kids, have a successful career, raise those kids into young adults, be able to see them do the same, have grandchildren, and so on. That's a fairly average, normal script for life that many people try to follow with a reasonable level of expectation. But when crisis occurs, when life's blueprint gets altered (an unexpected illness, divorce, loss of a job, or death of a child), those who are deeply entrenched in the template of how life is supposed to be, without the ability to adapt or deviate, may find themselves quite lost during, and after, the crisis. We see this formula often in cases of murder-suicide.

I investigated a case where a young couple followed that exact script. By all accounts, they were in love, happy, and expected to start a family. What they didn't plan for was the possibility that one or both couldn't have children. This was a blow that devastated the husband so much that one night, he plunged a knife deep into his unsuspecting, sleeping wife's chest. She died on the floor trying to get out of the bedroom. The husband then pulled a cord from the back of the television, fashioned a noose, and hung himself from the ceiling fan in the living room. A family friend found them the next day.

In a recent case I was involved in, a middle-aged man, grappling with the loss of his relationship, which he had scripted to last forever, made the horrific decision to end his life and his former girlfriend's. On a hot summer evening, he attended her home on the eighteenth floor of an apartment high rise, tied her up, and flung her off the balcony, much to the horror of many witnesses below. He then did the same to himself. Teetering on the railing for only a moment, his final act of suicide was captured on video by a multitude of onlookers. Grim.

These are drastic examples, but refusing to stay flexible and adaptable, can put you into a detrimental space if things don't work out as everyone had planned and expected. Having an awareness that you can edit your own script, that we can all choose to recover and regroup when life goes off the rails, gives us all the power to own our own path.

A beautiful example of the ability to edit one's own script comes through the story of a young woman I met several years back after her mother had been found murdered. Born into a criminal family, most would have written her off as a lost cause. Several of her family members had either been murdered or were murderers themselves. Throughout her life, she had been surrounded by people afflicted by alcohol, drug abuse, and the hell those demons bring. The deck was stacked against her to live a very different life if she chose to follow the script others expected of her. She didn't. She chose her own way. She went to school, studied hard, earned a job, and stayed sober. By putting herself on a positive path, she became the stability in an unstable and unsettled family. She could have easily fallen into the expected harsher path, and no doubt has stumbled against it a few times. She is an inspiring example of someone living her life her way.

Success

I believe success is a choice. Every day, each one of us chooses our own actions and attitudes that will either support or cripple our endeavors.

Our relationship with success, not unlike happiness, is really up to us.

Success is a mindset that requires effort and actioning opportunities. I am fortunate that so many of the people I have worked with over the years were highly motivated. We worked long, often grueling hours to resolve our cases. We advocated for our investigations and our victims' families and were constantly striving to improve and learn from each other through our achievements and our mistakes. In a concerted effort to always raise the bar, we sought innovative new approaches, technologies, and strategies to ultimately create better ways. It is for these reasons, I would argue, that I worked with a lot of successful people.

I know not everyone is interested in that same level of effort. It is a tireless dedication and commitment to results. But that effort matters and is part of the listed ingredients found on the back of every box of serial success I have ever read.

Several years ago, I sat in on a presentation given by a constable from our service who recognized that his background as a mechanic and car enthusiast could provide vehicle identification support when a suspect's vehicle had been captured on closed-circuit television. It can be challenging to accurately identify the make, model, and year of a car speeding through several frames of recorded time. Finding a vehicle expert to do this necessary step in our investigative process is a blessing. This officer gave a compelling presentation that demonstrated he had the ability to do this type of work, and we were all leaning forward in our chairs, recognizing the obvious asset.

By actioning his idea that day, he established himself as the go-to guy to provide support in this area. This has allowed him to work within his passion and the opportunity to work on some of the most sensitive police investigations in our city's history.

Other officers I have worked with have also identified unique skill sets, sometimes with training at their own cost, and are experts in their chosen fields. Within our unit, we have investigators and crime analysts who have taken it upon themselves to become leaders in the field of child death, missing persons, gang investigations, and cellular telephone analysis, to name but a few. By doing so, these individuals remain relevant and vital to the effectiveness of the team. It can also be argued that, by taking these extra steps, they become irreplaceable.

In police work, I believe our lucky breaks and successes come as a result of real action. I will submit that sometimes that action is seemingly helped in inexplicable ways, call it divine intervention, or maybe karma—sometimes it seems like the universe helps. However, something has to be set in motion:

A lucky break has to have someplace to land.

Successful people understand this. Just like you can't win the lottery if you don't buy a ticket, taking relative, viable action is necessary if you are to expect any measure of success.

Years ago now, a deranged man committed a heinous triple murder. He planned the homicides for months, right down to the smallest of details, like the specific doors and locks he would have to know how to breach. What he did not account for was the possibility that local surveillance cameras were present and would capture him on video coming and going from the victims' residence the night of and the morning after the murders. Once discovered, this lucky break was the first piece of evidence that linked the accused to the scene and led investigators to his home, where damning evidence was found. This would have never happened if investigators hadn't sent officers out to do extensive canvassing of the neighborhood, discovered the video evidence, and reviewed the footage in a timely manner to find that lucky break.

We are blessed to have a weather phenomenon called Chinooks that periodically blows into our city. These are a type of gusty wind that occurs on the downward slope of a mountain. Being tucked in the eastern shadow of the Canadian Rockies, we can experience these winds fairly often. When they hit in the winter, they can create balmy spring-like temperatures that quickly melt snow. With these melts, things under the snow become visible, like people who have been missing.

Prior to my time in homicide, there was a case where, following one of these Chinook events, the naked body of a woman became visible in the parking lot of an abandoned drive-in. With nothing on her to identify her remains, investigators received their lucky break when one of them noticed a receipt flapping in the wind off one of her buttocks. Remember I mentioned sometimes it seems like we get inexplicable help? That Chinook wind had bellowed in, melting the snow that led to the victim's body being discovered in the first place, yet the receipt didn't blow away. That little piece of paper was key to solving the case; investigators followed up on the information printed on it, which quickly led to the identification and arrest of the suspect. The receipt was loaded with potential, but that potential had to be realized by the investigators and relevant actions taken.

In another case, a killer who had just murdered a teenage boy lit the victim's car on fire, leaving the body to burn inside the makeshift crematorium on wheels— or so he thought. After dousing the vehicle with an accelerant, he lit a match and walked away without realizing fire needs oxygen to burn. Minutes after he left the scene, the fire extinguished itself. Smoke, melted seats, and plastics were left behind. So was the intact and processable evidence, including the DNA of the perpetrator and the murder victim. To harness this lucky break, investigators still needed to carefully process the crime scene and diligently examine all of the exhibits collected. The break was always there, but it was up to the investigators to give that break a place to land, turning loaded potential into success.

In another case, a phantom camera operator was our lucky break. The cheer from New Year's was just beginning to wear off as we entered the second week of 2018. But not for everyone. An impromptu house party at a residence across from a large retail space was a testament to that. On this night, six people were in the house when two party crashers arrived. The two late attendees—uninvited—made some of the guests uncomfortable.

These individuals were different. They had history, and everyone knew it. They carried themselves differently, walked like they would in a prison meal line, and even from across the room, you could see the chips on their shoulders. The host's decision was to leave them be—*Don't poke the bear.*

To this day, it is not clear what lit the match, but whatever it was, it led the uninvited guests to brandish mace and knives inside the home before chasing and stabbing two of the legitimate guests out into the snow—one suffering fatal knife wounds.

An exterior, motion-sensitive security camera installed to patrol mall parking captured the action. Set to sequence over the course of two minutes through multiple angles, including on the street in front of the residence, this camera panned and zoomed without operator control. The results were remarkable.

As if it was being controlled from the grave, the camera recorded the attack as it unfolded. The first victim was an aspiring MMA fighter with a bright future. He was stabbed multiple times in the street by both offenders while the second victim ran for his life and found refuge in the entrance to a tanning salon along the mall's west side.

The automatic camera zoomed in and panned out at perfect times to capture the entire violent assault, seemingly better than if someone had been operating it themselves. Although the video's night resolution was insufficient to exclusively identify both accused, it helped the members of the court see the level of participation of each accused in the murder. If this wasn't enough, the camera continued its two-minute cycle to record the stabbed victim staggering across the street to the mall entrance, where he collapsed—again zooming in as if needing to capture his last breath for the absolute record.

In another lucky-break case, one dreary January morning, a group of intruders with vendettas forced their way inside the residence of several college students, stabbing one student critically and the other fatally. We learned that the murder weapon had been thrown from the suspect's moving vehicle. To complicate matters, earlier that day, we had received a heavy snowfall, and the roadway where we expected to find the tossed knife had just been plowed. We knew recovering the knife would be like finding a needle in a haystack. Still, plans were put in place, and a two-block search radius was identified. It didn't take long. Police vehicles moved into the community to set up for the search, and one became stuck in a large snow bank. Tires spinning, the driver attempted to free the vehicle from the drift, and the knife we were looking for spit out from the back wheel and landed at our feet.

By giving the lucky breaks in our lives a place to land, we create opportunities that can help us toward our pathway to success.

The differences between success and failure are the words "try" and "do."

For me, trying indicates a thought, while doing is

the action that brings thought into reality. Success, personal growth, and the accomplishment of goals come from action, not wishing action. Successful people know this and practice it religiously. This is also why they consistently outperform others. Statements like: "I am going to try and solve this problem" versus "I am solving this problem," or "one day I am going to…" versus "today I will…" are two entirely different things. I've so often heard from suspects: "I am trying to be honest with you." Translated, that means, "I am not being honest with you at all, but I would like to be." When you want to do something, trying isn't an option.

Several years ago, you would have heard me say, "I would like to write a book one day." Now I can say, "I wrote a book." Back then, I had my own set of fears that kept me daydreaming instead of writing: fear of failure, fear of ridicule from my peers, fear of my police service not supporting a project, and fear of upsetting or offending people. It is not easy putting your thoughts, feelings, and opinions out there for others to read and judge. Writing a book my children can read would never have been realized if I hadn't jumped into the deep end of the pool. The fears are still there, but I have the confidence to know I can weather all of them. That thing I had always wanted to try is now a reality. Sarah helped me get here, but I had to take those first steps and then keep going.

I didn't realize how many drafts it would take to write a book. Weaving multiple concepts into coherent chapters, recounting stories from which I had learned lessons, and crafting all of the pieces in such a way that you, the reader, would understand. It took a lot of tries to get the book to a place Sarah and I felt was right. We did not let anyone see our initial scribbles while we found our footing, and those early drafts could be considered failures. Sarah and I both prescribe to the perspective that:

Failure is part of the evolution toward success.

We needed those awkward first sketches to brainstorm, to test the waters, and to figure out what we wanted to create. I believe that in people driven to be successful, failure is part of the equation. For those not driven, failure becomes a reason to quit. Knowing that, with each failure, we get that much closer to the solution can have a profound impact on our perseverance.

If taking action is required to generate our luck and successful outcomes, why is it so hard to move from trying to doing? I believe it is fear of unknown consequences, of failing, and even of succeeding. Successful people do not let fear stop them from action. That isn't to say they don't also feel fear. They just refuse to be paralyzed by it. When we move from trying to doing, there very well may be obstacles and roadblocks to overcome. The path to success is rarely straight and narrow, but by committing ourselves to our course of action, we are in the mindset to maneuver around any hurdles that come our way. Success is a mental game.

People live colorful lives. I have become keenly aware of this. What people kept hidden or not well known while they were alive—the skeletons in their closet—often come to light during the investigations into their deaths. Not all of these skeletons are ominous. Still, we pay attention to them during murder investigations as we work toward identifying the persons responsible. Moving through a murder investigation inevitably leads to the identification and subsequent elimination of persons of interest. This cycle of try/fail can be frustrating, but eliminating persons of interest is simply the evolution of an investigation moving forward.

Early in my homicide career, I was called out on a Sunday morning after a young man had been found dead in the parking lot of a strip mall. In the investigation that followed, we learned a lot about this victim and his life. First, he was a low-risk victim, a simple man who had lived with his parents, had several adult siblings, no girlfriend, and no criminal history with the police. However, he'd had an entrepreneurial spirit, and although not a lawyer, he'd provided legal advice to people who were navigating the legal system to sue others. In some of the cases he took on, his associates had shady backgrounds.

When we examined the scene, several details suggested that robbery could have been a motive. The victim's clothing was in disarray, and some of his property was strewn away from where his body was found. While canvassing the neighborhood, the information suggested other dark possibilities. A residence directly behind the crime scene was a suspected drug house with unsavory characters coming and going at all hours, and a second nearby residence housed two known criminals. After timelining the victim's last known movements, we learned he had been at a bar earlier in the evening where he had met with several different women.

We had a lot of information, many leads to follow, and eighteen persons of interest to either eliminate or focus on more closely. We began the process of systematically investigating each: interviewing persons of interest, checking alibis, establishing timelines, and reviewing forensic evidence to assess possible links. The list eventually dwindled to the two known criminals.

This may seem like a lot of work, and it is, but almost every case requires it. The case against the two individuals became stronger every time one of the other eighteen persons of interest was cleared. It was through this process of "failure," eliminating sixteen of the original eighteen persons of interest, that the evolution of success could happen. We can look at failure as simply a stepping-stone on our path to success.

Another secret to success is to:

Surround yourself with successful people.

For instance, I suspect it is more beneficial to take marriage advice from a happily married person than a recent divorcee still raw and hurting. It makes sense to seek out someone with experience making their marriage work who can share sound, practical advice. Unless divorce is your intention, then the latter is your go-to expert. There are exceptions, and we can all learn valuable lessons in unexpected places, but set yourself up for success. Who is best able to model and advise on the outcome you desire? When you make the conscious decision to surround yourself with people who are living the success that you desire, you are better positioned to learn and be in the right place at the right time when opportunities knock.

When I had less than two years on the job, I was dispatched to a nuisance complaint in a trendy area of town. When I arrived, a petite, scared young woman met me. She reported that she had caught a peeping tom peering into her window as she was in bed with her boyfriend. Originally unreported, the victim went on with her daily routine for the next several weeks but noticed pornographic and sexually explicit literature around her building and vehicle. What terrified her into calling the police was when she received a telephone message from an unknown male detailing her and her then-boyfriend's sexual activities.

Over the course of the next several months, the

victim called back multiple times to report each new piece of evidence showing the perpetrator was still returning at night. She found lipstick messages written on her vehicle, explicit materials left where she would see them, and she continued to receive frightening phone messages. After months of fear, she eventually moved from her apartment.

I was struggling. A nighttime stalker was terrorizing a young woman so badly she had to move to get relief. My inexperience wasn't getting the job done. I sought advice from successful police officers who gave me new tools and approaches. I also met an incredibly gifted officer who provided me with insight and experience that led to solving the case, including baiting the offender so he could be apprehended.

Surround yourself with other successful people. Pick the best people you can, those who insist on excellence, and stick with them. With a solid team, you are greater than simply the sum of your parts, a lesson we will discuss in chapter eight. It's amazing that, to this day, I continue to work with a lot of the same individuals in a variety of areas. This is not a coincidence; this is our recognition that we need one another to be able to keep improving, keep learning, and keep growing.

It was in my recruit class that a wise training officer said,

It is not hard to be a bit better than average.

In my view, the best police officers, and anyone wanting to achieve success, know this, and their decisions reflect this insight. Effort builds careers. Apathy disintegrates them.

In my world, a deceptively simple way to be better than average is to call back complainants, victims, and other stakeholders. This is how relationships are built instead of busted and how unexpected leads and information can come in. I have been told multiple times in our agency that the number one complaint received against officers is that members have made no attempt to call back complainants. Imagine if, after every call regarding a suspected drunk driver, the officer did a quick follow-up with the complainant to advise of the outcome. How much more likely would these individuals be to call back again the next time they had suspicions or concerns? It takes thirty seconds to make the call and creates a positive presence that lasts infinitely into the future. Do the math: a thirty-second investment has a payout of improved community relations and encourages the community to try to contact the police when they have information or concerns. I have seen those returns pay off so many times in my career. The results are incredible when police officers and the community, together, put in effort.

One of our homicide team members is a master at creating this positive presence. His effort has paid off in spades. From the outset of each new case, he works to build relationships with the victims' families. A potent example of this started years ago when he was investigating the murder of a woman who had been bludgeoned to death and discovered under a pile of clothes in the laundry room of her rooming house. Missing for days, a roommate came across her body after noticing her blood-soaked hand peeking through a pile of clean linens. The surviving family members had a longstanding disdain and distrust of the police. It took some time for them to warm up to this investigator's tact, but they did. Over the course of the next few years, he became a sounding board and friend whenever they found themselves in a new crisis, which was often. Through compassion and an understanding of the complex dynamics of their needs, he built enough trust to help other investigators develop their own rapport with this complicated family.

This is not the only time where his mastery has shone through. As you can imagine, investigating the death of a colleague brings with it a range of strong emotions. Bad guys know this, too, and after killing an officer, there can be a fear that turning themselves in could be dangerous.

During the investigation into the murder of Sergeant Harnett introduced in chapter one, as the manhunt intensified, our suspects' pictures were plastered all over the media. Both offenders knew it was only a matter of time before they were caught and sought counsel early. They both asked their lawyers to help negotiate their surrender. Going through their own professional Rolodex, the lawyers contacted this investigator to arrange for their clients' arrest in a manner safe for all involved. The lawyers trusted him; his years of service and his reputation gave them the confidence each needed to make that call. The resulting surrender was uneventful, tactful, and, most importantly, legal.

The police officers who are better than average know they must treat every complaint seriously and own the investigation from the outset. They treat people as they would want their own loved ones treated if they were a victim of crime or the subject of any police interaction. They recognize that the theft of a garden gnome from a little old lady is not a lesser event than the theft of a vehicle from a business executive. They treat both with the same diligence and respect. Yes, we live in a world of priorities, but remembering that on this day, the garden gnome is her priority will take you way past average.

In my world, it is embarrassing if an officer goes to a complaint, and an hour or two later, another call comes in from the same place. The assumption is that the original problem was not dealt with properly. No matter how diligent or well-intentioned we are, sometimes we make mistakes. Knowing failure is a stepping-stone to success doesn't always make it easier to swallow.

I once went to a shots-fired complaint that originated at a house party. Upon arrival, my partner and I, as well as several other police units, were confronted by a large group of drunken teens who told us that someone at the party had brandished a cap gun and fired it as a prank. After finding several expended cap gun cartridges in the alley, the story held some weight, and we spent the next few minutes shutting down the party and sending the partygoers on their way. About an hour later, our dispatcher advised that a teen had just been admitted to hospital with serious gunshot wounds received at a house party—the house party we had just attended—the house party we had just cleared of witnesses. We returned to the area, embarrassed that we had missed the shooting scene, and discovered the missing shell casings underneath our police van's previous parking spot.

Public shaming is a strong motivational force, and there is no doubt of the power it has. No one wants to be perceived as ineffective at their job. There is the acutely uncomfortable experience of being somewhere, maybe at a party or event, when people learn you are a police officer and someone says, "I had to call the police once." Then you get that lump in your throat because, for a fraction of a second, you don't know if it was a positive experience or not, and you feel the weight of every decision, good or bad, that every cop has ever made. When we work with people who own their path, that lump is still there, but it is a lot smaller.

By owning your investigation (or your life in general), you make yourself available to others. Back in the day, I quite enjoyed working simple shoplifting complaints. Through these seemingly uncomplicated files, I learned much about core investigation skills. Interviewing offenders when the stakes weren't lethal was excellent practice for when the stakes literally would be life or already dead. After attending several of these complaints from a particular department store, I became known to their loss prevention officers. At my urging, they would also call me when they had more interesting case files appear on their radar. When they identified significant internal theft rings, I got the call. These cases provided even more opportunities to learn and, quite frankly, practice. I was developing investigative skills that I still use today.

Perhaps the greatest secret to putting yourself onto a successful path is to:

Define what success actually means to you.

Life is more about the journey, not the destination. Where I stand, we're all going to die in one of four ways—naturally, accidentally, by suicide, or by homicide. Equating material things as your yardstick for success is limiting. The fullness of our experiences, the passion we have toward our partners, the love we have for our families, and the positive differences we make in other people's lives are all more accurate measurements of our success. The most successful people I know will tell you that their achievement comes from their connections to others and the experiences they seek in life.

A while ago, I realized that I do not have the power to make someone feel a certain way or do a certain thing. I can't make someone feel happier or change another person's perspective. I don't have that control, nor should I. With that awareness came the understanding that I should not give this superhero power back to anyone else, either.

I own my feelings, frustrations, and actions. I do my best to not let someone else's behaviors affect my own. If I want to be sad, then I'm sad; happy, then I'm happy; angry, then I'm angry. My feelings are not derived from an external source but rather an internal state. It is my choice how I roll with life. Yes, I am influenced by the people and circumstances around me, but I am in control over their impact and duration. This is one of the ways I have chosen to own my path and how I live my dash.

Many in a life of service take an oath, a promise to do the best job possible. Satisfactory is not satisfying at all. It is in each of us to be better than average. Making the decision to do so is owning your path.

> "*I swear that I will be faithful and bear true allegiance to Her Majesty Queen Elizabeth the Second, her heirs and successors according to law, in the office of police officer for the City of Calgary and that I will diligently, faithfully and to the best of my ability execute, according to the law the office of police officer, and will not, except in the discharge of my duties, disclose to any person any matter of evidence that may come to my notice through my tenure in this office, so help me God."*
> —Calgary Police Service Oath, 1998

Gray Matter

*"Discretion is the perfection of reason,
and a guide to us in all the duties of life."*
- Walter Scott

Discretion

Policing has taught me that there are very few certainties in life and

Just because we can do something doesn't mean we should.

Our actions, even if by the book, can have unintentional yet still incredibly damaging consequences. Discretion allows us to make wise, thoughtful decisions, with or without a manual that says it's okay. It allows us to mindfully go about our business and problem-solve at our best, not just when it is easiest. Discretion is intangible, and perhaps that is why it is so often underestimated. Its very nature introduces gray; few things in life are as simple as black or white.

In the moment of a crisis, people living within it often don't have the ability to see outside of it. A lot of the decision-making processes are muted or even corrupted because of the crisis. This next case is an extreme example.

A couple of years ago, after more than a month of not hearing from an elderly woman who lived with her son, family and friends became concerned and called the police to attend her home and check on her welfare. After door knocks went unanswered, police forced entry into her home and found her decomposed to the point her corpse had naturally mummified in the apartment's bathroom and found her emaciated son still living in the suite. It was a suspicious set of circumstances, to be sure, which led our homicide team to become involved in this case.

It did not take long to ascertain that what we were dealing with was a middle-aged man who had struggled with facing the death of his mother to a point that he simply didn't. He muted it. He carried on living within the apartment while she lay deceased on the bathroom floor. Surviving only on ketchup, his body had deteriorated so much that he himself was under a hundred pounds and in need of immediate medical care. His explanation for all of it was that he was simply overwhelmed—overwhelmed with the passing of his mother and overwhelmed with the prospect of preparing a service for her. In the end, he was apprehended under our province's Mental Health Act and sent into care for treatment. At autopsy, it was determined that she had died from natural causes, just as he had said.

Finding lawful, creative, appropriate solutions can mean the difference between surviving a crisis or being debilitated by it. When discretion is used for sound, compassionate reasons, how could its application ever be critically judged?

Discretion is making decisions in the gray.

When I was a young police officer, I attended a call of an unexpected infant death. Upon our arrival at the home, the mom came to the door, her deceased baby still cradled in her arms. There was no resuscitation option for the infant; this little one was the kind of cold that only dead can claim. At the time, I had no idea how the baby had died. I could be dealing with a woman who had just harmed her infant or an absolutely devastated mother. My training shouted within me. I was supposed to get her to put the baby down. The rigid structure of police procedure dictated that I had to protect the body and protect the scene — but what if there was no foul play? Images of a tug-of-war flashed through my mind, definitely not anywhere I wanted to go. It must have only been moments while my mind raced to find the best course of action with the limited information I had. She had already been holding the infant. Would a couple of more minutes impede the investigation? Would a strict interpretation of securing the body and scene make an already tragic situation that much worse?

In the end, we (the other first responders and I) provided the mom time to hold her deceased child. Later, it was confirmed the infant had died of natural causes. I believe we live with the choices we make. I don't know if we left this mother better than we found her. I imagine that would have been impossible. But by choosing to use discretion in a compassionate and empathetic way, we did not leave her worse. I also learned a valuable lesson—discretion is considerate. This is a lesson I have sadly had cause to apply a half dozen times since when investigating the deaths of children.

In another case, on a hot summer afternoon, a heartbroken and sad thirteen-year-old boy pulled back his shower curtain, took off his slippers, removed his shirt, and shot himself in the head while his older sister was watching television downstairs. The gun the boy used was his father's, originally stolen, and from a cache of firearms found unsafely stored on the premises. If charged and convicted, the father was looking at a minimum mandatory sentence of three years in jail. This would be after we sorted out the tragic suicide of his son, who had used a gun the father should never have had in the family home to begin with. For black-and-white thinkers, the father should face the full criminal consequences for his carelessness, regardless of the fact he realized his own grave mistake had ultimately contributed to his son's death.

Taking a step back and looking at it from a broader perspective should be considered. We obviously didn't want this to happen again and judging by the father's reaction, it could, this time with him being the next suicide victim. Consideration for public safety, including this family's, was first and foremost on our minds. If we were to permanently seize the firearms and prohibit the father from ever owning guns again, we had to charge the father criminally. In this case, that would come with an automatic three-year sentence of incarceration. None of us felt good about that outcome. The father was the primary breadwinner. If he went to jail for the next three years, there would be significant consequences for the rest of the family already grappling with the unfathomable loss of a brother and a son. How to proceed with this case weighed heavy on all of our minds.

Another investigator close to the case reasoned there must be something that could help and pored over the criminal statutes. He found a section within the law that was rarely used, but that would accomplish our objectives. Removal and destruction of the guns would spare the father from incarceration but still prohibit him from ever owning guns again. It did require extra work writing applications to the court, and something we had never written within a context like this before. For all of us, it felt like the right thing to do. Our actions were affirmed a decade later when I received an unexpected call from the father. He just wanted to touch base and say, "thank you," closing the loop for me and this story.

As mentioned in chapter two, successful people come up with alternative solutions to difficult problems. That is exactly what this investigator did. Because of his efforts, the family could pick up the pieces of their lives together, with nobody going to jail. There are times when discretion can make an immeasurable difference in a person or family's life. This was one of those times.

Policing 101 teaches us that when it comes to the management of witnesses, it is a best practice to keep them separated until investigators have had an opportunity to speak with each. This is sound logic in a lot of cases because it avoids the potential for contamination of their statements and their evidence. In many cases, police witnesses do not have to be eyewitnesses. In homicide cases, most people who provide information are actually providing evidence of the backstory. Witnesses may have information about the last time they saw the victim alive, problems they may have had with other people, or criminal behavior. What happens when witnesses are also victims of a crime? Should the rules learned in Policing 101 still hold true?

Several years ago, I was involved in investigating an extremely sad and brutal case of murder. It was an early spring morning when a father of three came home from work to discover his wife and youngest child had been slain inside the family home. The husband first found his wife, still in her nightgown, lying motionless on the kitchen floor while cartoons played on the main floor television. It was clear she had been the victim of a vicious stabbing. On the edge of the kitchen counter was the little one's lunch still packed for preschool. Racing through the house and calling out his youngest's name, the father ran up the stairs and into the master bedroom, where he found his little one massacred on the floor. Armed with only a back scratcher, the five-year-old had been no match for the knife-wielding intruder. When we arrived on the scene, we brought the husband in for questioning to hear his backstory (typical protocol). The surviving children, who were all in school when the murders occurred, were also brought to our headquarters for the same purpose. Once at the station, each was to receive the news about their mother and youngest sibling's passing. It became the discretion of our investigative team on how best to do this. Should investigators have all the family members brought together for the delivery of the news (discretionary choice), or should each be told separately (by-the-books protocol)?

For all of us in the unit, this was a no-brainer. In this instance, the need for compassion for the surviving children far outweighed following the protocol of witness management. The horrible news was delivered to everyone together. Does the use of discretion in this way affect the investigation in the short term? It does. But regardless of this fact, in this case, and cases like these, putting others before ourselves trumps everything, and I am blessed to work with a group of people who see it that way, too. How do we know we made the right decision in this case? Because the alternative wasn't conscionable. Imagine the outcome if, after each child had been told the awful news, they were left to deal with it on their own, sobbing in a room while a stranger looked on.

Something I learned long ago from one of my old-dog mentors is that you should never mind being in the news but never have your actions make the headlines for the news. If discretion had not been applied in the cases above, what could the headlines have been? Asking myself this question is a simple exercise that has always helped me identify if I am doing the right thing.

This, no doubt, seems like common-sense stuff, but if people lose sight of common sense by being policy-driven or only thinking in black and white, they can forget the big picture. This can lead to the uncomfortable position of making poor decisions.

Long before I was ever a police officer, I was a sales associate for a large retail outlet and remember watching in dismay as a shocking scenario unfolded. A mother whose baby had been stillborn came into the retailer to return the unused car seat and baby swing, both in the boxes and with a receipt. She was approximately two weeks past what was printed on the refund and exchange policy, and the sales associate, citing store policy, refused to complete the transaction despite her story. What were the consequences of his decision? An upset and sobbing customer, a bewildered store employee (me), and no doubt the life-long loss of that customer and anyone she ever told the ordeal to.

When it comes to applying discretion, police and prosecutors use the law and precedents as guiding principles. This can seem quite subjective, but it is an important first step when considering the application of discretion. Before a charge is laid, certain questions need to be answered. Are there reasonable grounds to believe an offense has been committed? Is it in the public interest to lay the charge? What is the reasonable likelihood that the accused will be convicted? The answers to these questions are where the circumstances of a case and discretion can meet.

Several years back, I was involved in an investigation where a police officer was attacked with a tire iron. In the melee, the officer fired his gun, paralyzing but not killing the offender. The injuries the officer received were minor compared to what the offender sustained, arguably because the officer took the action he did. In comparison, the offender received a debilitating injury that put him in a wheelchair, changing his life forever. Consideration was applied in determining what the offender's fate after attacking an officer with a tire iron should be. While I deliberated with the crown prosecutor, we considered whether it would be in the public's best interest to prosecute and potentially incarcerate the offender, considering the extra care this person would require in jail. What would the cost be to society versus the benefit? The offender had also already paid his pound of flesh, and then some, and would likely not serve more than two or three months if convicted. The charges for the assault against the police officer did not proceed further, and the officer was cleared of any jeopardy, as well.

I have also been involved in several cases where homeowners have killed intruders and were later determined to be *non-culpable to homicide*. In these cases, the concept of *reasonable likelihood of conviction* was weighed against the right to defend oneself. In Canada, the police and the public have a right to defend themselves or others from imminent harm or death. Self-defense is a viable defense when evidence and circumstances support this conclusion. As such, prosecutorial discretion can be applied to avoid a trial where the accused would argue for protection of himself or others.

A few summers ago, I had a case where this happened. A house in the south end of our city had become a place where drug users would often congregate. They'd get high, wake up, and do it all over again. Residences like these, referred to as "trap houses," do not just attract those suffering from addiction. They also become known locations where money and drugs can be found and become attractive targets for home invaders. In this case, an individual with an extensive history of violence made the fateful decision one August morning to visit the local trap house with plans to rob those inside of money and drugs. He approached the home from the west, made his way up the concrete stairs to the front door, and, with one kick, forced himself inside. He sprayed the occupants inside with bear mace while also brandishing a firearm. He made his way through the home, ransacking it as he went, until one of the occupants got the better of the situation and plunged a knife into his chest as he descended the basement stairs. Moments later, he succumbed to his injuries at the base of the stairs. The actions of the stabber were determined to be justified within the context of the law, and no charges were ever laid.

    This case is not unlike another I remember. A nineteen-year-old kid (the drinking age in this province) had been out with his girlfriend at a community pub. He had chosen not to drink and had offered to drive his girlfriend—who had consumed alcohol—home in her vehicle. Unacquainted with the nuances of her car, the kid fumbled through, starting the engine, popping the clutch, and stalling it before even leaving the parking spot. A group of bar patrons outside for a cigarette interpreted his clumsiness as a sign of impairment, and the initially well-intentioned group converged on the couple still inside the vehicle. Things escalated when one of the bar patrons opened the passenger door of the car and began striking and pulling the young female's hair, ripping out an earring when he pulled her from the vehicle to the pavement.

Fearing for his girlfriend's safety, the young man got out of the car to go to her aid. Another bar patron stopped the kid, pushing him back from the melee. The kid lashed back and took a swing at his aggressor, connecting with a single solid hit. The bar patron lost consciousness before falling and hitting his head on the pavement. The head injury was fatal. The kid called the police, checked on his girlfriend, and attended to the victim with first aid until emergency crews arrived. Because the boy was defending another, this tragic set of circumstances—based on these facts—was deemed justified, and he was spared a criminal charge despite a fatal outcome for the victim.

Discretion is not limited to tragic situations with high stakes.

Consideration creates a positive presence.

This is true. One Christmas holiday, I worked with a senior police officer who had the novel idea of handing out candy canes instead of writing traffic tickets on Christmas Eve. The motorists we stopped, happy to receive warnings and peppermint sticks instead of violation tickets—not to mention having a jollier story to be shared around the holiday dinner table—appreciated the initiative.

Another example where gray mattered was when our city hosted several large conferences that attracted large numbers of people protesting global issues and the conference topics. In a free and democratic society, peaceful assembly is an important right that, in my view, the police have a role in maintaining—for the safety of all that attend. So why, in so many instances, do these events end in rioting? In some cases, criminal elements who follow the protest groups and hide among the masses are to be blamed. In other cases, the absence of discretion by the police can ignite, instead of calm, agitated groups.

In the early 2000s, I was a part of the crowd management teams that attended to public safety during one of these contentious conferences. I witnessed firsthand how these protested events began and ended peacefully. Incident commanders masterfully made decisions that put officer discretion first and foremost. As large crowds marched through the streets, they did not encounter police wearing helmets and carrying shields and batons but instead were flanked by uniformed members on bicycles who tirelessly pedaled with the crowd and blocked intersections for safe passage, like they would for any other dignitary event going through the city. If the crowd took over an intersection, this was not met with resistance. Instead, it was accommodated like it is whenever police shut down an intersection following a serious accident. In the end, these discretionary actions led to peaceful assemblies in both instances, and not one window was broken or a can of tear gas deployed.

Discretion does have boundaries. I remember when the option of discretion was taken away with the bat of an eye. I had pulled over a car of flirtatious women whose attempts at flashing a little skin to avoid a ticket did not go unnoticed. I knew that anything other than issuing a summons that day could be perceived as something to do with their false adorations, and the driver received two tickets before being sent on her way.

Sometimes discretion can be eliminated due to the seriousness of a crime.

Nearly a decade ago, police were dispatched to a sudden death of a woman in the city's deep south. Once on scene, officers concluded the evidence, or lack thereof, left only one conclusion. Homicide.

The woman had an extensive psychiatric history of depression. She was found in the basement of the home, fully clothed, and lay deceased in the laundry room, suffering from multiple gunshot wounds to her body. The walls of the room had been wrapped in plastic—a clue which suggested the killer had been considerate of the mess his actions would make and potentially any evidence he would not want to be left behind. No firearm was present, but judging from the size of the gunshot injuries, it was a small caliber weapon, likely a handgun. The victim's eyeglasses had been removed and neatly placed on the top of the washing machine, a behavior I had personally seen many times in cases of suicide, not homicide.

The wrapping around the walls was also consistent with behaviors I had observed in past cases of suicide because of the deliberateness of consideration for the clean-up. However, with no weapon present and the victim shot multiple times, homicide was the only logical conclusion.

It took months for this case to ultimately reveal its truths. The primary investigator identified her assailant from a polygraph examination. The man had been this woman's lover for many years—a man who had cared deeply for her—had been the one to carry out her final wish, to end her life, thus removing her from the pain she had felt so sharply in this life. The pair had meticulously planned her death to the last detail, including a video she had made explaining her desire to die and her wish to have him kill her. The problem with this scenario is that although our country has recently made allowances in the law for doctor-assisted death for people suffering from extreme medical conditions, this was not doctor-assisted, and the illness was not terminal as defined by the law. Presented with this, the crown had a difficult decision to make, but it did. Her death was a result of one person taking the life of another, a homicide. The multiple gunshot wounds he inflicted on her body signaled intent, which means murder. Her death was planned and premeditated, which is first-degree murder, and there ends any discussion of discretion.

In the end, through litigation in the courts, this love-struck man eventually pleaded guilty to a lesser offense, though the ramifications were still catastrophic on his life and hers.

Another case where our ability to use discretion

simply wasn't possible occurred a few years ago. A mentally ill man attacked his sleeping wife, believing she was an intruder in their home. The couple had been married for decades and, by all accounts, still happy and in love when the husband was afflicted with dementia. Our hands were tied. We all felt helpless when the only remedy to secure the man the care he needed was to charge him with his wife's murder. (*Not criminally responsible* is a defense that can only be raised at trial. The police do not have the authority to make that call.) None of us were happy with that outcome. He would live out the rest of his life in the hell his mind had created, and we all hoped not in a jail cell. He is currently in a secure care facility with the support of his family.

When discretion is either ignored or applied at the wrong moment, its wisdom is missed.

I once watched a news story about a father who was distraught over a police officer's ill-placed discretion, which prevented him from holding his dying daughter's hand. The father and daughter had set off on a bike tour and were traveling south on the highway, just outside the city limits, when the daughter was hit by a vehicle that caused catastrophic injury. While his daughter lay dying along the roadway, the well-intentioned first officer on the scene went to the victim's aid. He asked the father to step back from her side, something the older man was not willing to do, and was then physically restrained. He could only watch helplessly as his daughter took her last breaths with a stranger. Later, the officer explained his actions. He had not wanted the father to experience further trauma. There was noble intent behind the censorship, but this case illustrates that.

We get into trouble when we assume we know what is best for another.

Making decisions for people in this way is not the business of police, or anyone for that matter.

As ambiguous as discretion can be, taking it away isn't a remedy. Many people bristle at photo radar, seeing it as a cash cow. I wonder if the more pertinent frustration is that it lacks discretion; there is no gray option. People want a chance to be heard, to share their side of the story. Why were they speeding? Why did they run the yellow light? Discretion can balance the lopsided power dynamic between driver and officer. A picture snapped of your license plate doesn't afford that connection or chance to relate.

Just as discretion has a firm place in law enforcement, so too does it pertain to everyday life when there are power dynamics at play. The one and only time I received a bench misconduct in hockey was when I was coaching my son's team, and we were getting a thorough trouncing. The score was ten to zero midway through the third period. When the eleventh goal slid into our net, our goalie became frustrated.

Before the puck was dropped again at center ice, he skated from his crease to the corner boards, smashing his stick into them. Now, this is not a move we, as coaches, would ever condone, but it was something I also understood in these circumstances. Still, the action needed addressing properly, and the next break in the game would be a good opportunity. Unfortunately, that option disappeared when the adult referee blew his whistle and assessed our goalie a misconduct penalty. When the referee skated toward the penalty box to provide our player's number to the scorekeeper, I asked him if we could have a moment with our player to speak with him. His narrow-minded response was to get one of our players off the ice to serve the penalty (another player serves the penalty, so the goalie remains in the game). I pleaded my case further and reminded this official that just because he could didn't mean he should, empowering him to look at the lopsided score. This middle-aged weenie's response was to shoo me from the bench with a couple of hand gestures. At this moment, I took on a new motto: *if you're going to do the time, you might as well commit the crime.* The blast doors came off, and I earned every repercussion that followed. The lesson of this story is not that I was a fiery coach who lost my shit after someone chose not to even consider discretion (let alone the way I would have). The lesson is when discretion is not applied appropriately, it can spark unnecessary tension. I know I made the wrong choice in that circumstance. It is a great example of how the lack of discretion can become a flashpoint. We can't make someone use discretion, but we can decide how we will react (and I know I blew it).

> *When we only think in black and white, we can become narrow-minded to the greater game playing out before us.*

Several weeks later, I was attending a friend's son's hockey game, the city championship game final. Both sides were there to win. I was standing behind the opposition goalie's net when the first goal of the game went in. Devastated, the goalie lay there in his crease, refusing to get up and kicking his pads into the ice. The thirteen or fourteen-year-old referee skated over to this young man, placed his hand on his back, and said, "It's okay, buddy; there is lots of time left, and you have a good team in front of you." There was no penalty assessed, and the goalie took the opportunity this young—yet official—discretion provided. He puffed himself up and stood in the net to finish the game.

I think we all know what it feels like when someone does something to us just because they can and also when someone chooses not to.

Absolutes

> *Absolutes can be dangerously limiting.*

By choosing to see the shades of gray, we don't

paint ourselves into corners with no graceful way of getting out. It is not fence walking; it is recognizing that other possibilities may exist. The truth is we don't have to win every argument, and it's okay to agree to disagree. In the courtroom, defense counsels make short work of black-and-white thinking; there are simply too many variables to successfully defend an absolute. Good lawyers know this and obliterate those who have boxed themselves in with certainty when uncertainty could exist. They may ask questions such as, "Officer, is it possible the fingerprints were left behind from another time and are not related to this incident?" Or, "Officer, is it possible that the witness misheard what was said?" Defending either one of these questions with an absolute "no" is erroneous. The possibility could exist.

A firmer footing is to recognize that the possibility may exist but to provide your reasons why that would be unlikely or improbable.

For example, if the question was posed to an investigator on the stand, "Is it true that DNA cannot be dated?" A black-and-white thinker may simply answer yes and then move on. Would that answer be the full truth of the evidence they are providing to the court? The following would be more comprehensive. "Yes, I would agree that the victim's DNA cannot be dated; however, the victim's DNA comes from blood swabs taken from the scene. The scene showed there had been a major bloodletting event inside the residence, and at autopsy, it was determined that the victim had suffered a major injury that would have caused substantial bleeding. I believe it is unlikely the DNA comes from a time different from the time of the crime."

I have plenty of practice understanding how this questioning can go in court. Not everyone has had the same opportunity. I investigated a liquor store robbery where it was alleged that the gloved-up and disguised perpetrator had entered the liquor store with the intention of robbing it. The robber asked the store clerk to put the money in the bag as he held open his jacket to reveal the butt of a gun sticking out from his waistband. Scared, the clerk complied and filled the robber's bag with the day's earnings. The accused then turned and ran out of the store.

At the trial, the defense counsel asked the clerk if it was possible that the robber had been asking for something other than money to be put into the bag and that, instead, the panicked clerk had misread the intent of the "customer" and complied with a direction that was never given? The clerk truthfully answered, "I guess so, maybe." She stopped her answer there, leaving the argument open that it was all just a big misunderstanding. After recognizing that the possibility did exist (which was her honest answer), the clerk could have shared why she didn't think that was likely. "I guess so, maybe, but I think it unlikely because along with the words that I heard the accused say to me, I also noticed that he was disguised and wearing gloves, handed me an empty bag, showed me what appeared to be a gun in his waistband, and left the store running. All of these circumstances led me to think I was being robbed and that I did not misunderstand what he had said." That answer may have closed the door on any reasonable doubt arguments later.

Never fear other possibilities could exist.

We just need to be clear and share what we believe actually happened. In that way, accepting other possibilities is not at the expense of the whole truth as you know it.

Early in my career, I had the opportunity to watch another officer give evidence on a drug case in court. In this instance, the accused was alleged to have left cocaine in the police cruiser. It is a common procedure for police officers to search their vehicle each time a person is placed in the back. This is to ensure that things like drugs and weapons are not disposed of before the arresting officer discovers them. In this particular case, the officer testified there was no cocaine in the vehicle prior to the accused being placed in the back and that it was there after. Naturally, the officer was asked if it was possible he had missed the cocaine from an earlier search. It was awkward to watch as the officer insisted that there was no possibility he could have made a mistake, that it was absolutely left behind by the accused. The officer was answering the questions asked of him truthfully as he saw it, but he failed to see that the possibility did exist. In the end, the accused was acquitted, and I realized the danger of an uncompromisingly strict view.

Interviewing suspects or persons-of-interest is another great example of harnessing the wisdom of gray. Those in an interview (some still call it interrogation) are more likely to keep their mouth shut if you are openly judgmental. In my experience, when you let them know you are open-minded, that you recognize possibilities and hear them in the gray, it encourages them that you might actually understand.

> *People will say extraordinary things when given the space to be heard.*

When you have listened, resisted tunnel vision, and avoided putting blinders on, you may be given unexpected but no less honest answers.

I now know boxing ourselves in makes us less effective in communicating our points, let alone winning any argument. It can eliminate real dialog—closing off potential information and insights—and does not lend itself to having the time or the inclination for other people's opinions. This can lead to isolation and frustration.

What's right isn't always popular, or even what the "rules" say. For instance, police protocol has always been to give a scene back the way the police found it. This makes sense from a budgetary perspective. But sometimes, there are valid reasons to break with protocol.

I worked a suicide scene with a medical examiner who understood this point better than most. After we had finished at the home from a procedural standpoint, this medical examiner looked at the violently splattered bathtub—a sharp contrast to the otherwise pristine house—and recognized that we couldn't leave the scene the way we found it. Armed with a bottle of bathroom cleaner and some paper towel I was able to scrounge up, I held open the garbage bag while she meticulously cleaned that bathtub. Attending to the haunting task wasn't just relieving the family of it. It was identifying with the victim and the victim's family. In this case, it was clear the deceased had made an effort not to make a mess for others to clean up, choosing the bathtub and pushing all the bathroom accessories to one corner of the room, as far away from the tub as possible. The medical examiner did what she could to make an incredibly difficult situation fractionally better for the family members who would have to return back to their home.

In another of my cases, an adult son had borrowed his father's vehicle and, while out, had been beaten to death. The vehicle was impounded as evidence at the start of the homicide investigation, and the father quite reasonably wanted it back. There was no washing facility at the impound, but how could this vehicle simply be released to him? His son's teeth, hair, and biological material were still on the car. A cleaning service was called, and a month later, when the bill came, a co-worker suggested that the decision to clean the vehicle "set a bad precedent" for everyone else in the unit.

The existing protocol was a bad precedent and didn't consider the traumatic implications of such a restrictive policy. The prescribed process of doing nothing was ill-conceived. The decision to clean that vehicle should not be regretted—it came from a place of empathy, compassion, and understanding. It isn't always popular to do the right thing, but that is how positive change is given a chance. Visionary people understand the value of new ideas and that doing the right thing is an ever-changing scale of discretion. During my time in homicide, I have seen this beautiful shift. Remember,

Just because something has always been done one way doesn't mean it is the right way.

White Picket Fences

*"Human nature is so constituted that all
see and judge
better in the affairs of
other men than in their own."*

- Terence

Not everyone lives behind white picket fences.

Not even close, I saw this first-hand as a member of the Organized Crime Section (OCS); the first three years, I was on the Drug Undercover Street Team, and the last two, I was an Organized Crime Investigator. I was involved in purchasing illicit drugs from mostly street-level traffickers. In this world, we were like chameleons, changing our appearances and mannerisms to blend into different environments. That camouflage allowed us to witness a unique perspective, to live in two worlds. At the time, I didn't know I would become part of my own social experiment. A workplace can provide a breeding ground for experience—that's true anywhere, but I had no clue of the depth of the social lessons I would learn here. Reflecting on it, I now realize the profound effect this experience had on me.

We all have a story. What happened, or didn't happen, that led us to where we are today. What I saw, especially during my time in the OCS, is that most who are marginalized didn't earn it on their own. They had help from others, those who abused them, those who hurt them, those who betrayed trust or set them up for crippling blows—or they fell to the staggering challenges of mental illness. I also learned that within this world of beaten, weary souls, there were many predators ready to exploit a person's vulnerability for their own gain.

Some turn to the street to live a fantasy that their life can be like the music videos, where gang life is glorified, and belonging to a group—any group—brings instant happiness. It may be hard for some to understand, but this scenario of belief actually happens. This type of messaging—the possibility to score big and score fast—can be an overpowering out to those who come from incredibly challenging circumstances. They want to buy those gold chains, fancy jeans, fast cars, and party with the prettiest girls. Several Hollywood movies have exploited this same notion further—have sex with strangers for money, and you will find your Mr. Right. Many in the drug and prostitution subculture (they go hand-in-hand) don't often become aware of the reality until they face jail time. That's when the *oh-shit moment* dawns, and they realize just how far down the rabbit hole they let themselves fall. By then, it is often too late to make an "easy" break, and any life choice adjustments will come with steeper climbs.

I had been working undercover in the city's downtown core for several years and had become familiar to many in that world. One thing I figured out pretty fast is that reading something in a briefing or a textbook doesn't give you the same nuanced data as observing it in person. You see things in living color.

One evening, I entered a particularly notorious drug corner where our intel had directed us. As we sat in our undercover vehicles before work, with the windows providing a full 360-degree pan around the vehicle, we could see the brief flashes of lighters flicking on and off in the darkness as people took "hoots" of crack cocaine from their pipes. The frequency reminded me of watching a dark field with fireflies—that subtle yet constant flickering light. Clearly, we were in the right spot, but the sheer volume of the flashes of flame confirmed the problem here was worse than our information had suggested.

This was not the only time I had an opportunity to see how bad it could be for some. Years ago, I was presenting at a Western Canadian Gang conference in Vancouver, British Columbia, and had the unique opportunity to spend a night shift with two extraordinary officers who worked the city's East Hastings area. The district was notorious following the capture of Robert Pickton, a serial killer who preyed on vulnerable women working the strolls in this community.

Pickton wasn't the only thing that put East Hastings on the map. It remains notorious for massive opioid consumption. Heroine, methamphetamines, fentanyl—these drugs are responsible for taking catastrophic numbers of lives. They destroy families and annihilate the people suffering from their addictions. East Hastings continues to be the last stomping ground for anyone suffering from addiction's grasp, and in my view, it is really a place where people go to die. Despite this, community efforts to curb this trend, such as safe consumption sites, are also prevalent in the area.

On the night of my walkabout, I remember showing up at the station to meet the officers I was going to walk the beat with. They were young, enthusiastic, and kind—definitely the right temperament—who could be entrusted to help serve this very difficult community with specialized needs. Policing in this type of situation requires an ability to ignore the more shallow offenses—it is unlikely you would get thirty steps from the police station before coming across something minor that could result in an arrest. In a policing scenario like this, shallower, nuance-type crimes are ignored to allow officers to sink deeper into this world and access the most serious crimes plaguing the area.

I remember at the beginning of the shift, as the officers were at the equipment counter, they were provided their Tasers, pepper spray, radios, and a package of cigarettes—these would be dispersed to anyone they came across that may help them with the latest street gossip or rumors. This tact seemed to work. I watched throughout the shift as the partnership was approached, often by those in the final swirls of addiction, willing to provide a little bit of information about "bad dates"—the gangster drug traffickers and those who preyed on the most vulnerable in this community—for a little tobacco.

What stuck with me the most that night was the alley walk. Behind the rundown hotels that lined the front street, in the alleyways, the really bad stuff happens. Walking carefully down the center, the smells of human excrement were foul in the damp urban air. Along our route, on both sides of the alley block, people slept under thick blankets to stay warm. As we slowly made our way down the corridor, each officer made sure to check each person along the route with a little tap on the foot with their boot to make sure they still stirred. As they did so, I was shocked that sometimes a rat—or three—would scurry from the warmth of their human counterpart and take off down the alley. It is hard for me to believe this could even happen in our country. But it does, it does happen. Addictions, undiagnosed or unchecked mental health struggles, a series of bad choices that spiraled out of control—it is real people living in those tents and makeshift shelters that we hustle so quickly past. Some are dangerous, absolutely worthy of our wariness and a wide berth. Others, if given a different context, we would smile at in line for a coffee or as we check out our library books. But East Hasting isn't a library, and living on the streets, there is a death sentence.

I am grateful for those two officers who took me on that night shift—providing me with experiences I had never seen during my own tenure undercover.

In my world, it looked like men often destroyed themselves from the outside; they were more aggressive, more abusive, and more violent. Women appeared to be more apt to destroy themselves from the inside; they were promiscuous, seeking love from anyone who would pay attention and often selling their bodies for sex—for that next high. From my experience, the street pricing of drugs directly correlated to the street pricing for sex. It's a brutal reality for many.

The years I spent working undercover, I saw a lot of things, some pretty bad. I expected to see that that's what you prepare yourself for. I didn't expect to make personal connections with people cast aside by the rest of society. One particular instance of this was Niki. I first met Niki in a bar where she had entered that night seeking warmth, and I mean literally. It was a cold night, and she had been selling herself on the street. Her vice was crack cocaine, which she was getting and selling for the target of our investigation. Niki was likely a very attractive girl back in her day; she had blond hair and delicate features but was now very thin, gaunt even, likely from the dope. Her cheeks were hollow, and I remember her eyes. They were sad and held way too much resignation. Over the next several weeks, Niki would often return to the bar, flip her hair, and pick up her supply of dope, but before she would head out, we would always have a pleasant little conversations about her day or night.

Then, one day, I was hanging around another drug trafficking front, this time at a local grocery store. Unknown to me at the time, Niki had been spotted by members of the surveillance team. They saw her walking along the sidewalk toward me and then quickly dart off into an alleyway. Once in the alley, Niki took off all her clothes and reached into her backpack. Standing there stark naked, Niki pulled from her pack a fresher, prettier dress. She put it on, spritzed herself with perfume, applied makeup, and left the alley, heading directly toward me. That day, I had a lovely conversation with a really confused, messed-up girl I knew was seeking more than just friendship. She was smitten because I had been kind to her. Looking back on it now, this was one of the more flattering moments of my life, but it was also sad because it showed the vulnerability of people like Niki who live on a street full of predators. I realized the important lessons Niki provided me. Even the drug-addicted, marginalized members of our communities still seek the things all of us want: comfort, companionship, love, and the recognition that

Often, those who are not the easiest to love are the ones who need it the most.

First Impressions

I've always known how we present ourselves matters. It can communicate more firmly than words who we are and what we want people to think or know about us. Even understanding this, the first six months of my undercover career had a steep learning curve. I felt like a rookie all over again. I had to lose the polish a uniform provides. I needed to learn a new language and a different way of carrying myself—slouching instead of standing tall. I also learned an important lesson about keeping things simple.

My sergeant at the time was a wise, veteran police officer who had spent years working within the shadows. He had advice for us younger officers when it came to putting into play our fictitious backgrounds or cover stories—sometimes less is more. He used a prophylactic analogy to make his point. "When someone buys a pack of condoms, the guy doesn't get into it with the store clerk about what he is buying the condoms for or what his intentions for the night are. Buying condoms is embarrassing, and for a lot of people, so is buying drugs." He asked, "Why do we need to go and explain ourselves on the reasons we are buying dope or what we're doing with it later? Most people suffering from drug addictions don't, and neither should we." He was right. In the environment we were working, less was more and impressions everything.

Daily, I took on the tasks and challenges of living in this fictitious role. I grew an unkempt beard, changed my clothes, and acted the part. It was like a puppy growing up, one day, you just wake up a dog. As I moved through this process, something else was occurring. The community I had always been a part of was also changing, at least toward me. People would move across the street to avoid me. They stopped approaching in the grocery store or asking for directions. When I crossed an intersection on foot, I could hear the locks of people's cars click.

It took about a year to really master this persona that masked the real me. My beard had grown long and straggly, hanging well down my chest, my ears had numerous piercings, and many of my shirts and hoodies were adorned with heavy metal icons. I learned what it felt like to be marginalized by my community. My children, by association, learned it, too.

My family and I were fortunate to live in a nice middle-class neighborhood where appearance and status mattered. One day, my three-year-old son and I had been sent to run errands and pick up groceries for the week. Like any other day, we entered the store and went about our business, selecting our eggs, milk, meat, and cereals. Happy, my son sat in the cart as we made our way through the store. As we turned down our next aisle, I heard a young boy say, "Look at that guy, Mom." My son and I both turned to see a young boy with his well-groomed mother pointing at me. "Look at that guy, Mom," he repeated, this time catching his mom's attention. As her eyes met mine, I saw them widen before an expression of fear or disgust flashed on her face.

"Quiet," she said to him, and they promptly fled the aisle.

Without missing a beat, my boy, realizing what had just happened, put his hands on mine and rubbed them, proclaiming, "You're the best dad ever. I love you."

That day stayed with me, my son's innate social wisdom and compassion, and the knee-jerk reaction of the well-heeled mom and her son. That response became our new normal. Whenever I was with my spouse and kids, at the zoo, the mall, or an amusement park, people stared. The judgment and disapproval were clear, *those poor kids*. When they saw the pretty brunette with me, I could only assume those confused stares meant they were trying to figure out if she was my sister or maybe my parole officer. I'm certain they never suspected she was my wife at the time.

These experiences were damaging to all of us. I understood when I was asked not to pick the kids up from school or when my family would whisper quietly to neighbors my real persona. They were embarrassed by me. This world took a toll on all of us and only compounded with time. The family unit, after being pushed and strained too far, sadly began to unravel. Living that experience taught me important lessons.

> *We should resist comparing our life to others, we really have no idea what their path is.*

It also taught me to be much more empathetic toward the marginalized and disadvantaged. In the past, I had often thought, "Why can't these folks get jobs? Why aren't they working? Why is he wearing his underwear on the outside of his pants?" Now, I know that's easy to say if you are a person who adheres to the traditionally accepted undergarment layer order, or you have an appearance that is inviting instead of off-putting, or you just naturally know how to walk tall and speak eloquently. Now I know first-hand if you are not those things, some in society will devalue and judge you harshly. I also learned you must care for yourself if you wish to have others care for you. Like it or not, first impressions count.

> *If we want to influence how others view us, we must match our actions to our intentions.*

What surprised me the most was my isolation went relatively unnoticed until the day I left undercover work. I shaved off the overgrown beard, put on a suit again, and walked out the door, this time back into the real world, or at least what had been my real world before the undercover work. What had taken months, that incremental slipping until I was a shunned character of society, was gone in moments. When people smiled at me again or just said good morning, I reeled from the culture shock.

This was the greatest eye-opener of my life. I realized with unexpected clarity how isolated a person can be from their larger community simply because of how they dress and carry themselves. Not everyone can take off the mask. They might not know how, or have the means to, or simply have the desire, so they stay isolated and alone in a city of a million and a half.

Respect

Respect is a currency.

Regardless of the social standing or segment of society in which we find ourselves. It is foundational for building trust and relationships, not to mention ingratiating yourself into groups of people—which is a key component to successful undercover work. Maybe it is even the keystone because in the darkest corners of our society, respect matters. It was once explained to me by a career criminal type that when people give you their word on the street, it is an incredibly potent gift because they have little else to give.

On the street, if someone went against their word or disrespected another's view, things could boil over quickly. I was part of an undercover drug purchase in a high-intensity drug-trafficking area. These areas earn the designation due to a high volume of drug-related crimes and tips from the public describing illegal drug activity. Obviously, these high-intensity areas became important to target. One night, a member of our undercover team learned the value of respect when he tangled with the wrong female. She had tried to short him on a drug amount and, thinking he was playing the part, he called her an inappropriate name. She struck him on the back of the head with a whiskey bottle for the disrespect he had shown her. In her world, it was okay to short him on the drug amount; he had not yet earned her respect and was fair game to be swindled. The greater misstep in her view, and worthy of violent reprimand, was him calling her an inappropriate name. In that world of heightened sensitivity and high stakes, there were rules of honor that strictly dictate conduct or consequences. We learned fast that words like "goof," or a belief you were a "snitch," could get you a knife in the back—quick.

Around the second anniversary of my time with the Drug Unit, our team heard quiet whispers on the street about the horrific death of a sex trade worker who had been erroneously identified as a snitch. It was alleged to have happened at the white house around the corner, the place where she was taken to be brutalized by a group of three girls. After several days of confinement and torture, they dumped some of her remains in a garbage bin near the home. Investigators, wary that these rumors were true, searched the dumpster near the house and found, among the bags of garbage, the scalped ponytail of the victim—with the hair tie still attached. After an intensive search that lasted weeks, the rest of her body was found inside a hockey bag at the city landfill.

In the shocking analysis of the case, we learned she had been viciously killed because they thought she had ratted out a couple of drug dealers several weeks earlier. She wasn't a snitch at all. She was an addict looking to buy drugs, with the seriously bad luck of being in the vehicle when the dealers were traffic-stopped and arrested by police. In the street conspiracy that followed, a few assumed that she had set up the dealers, which led three people to take it upon themselves to savagely reinforce the street code that *snitches get stitches*, leaving her as another murder statistic.

In the non-criminal world of business and family, disrespecting someone will probably not get you killed, but it could get you fired, passed over for the next big deal or promotion, or an earful from Aunt Mildred. The bottom line is respect—some see it as integrity—is a currency. It can be cashed in for preferred treatment or cashed out with appalling consequences.

Support Systems

Support systems are our parachute, our sanity check, and the warm blanket when we've gotten too cold. Undercover work requires them. Especially when your full-time job demanded mastering the dark arts of lies and deception. Anxiety and fear were normal working parts of the job, and isolation from the community was not only a side effect, but it was also a performance indicator. Our new normal was a world of sex (not that we could partake), drugs (couldn't do that either), and rock 'n' roll and rap (which we totally blasted in our cars all the time).

The team I worked with consisted of a supervisor and six constables. We were a band of brothers and one sister. The importance we placed on each other was high—it had to be. We relied on each other to ensure the safety of all, and our bond was tight. Through the years, we were there to support each other through the passing of loved ones and the births of new ones, all the while knowing it was our responsibility no one went home worse for wear. We all understood what the others were going through, and when a member of the team expressed concerns, we all listened.

In this high-stakes game where reality was troubling, dangerous, and often sad, I came to learn that having support mechanisms was critical to my overall health and well-being. Unlike the Hollywood concept of having a handler tame the too-deep undercover operator, our support mechanism came by way of regular debriefings within the team itself. Each of us had strong, confident personalities, and our debriefs were rarely about butterflies and hugs. We would often disagree about how things should be done and openly share our critiques of how each did. These were always honest and, for the most part, healthy discussions. At the end of the day (or night), our practice was to debrief each other—and air out any dirty laundry in what I affectionately came to know as *big-boy debriefs*.

Leaving pride and ego at the door, we would all meet in a safe location to discuss the day's events. Feelings would sometimes get bruised, and guys would fall on the sword if they needed to. But being able to just say it as it was, diplomacy and fear of political correctness aside, was our way of ensuring that we all were performing at our highest levels and learning through our mistakes. There was never mincing of words, which was a good thing, and those debriefs kept each of us on our toes and, perhaps more importantly, kept us honest with each other, even if sometimes our pride got battered in the process.

Those debriefings taught me the risk of offending should never outweigh the value of learning from our mistakes and honestly sharing what we are feeling. It is a valuable lesson I still take with me to this day, and I know—

Grudges have room to grow when we are not free to speak openly.

Big-boy debriefs taught me a lot of things: support systems matter, not everyone needs a trophy for participating, and honest communication can create harmony, whether that be within a work environment, a hockey dressing room, or even the family unit.

Adaptability, Boundaries, and Chasing the Shiny Object

Two of the biggest issues that arose during our briefings and debriefings involved setting parameters and keeping the investigation focused by not chasing shiny objects—when investigations produce bigger leads to follow, often at the expense of the original investigative goals.

In an undercover operation, there are controls or parameters put in place for safety reasons, but if those boundaries are too strict or too loose, they can cause issues. As we discussed in chapter three, absolutes can be problematic, and this applies especially to undercover operations.

I was once involved in a case where, after making several drug purchases from an individual with an extensive violent criminal history who was known to carry a gun, it was decided that this particular day would be the takedown. The target would be arrested after my final meet. In the briefing prior, I was informed that I would need to be at a specific location, at a specific time, so the arrest could be made—a simple enough plan if the target agreed. That's a big if. As the operation unfolded, it became clear that he wanted to meet somewhere else, and we argued. In the end, I was successful in getting him to go where we needed him to go, but when he did, he was pissed. Very pissed. The parameters meant to keep me safe now placed me in extreme danger as he reminded me in not-so-kind words that he was doing me a favor. The arrest team moved in and took the target into custody, but not before I was placed at unnecessary risk by the inflexibility of the parameters set out.

On the flip side, I also remember a case where, after infiltrating a new drug target, a member of our team was given less stringent parameters, and we were all caught off guard when he got into the suspect's vehicle, and it took off at a high rate of speed. Scrambling to keep an eye on our member, the suspect vehicle's taillights disappeared from view a number of times—which meant we had lost eyes on our guy. Thankfully, everything worked out, and our undercover made his drug purchase without incident.

Parameters can be so loose as to be dangerous. Finding that happy medium can be difficult, but it is necessary to set rules with contingencies that allow for appropriate adaptation.

Staying adaptable gives us the agility to see our choices.

The second big issue, chasing shinier objects, challenges many organized crime and narcotics investigators. Investigations, like so many things in life, can get away from us when they grow disproportionately fast. Staying on task and adjusting goals as needed keeps the operation in check. The investigation of criminal groups usually starts with focusing on one or two primary targets. However, the tendency is that as the operation picks up speed, more and more people (targets) are added. When this happens, the initial targets become less and less the focus because the investigators begin chasing the newer, shinier object. This simply does not work out the way it is intended, and months can go by before someone steps up and realizes that the operation is doing a hundred different things—but nothing particularly well.

I remember several cases where we observed large drug trafficking operations and decided not to act immediately because we didn't want to jeopardize a larger drug score from a future investigation. Sometimes, that future larger shipment never arrived, and the original drug trafficking operation did not produce the expected results. Similarly, working with lower-end criminal groups led us to places where higher-end groups and gang members were often seen associating with our lower-end targets. The investigations would then shift focus to those higher-impact individuals. That didn't always pan out, and in the meantime, the lower-end individuals had slipped our radar. We called these diversions *chasing the kilo fairy*.

As in life, taking smaller, manageable slices of a big pie will help keep the focus on what the original mission or goal was. Taking on too much will result in spinning wheels and can often lead to either no results or less than desirable ones. Shiny objects should not necessarily be dismissed, but it is important to be aware they can quickly modify focus and our resources. It's a balancing act. Like the example from the East Hastings officers, know your goals and pivot appropriately.

Loyalty versus Secrets

> *"If you reveal your secrets to the wind, you should not blame the wind for revealing them to the trees."*

Artist and poet Khalil Gibran wrote those words that bring to mind my undercover days. I imagine, for some, there is a struggle with the whole notion of undercover police work. It involves trickery, deception, and eventually breaking the bonds of friendship when the target of an operation goes to jail because of secrets shared in confidence with a person they thought they knew. I don't know if this helps, but there are rules (laws) that we must follow. Trickery must pass a public shock test, meaning: would the public be shocked at the conduct of the trick? For example, filling a syringe of saline solution, injecting it into an accused's arm, and calling it a truth serum would not pass this test. Neither would actions that violate the sexual integrity of a person, actions that could cause substantial damage to property, or those that place people at imminent risk of danger. Police must also be able to pass a random virtue test, meaning investigators have to explain why a person was targeted in an undercover sting in the first place. There must be a justifiable reason to commence an operation. In other words, randomly selecting a person off the street and running with it to see where it goes wouldn't pass the sniff test.

Knowing these rules exist will hopefully help put some minds at ease, but perhaps it is the deception of the fictional friendship that is so offensive. The betrayal of trust is a serious social injustice that most of us recognize, and it goes without saying undercover work creates these situations where, in the end, trust will be betrayed. As a former undercover cop, I had to reconcile with my social conscience that what I was doing was right, even if I felt like shit about it. I developed my own philosophy around secrets and trust, and today, when I speak publicly on this topic, I address my personal feelings around this issue.

I hope we all have a confidante, someone with whom we share what is too personal for general consumption. Someone we trust. When we share these private thoughts, desires, and secrets with them, it is either expressed or inferred that it is not to be broadcast to the world. If it is released, of course, there is a sense of betrayal. Most of these cases are what I call *good secrets* and, for the most part, benign. Things like "I have a crush on that boy" or "I called in sick today to sit on a patio with some friends," in the grand scheme of things, are not what I would consider a big deal because, if kept, they would not harm another. When people breach secrets like these, I agree they are, in fact, snitching.

On the other hand, *bad secrets* are exactly that—bad. If kept, they will compromise someone's safety. "I am scared to go home because my father hurts me" or "my boyfriend is committing armed robberies" are obviously secrets that compromise people's safety and need to be reported, even if that fractures the relationship. This is not snitching. It is being a courageous friend or a concerned community advocate.

Being willfully ignorant of dangerous behavior is bad secret-keeping.

For parents or those with young people in our lives, this lesson may resonate more than we are comfortable with. While watching our children grow up, how many of us have been exposed to a bad secret involving a friend of our children or a parent to one? When this happens, of course, it is uncomfortable, and in many cases, that uncomfortability will cause us to do exactly what we shouldn't—nothing.

Today's generation of children are routinely messaged to come forward when they have heard or seen something they know is not right and to tell an adult. When they do, the buck stops with the adult they told. That could mean us. Whether we like it or not, it is our responsibility to take further action, though I suspect sometimes we don't because sharing bad secrets can be scary. I have a story that sadly demonstrates my point.

When I was in elementary school, a classmate demonstrated actions daily that, as kids, we didn't understand. We only knew something seemed off, but any adult, I am certain, would have seen some of these same things as major red flags. To be clear, I don't have specific recollections of adults witnessing her behaviors (drinking, smoking, inappropriate humor). However, I suspect that among a bunch of hyped-up grade-six kids, rumors were likely rampant about her activities. For this reason, I believe some of her most concerning behaviors would have landed in the ear of an adult in a position to address at one time or another - but didn't.

One such instance of alarm occurred when the young girl in this story stood in the middle of the school playground and allowed a line of boys to wait their turn to put their hands down her pants—an action that would signal to most adults that something was very wrong, something deeply troubling and symptomatic of a bigger issue likely going on at home.

On that day, I stood back on the sidelines and witnessed something I knew wasn't right: a bad secret. I am not sure my eleven-year-old self knew what to do, and forty years later, I realize I likely did nothing—a regret I have to this day and think about often. You see, this young girl grew into a young woman who, in our Grade ten year, left our school and went on to support herself as a sex trade worker. In the early nineties, as we were all graduating from high school, she went missing, only to be found murdered on the outskirts of our city a few months later.

Her cold case homicide file still sits in our file room, a haunting reminder to me of the devastating consequences of not actioning bad secrets if and when we receive them. We can all:

Do better. Be better.

If we are to live in vibrant, strong, safe communities, we must not turn a blind eye and pretend we don't notice the swollen lip and black eye of the kid who just walked past. Truthfully, some of the saddest child murder cases I have investigated uncovered witnesses (after the fact) who chose to ignore the black eye of the little girl whom they had seen playing in the front yard a week prior to her death, or what they believed could be signs of abuse and neglect of a boy who looked gaunt and unwell.

While undercover, I received and actioned bad secrets. We all did. If someone was selling cocaine, I told. Why? Because, by not telling, it put the greater community at risk. Were there people I liked in this world? Of course. But that did not stop me from doing what was right for the community and sometimes even the target. I'm still sheepish to even admit this, but remember the story of Niki? She was one of those people I liked, and I felt terrible the day I learned arrest warrants had been issued for the drug crimes I had seen her commit.

Dark Places

Perhaps the greatest universal lesson I took away as an undercover operator was,

Staying out of dark places keeps us safe.

This also works as a powerful metaphor that can apply to all aspects of life. Many times, bad people would use the cloak of night to carry out crimes against our team. Often, there would be lures to go a little deeper into the alley or go for a drive to an unknown location, someplace visibility, exit options, or assistance were compromised—and our boundaries were pushed. Trusting our instincts, remaining adaptable, and staying within our parameters kept us safe. When we didn't, we opened ourselves up to being scammed, assaulted, robbed, or worse. This was more common than you may think, and we needed to be careful when we were in places the light of civility did not reach.

Addiction is a powerful force, and I witnessed many who took significant risks for their next high. One of the more common scams some would try included holding out pebbles or paraffin wax as crack cocaine, hoping the unsuspecting customer would not notice—and not adversely react—until after the pebble trafficker was gone with a fresh forty dollars in his pocket and on his way to buy his own real rock of cocaine.

In the early 2000s, cocaine was, without a doubt, the drug of choice on the street. Every day, we would leave the safety of our office to buy and infiltrate the groups trafficking it. There were other drugs, like methamphetamine and heroin, that were also very much a part of the city's drug scene. We knew if we could hook into a meth or heroin downline (the path drugs take to get to the street), it would help keep a finger on the pulse of the full drug scene and allow us a wider undercover experience—you learn different things through different experiences.

One day we decided to focus our efforts on finding a crystal meth dealer and maybe even a lab that produced what was known on the street as *jib* or *ice*, although a more accurate name could be *this-shit-will-blow-up-your-lif*e.

Up for the challenge, I volunteered to try my luck first. That night, I started along one of the frequented prostitution strolls—sex trade workers traditionally have a lot of street intelligence and know a lot of dealers. With that in mind, my first stop of the night was for the *boys' stroll*. The first person I met was a young male prostitute. He said he knew a good jib dealer and would call if I had the money, forty dollars for four-tenths of a gram of the drug. Wanting to see the deal happen, I produced the money, and without missing a beat, he grabbed it from my hand and, before I could blink, took off like a shot down a nearby alley, never to be seen again.

Once bitten, but not twice shy, I wasn't deterred from this minor setback and moved to another area of the downtown core. This time, I picked up a female sex-trade worker from the stroll who offered to take me to a house a few blocks away where she said I could find jib. As we drove, nothing seemed out of the ordinary, and she made conversation. Apparently, the cold that evening had made it a quiet night, and before I came along, she said she had only turned a couple of tricks and was happy to be in my warm car. She directed me to a house several blocks away, and I parked in the front. She told me she would need to show *paper* (money) to get through the front door.

Feeling a little uneasy about letting her go in on her own, I suggested we could both go in the house together. She quickly answered, "No way, the doorman will never let anyone he doesn't know in." Convinced she could be trusted, I forfeited my twenty dollars and told her I'd give her the rest of the money if there was dope in the house. Agreeing to my terms, she went with a spring in her step up to the front door and in. Ten minutes passed, and I began to worry I had been scammed again. The front door opened, and out she came, bounding back to my car. "Where's my dope?" I asked as she got into the passenger seat and giggled uncomfortably.

"They didn't have jib," she explained.

"Okay, then where is my twenty?" I asked.

"Ummm, I smoked it."

I was not impressed that I had been taken for a second time in less than an hour. After an adequate scolding, I dropped my would-be BFF at the end of the street where I had found her.

A scraggly-looking mess of a man sporting a black eye approached my car, asking if I was "looking for food?" which is common street vernacular for cocaine.

"Not coke, my friend, I'm looking for jib," I said.

"I know a guy. I'll take you there."

I figured twice bitten should mean the third time's a charm, right? So, with that, I invited him to jump in my car, and again, I was off with yet another "helpful" individual along the elusive trail of ice.

"Turn here," he said, and as we rounded the block, things began to look familiar. It was the same house I had just been at. Pulling up in front, my new friend advised me I needed to show paper to go inside.

"Listen, bud, I've done this already, and she smoked up the twenty I just gave her," I replied.

"I know there is jib in there. Give me the money, and I'll grab it and introduce you to the owner after."

"I'll give you twenty, but I'm holding your jacket

and one shoe as insurance that you're coming back."

"Okay bro, deal," he said, and out of the vehicle he went. Twenty minutes later, I was still sitting in my car with no dope. Things were not looking good when my phone rang—it was the boss. "Did you front that guy money?"

Shit. "Umm, yes, why?"

"He just ran out the back door not wearing a jacket and with only one shoe on."

That day, the third time, was clearly not a charm. Scammed three times in an hour, I reconciled that this is what happens when ego, stupidity, and trust meet with people who live in the darkest of places. The social norms I took for granted and even counted on in everyday life were not always reinforced on the street—except for maybe one:

Only lend to others what you can afford to lose.

In my experience, the drug dealers who could earn the most were also the ones found in the deepest shadows. In the drug subculture, like in any other business, the stakes get higher when greater profits are pursued. The difference in the drug world is that this means a greater risk of danger—from theft, assault, or even murder from competition.

To stay in as much of the light as the street can offer, we lived by the motto *cash is king:* we paid our debts immediately and never bought on credit. Not everyone on the street makes the same decision, and the risk they assume is significant and very real.

Unsurprisingly, working undercover means hanging out in dark and uncomfortable places. Once, I was sitting in a bar with a fairly "big fish" in the drug scene. He was a large man, respected on the street, and only known by a nickname. He had taken a shine to my partner and me, and we were invited to his table whenever we entered his bar—his drug territory. That night, I was sitting with this individual when he found out a young kid had just come into *his* bar and was selling crack cocaine out of the bathroom.

As we sucked back our second beer of the night, we witnessed an unfolding murder plot right before our eyes. Angered by the turf intruder in the bathroom, our target called a friend to bring a gun to the bar so the kid could be dealt with. When he hung up, he shared his intentions with us. Concerned that I was quickly becoming involved in this plot, over the next several minutes, I looked for ways to stop the conspiracy from unfolding, even suggesting ways I could help bring peace to the situation. In the end, I committed myself to the simplest solution; I excused myself from the table, walked outside, and called the "real" police to intercept the male before he got to the bar.

Living in dark places really does put people in jeopardy. Dark places don't have to mean drugs. They include any sketchy enterprises. I have been involved in numerous murder investigations that, when we uncover the victim and offender's history, we find the murky places where they have been living: bad business deals, secret lives, and addictions are just a few. In my view, making decisions that keep us in the light goes a long way toward our own mental and physical self-preservation and protection.

Working undercover was a time of steep, and deep, learning for me, and in shockingly unexpected ways. Those years cannot be undone, nor would I want them to be. They fundamentally changed me, I think, for the better. Knowing that not everyone lives behind a white picket fence has helped me make better decisions throughout my career. Remembering that some places are darker than we can ever imagine keeps me on what I consider the right path and allows me to thank my lucky stars for all the blessings I have had in my life, starting with the family I was born into.

Thinking From a Different Box

"A miracle is a shift in perception from fear to love."
- Marianne Williamson

Not all of our paths in life will be easy. Sometimes, our choices or our circumstances create tricky routes to navigate. This doesn't mean impassible or even unwanted in some cases. When we have been tested by fire, hotter than we could have known was coming, and come through the other side—even if singed—there is the potential for perspective, personal growth, and maybe even that often-elusive peace. We can do more than simply survive life. We *can* find our way to thrive, even under challenging conditions.

Our mindsets and attitudes can either support or undermine us.

You don't have to be a homicide detective to smack headfirst into troubling or challenging situations. This chapter is about helping you choose positive mental approaches in your life that will help you thrive through crisis, whatever your concept of thriving is.

In my career, some officers will leave with physical scars and many more with emotional ones. By last count, I have been involved in just over seven hundred cases of suspicious death and/or homicide in my fourteen years with the Homicide Unit and have seen well over a thousand bodies, most at the medical examiner's office. It's staggering how many people that represents and how many lives lived. The truth is this is mentally taxing work. It can take a toll on our mental stamina, our faith in humanity, and even our faith in ourselves to solve the most complicated of crimes. Some of my closest colleagues have confided that certain things trigger or haunt their psyche. For one friend, seeing the small hands of a child troubles him. For me, certain locations can trigger gruesome memories and tragedy.

Despite these things, we cope and thrive in the world where we work. I am regularly asked *how*? and I believe there are a few reasons. Humans are incredibly adaptable, and we get acclimated to crisis through exposure to it. Our scale of what is morbid and what is possible to see in a workday expands through experience—it must. Our brains have built-in mechanisms for dealing with terrible things, but we can also actively train our minds to develop and implement effective strategies that allow for coping.

I have been asked how, as police, we can consider ourselves as thriving when our divorce and suicide rates are high. It is true that law enforcement is one of the fields which significantly taxes individuals, and the people close to them, sometimes beyond repair. Regardless of our career, we each adjust our own personal scope of what it means to thrive so as to have meaning in our own lives. The sense of thriving, not just surviving, is personal. Knowing happiness—that key ingredient for thriving—is possible, even with constant exposure to the contrary, is necessary.

Emergency workers get proficient at processing the sights, smells, and sounds of grievous injury and death. This doesn't happen overnight. It can take years to reach this place. In the meantime, day after day, first responders have experiences that both demand and allow for them to develop strategies that work for them. I feel strongly that anybody can use these techniques to overcome challenges in their lives. At the very least, we can train our brains to recognize and appreciate the good that surrounds us. That's actually a perk of this job; being around death so much has given me an acute appreciation of life. That open, positive outlook in the presence of challenging situations is the essence of thinking from a different box.

Aversion to Acclimatization

Naïveté is a beautiful and pure part of the human condition, something to be admired, not despaired.

I feel it is a good thing, maybe even imperative, that

our loved ones and our community don't understand a specific brutal event, let alone the effect of compounding years of them. It means the images or experiences that scar the heart of the police officer have not bled into those around us. For me, this means there still exists an innocence in the people with whom we have relationships in our lives; we spare them the details of just how ugly life can get. I suspect health care practitioners, other first responders, soldiers, or anyone who has experienced great trauma have also had feelings that some in the community, or even their own family members, don't understand. Again, thinking from a different box, I can't help but think this is a blessing. If someone wasn't holding down the "beautifully innocent and naïve" fort at home, where would we have to go after coming back from the dark?

As touched on in chapter two, most police officers go through phases in their careers. I was no different and acclimatized to real-world violence, negativity, and sadness. It is true, over my past ten years in homicide, I have forgotten more of the violent death scenes than I remember. There are about a dozen that stick with me to my very core, but most do not unless I am reminded of them. Conversely, I remember almost all the death scenes I went to as a uniformed constable, including the benign, natural passings—as a young, naïve officer, I was still acclimatizing, still developing the necessary coping strategies I now use every day.

The first sudden-death call I ever attended was the

natural passing of an elderly woman. Family members found her in her home. Upon my arrival, they directed me to the back of the house, where I was told I would find their aunt in a back room off the patio. I did as directed, entered the house through the rear patio door, and almost tripped over the dead woman. She was seated in a cushioned rocking chair, her eyes wide open, her mouth gaping, a knitted afghan across her lap, and a glass of rum gripped in her hand. I had expected to have to walk through a room, a hallway, something, before encountering the deceased. It was a jolt to find her *right there*. From that point forward, whenever I attended a scene with a dead body, I would start by squinting, letting my eyelids and lashes blur the edges of reality, giving myself a few moments to orient to the scene before blasting myself with a full look. Now, my comfort with death—through my repeated exposure to it—has the same effect as my squinting eyes did when I was starting out as a uniformed officer.

Imagine if you were driving to work or school and you heard over the radio: "Breaking news, police are currently on scene investigating a suspicious death in the city's south end." An image likely appeared in your mind. When I do this experiment with recruits, I ask them to take it further. "What does the house look like? Where is the body inside the house? What is the gender of the deceased? Is the body clothed, and if so, in what? Is there blood, and if so, how much?" Most recruits place the *male* victim inside the house either on the couch, in the bedroom or on the kitchen floor, in their pajamas, or under the covers of a bed. Some imagine a lot of blood, but more do not. Most people can't imagine truly horrific or gruesome details because they, thankfully, have never experienced truly horrific or gruesome events. When those police recruits eventually work a real scene, one that doesn't match what's in their mind's eye, there will be a steep learning curve because they have to abruptly recalibrate what they are seeing with what they were expecting. I still remember one of those scenes vividly.

Early in my career, I was the first responding officer to a fatal motor vehicle accident involving a semi in a parking lot. I am sure you can picture the scene. So could I, until I arrived and found something very different. A petite, twenty-something female truck driver had fallen from the cab of her truck while it was rolling away as she was stepping into it. No other vehicles in the parking lot were involved. The truck had been left idling in neutral, and the parking brake had failed on the slight incline the truck was parked on. Tragically, she fell from the steps that led up to the truck's cab in such a way that her head landed in the path of one of the front tires. Her crushed glasses were the only thing left to landmark where her nose and eyes had been. My expectation going into the scene was drastically different from the reality. At the time, I did not have the coping mechanisms in place that I now possess to process what I saw. That image has stayed much longer than they do now.

In the scenario above, where I discuss the breaking news of a suspicious death, did your mind turn to the idea that the deceased could be a child? Or that the victim was naked, exposed, bound, and blindfolded? Did you imagine the victim's blood was on every wall and surface leading to it? Or that the weapon was an ax lodged with an eerie precision between the eyes? Did you imagine the house was full of flies and the victim badly decomposed? Chances are slim that any of those scenarios crossed your mind. To some degree, we all are naïve to the reality of violence until we are in a position where we are routinely exposed to it and must acclimate.

Cynics could argue that exposure to violence has anesthetized my brain. Maybe. But if it allows me to do my job and hasn't deteriorated my ability for compassion and empathy, it's a side effect I can live with.

I'm not completely desensitized, though. There are times when my mind still gets rocked, and my knees go weak because the scene in my head differs from the reality in front of me. Several years back, the body of a female was found under suspicious circumstances in a ravine, and we were called to investigate. My job was to attend the autopsy the following day. I had been briefed on the discovery of the body and the crime scene, which had included several pill canisters. I was also told there was evidence of *some* animal activity on the body and that the coyotes had to be shooed away by police upon arrival at the scene. Armed with this information, I attended the autopsy the following day. That person's definition of "some animal activity" was completely different from mine. I stared in shock at the half-eaten corpse on the metal table.

Thankfully, this guttural reaction is not completely foreign to me. It has certainly played out in other instances and reminds me I am still human. It returned not long ago when I attended the scene of a suspicious death of a toddler. Walking into the home, I was not prepared to see this little one in the condition he was in. He had been burned by a pot of boiling soup, with burns to ninety percent of his body that had been left untreated for more than a week. On the car ride back to the office, it was the first time I think I ever wept on a case. What that young lad must have endured still wrenches.

It also returned when my eyes cast upon pictures of a teenage boy who had been starved to death by his parents—confined in his room for years, they believed that "air was his food." Most recently, it returned when my eyes strained to see through the charred wreckage of a car the bodies of three people who had been savagely murdered. All of it unconscionable.

It is not foreign to my colleagues, either. In this new age of policing, body-worn cameras capture the gasps and shock of our officers, who are thrust into incredibly difficult situations every day. One particular case comes to my mind. Several years ago, just before Christmas, we were contacted by an emergency room doctor who, earlier in the day, had a patient come into the hospital complaining of hemorrhaging. An hour or so later, she delivered a "full term" placenta—but no baby. Concerned that the infant may have been delivered at home and in need of medical care, officers were tasked by the doctor to attend the home of the woman to look for the newborn infant.

With body-worn cameras rolling, the officers approached the front door of her home and entered. As they made their way through the residence, they noted several areas where blood could be seen and found a pair of bloody scissors in the kitchen sink. Moving to the garage, a seasoned, veteran officer made his way to the hatch of the women's car still parked inside. As he began to open the plastic bags within the hatch, he noticed one that was tied. Carefully untying the bag, his body-worn camera captured the moment he opened the bag, and the distinct outline of an infant could be made out. Shocked, the camera footage captured him standing over the open bag for a moment before he began to close it again, not believing what he was seeing, then returning back to it seconds later. It was the newborn, lifeless.

Later that afternoon, I called the officer to check on him and talk about what he had discovered. He recalled the moment he first opened the bag and thought it must be a turkey—Christmas Day was only a few days away, until his mind un-tripped and realized what he was actually looking at was the infant they had been called to locate.

Over time, human beings can acclimate to most situations through acceptance and exposure. Acclimatization is not so much a coping mechanism but rather a lesson that

> *Experience and time can make difficult things easier to deal with.*

In the moment of crisis, acclimatization permits me to focus more on the job tasks at hand and less on the undesirable tragedy or the unfolding scene before me. In the quiet times, acclimatization has also given me opportunities to reflect and reconcile my own philosophies about life and death, with little need to go back to the images of violence seen that day. Compartmentalization and reframing help me with that, too.

Compartmentalization and Reframing

In 2014, my Homicide Unit experienced a deluge of unimaginable crimes committed by a vast array of people. Multiple murders, mutilated bodies, child victims, and several brutal domestic homicides rounded out a very trying year for the unit. A co-worker said during the height of the nonsensical violence, "Every time we go to one of these, we lose another little piece of ourselves." He was right.

Without some form of respite, our ability to continue working through crisis can become compromised. However, we also must be mindful to never make someone else's tragedy our own because this can result in the same compromised outcome. Of course, it is natural to have feelings of sadness or anger. However, we must take care not to adopt (or hijack) someone else's crisis—it simply isn't ours to inherit. This is not always an easy thing to do, but it is necessary as a professional law enforcement officer.

How else do our members deal with death, brutality, and all the other awful things that go with it? According to at least one doctor I have spoken with, it is a technique called *compartmentalization* that keeps us from not losing our minds.

Compartmentalization allows our minds to change direction, shift focus, and eventually lead us to be able to reframe a traumatizing experience. Exactly what it is and how a person practices it depends on the individual, but it's basically closing off traumatizing information into a room in our mind so that we can focus on a different or more pressing matter.

I utilize compartmentalization for those moments of respite and to function in the rest of my life. Depending on which side of the desk you're on, it's either a disorder or a coping technique. I'd say inherently, it may not be the best-case scenario because it could manifest itself later, but it helps people survive in these scenarios for a long time. Writing the first edition of this book was rather cathartic until our early readers asked for more grit and more detail. I opened those vaults, long closed, and suddenly, it wasn't so healing anymore. Probing my memory banks for the visceral details irritated the peace I had just found, but I learned a really important lesson:

> *We don't need to rehash the harsh details of a traumatizing event to allow ourselves to come to a place of peace or healing.*

That is good to know. Healing from trauma doesn't have to be traumatic. Some may believe that reframing is whitewashing an issue, but I would disagree.

> *Changing paradigms is like turning a coin to see the other side.*

The ability to turn the coin over can light the way out of some very dark places. You don't have to be in severe anguish for reframing to be of benefit to you. When we can do this with some regularity, I believe we are getting closer to being able to have an optimistic and supportive worldview—seeing the glass as half full, not half empty. Take divorce, for example. What changes if it is seen as a new opportunity, a chance to carve out your own path, maybe refocus on yourself, or even a mulligan for a chance at new love? What about job loss or bankruptcy? Would it help people if they chose to see it as a chance to change career paths for the better or as a clean slate to start fresh? Would they move forward faster? Or, even more challenging, the loss of a close family member? It can be excruciating, but I have seen people cope by looking at it as a new spiritual journey, as an opportunity to reunite with other loved ones who have passed before, or just accepting that death is a process of life.

Each of us chooses how we see and define the painful, tragic, or confusing experiences we all endure in our journey through this world.

My ability to use compartmentalization has helped me endure homicide as long as I have. Like any job, experience is an asset, and I keep my headspace as healthy as possible so my experience helps instead of hinders—I have become a master at it. One night, after getting home from coaching an evening hockey practice, the phone rang. It was a co-worker checking in. It had been one of those days where it felt like I had gotten nothing done, and I told him as much. My friend gently reminded me I had spent the whole day at the medical examiner's office for the autopsy of a child. Startled, my mind flipped back through the hours prior to the practice. He was right; I had attended an autopsy. In that minute, I realized how effective I'd become at re-cataloging harsh things to the back of my mind to refocus on something positive, like the evening hockey practice, to get that respite.

For me, it's about removing the emotion from an emotional event. When I attend a crime scene, I focus on the science; this helps me read the body and the scene like a book. Once I've read it properly, I'll understand what happened, and the science backs up my translation. I don't focus on the rigid, bloody hands of the victim in rigor mortis and imagine her last moments; instead, I focus on the skin and hair under her fingernails. I don't focus on the mutilated body; instead, I look for the likely tool or weapon used to disarticulate it. I want to identify a killer, not wallow in his crime.

Early in my homicide career, I worked a case where three dead newborn infants were found in suitcases inside the closet of a very tidy home occupied by a woman with a very messed-up mind. In the room where the three little bodies were located, pine tree air fresheners postered the walls. Their fragrance left us with the lasting impression that we had walked into the middle of an evergreen forest out of a horror movie, artificially rich and earthy but with an underlying stench of death.

In this case, my partner and I needed to understand why each little body appeared so different from the others. The mother's diary explained that each infant had been born in a different year, each smothered within hours of being born. The other evidence collected at the scene and the medical examination confirmed those claims. I experimented with smell abatement techniques with uncooked beef in bags to try and understand how the bodies had gone undetected for so long. We finished our case and presented our findings, but throughout this process, I never focused on the horrific hand those three had been dealt or replaced them with thoughts of my own children. My mind does not allow me to go there. This may seem unhealthy to some, but it is what has allowed me and others in my unit to continue doing the work we love to do.

Limiting my emotions in these situations helps in other ways as well. I am able to provide effective support to the victim's family members when called upon. It also allows me to remain open-minded and without perceived judgment when I interview the suspects in these cases—but it's a balancing act. Investigators need enough emotion to be authentic and supportive to the victims' families and the emotion required to connect with suspects in the interview room, which is essential to uncover the truth.

A few years ago, I investigated the murder of a man whose male partner came home to find him in bed with a woman. Livid, the accused argued with the victim about the affair while the girl quietly got dressed and left the apartment. Now, at a flashpoint, the accused, stinging from the pain of betrayal, grabbed a knife from the kitchen and chased his lover, viciously attacking him in the hall. He stabbed him over thirty times in the back, chest, and face. The man was *dead-dead*. The slaying, witnessed by multiple neighbors, was an open-and-shut case. Within a few short hours, the suspect was in custody, and I was assigned to interview him.

This crime was particularly brutal, and the offender was extremely callous in his attack. Several witnesses reported hearing the victim plead for his life multiple times, but that did not deter his partner's frenzied blows against him. Now, I'm a guy with a few sore spots. Extreme victim suffering, victim pleading, and overkill have always been hang-ups for me. So is the whole *if I can't have you, nobody can* thing. Exacerbating those sore spots was my unfamiliarity with same-sex partnerships, and I worried that I wouldn't be able to connect with him emotionally in the interview room. In the end, none of these factors mattered. I listened as the accused spoke for hours about his relationship with the victim. At one point in his statement, he abandoned his chair and lay on the ground on his side. Wanting him to continue his dialog, I simply got on the floor and listened, his back in front of my chest, in a maneuver now affectionately known around the office as the *murderer's spoon*. It worked. He continued to talk for several more hours, providing the evidence we needed to help secure his conviction.

All professionals require effective emotional distance. A dispassionate perspective fosters action, not reaction. In the case of the police and other emergency responders, a level head saves lives and solves crimes. Compartmentalization and reframing is the vehicle that allows us to have this perspective.

A medical examiner friend once said during an autopsy, "I don't know how you guys do it; talk to these people and not take these things home with you."

I smiled and looked down, "Said the woman

holding a refrigerated human spleen in her hand."

Catastrophizing

Ralph Waldo Emerson once said,

> *"For every minute you remain angry, you give up sixty seconds of peace of mind."*

I think Emerson was on to something. People have a tendency to catastrophize what they anticipate will be a negative experience instead of taking on the challenge and owning the problem or even flipping the negative into an accomplishment. Are things ever as bad as we dreamed they were going to be? Catastrophizing is the irrational thought that the worst possible outcome will befall us. It robs us of perspective and peace of mind. It can prevent us from moving forward and hinder our ability to reframe or remove emotion from an emotional event.

It is true that the things we don't prepare for, the stuff that blindsides us, are most apt to really change us in the moment. It's not the things we see coming. It's the ones we don't. This isn't a lack of planning, either. Sometimes, life derails us, and no amount of planning changes that, like what happened to a mother of three small children I met one morning. I went to inform her of her husband's murder on their oldest son's fifth birthday. For her, the night before was like any other, as she wished her hubby off for a good time on the town with his buddies. He was a normal, hardworking father who attended a house party with a couple of friends. Unbeknownst to the others in the group, one of them was not welcome. In the skirmish that followed, a knife was stuck into the father's chest without cause, and he died minutes later outside, cradled in his friend's arms, while the party raged on.

For me, these types of scenarios help bring perspective to my life. Are the things that plague me worth the worry? Realistically, will it matter in five years or even five days? We all have bad days, but my bad days at work remind me how fortunate I am.

When we are brand new at something and haven't figured out what stuff we should sweat, we have a tendency to catastrophize everything. Early in my career, I was summoned to my inspector's office regarding a call I'd attended that led to a complaint. A woman had threatened to swallow a number of pills (but hadn't) and called for police and the ambulance. After refusing treatment by our paramedics and being assessed as medically cleared by the ambulance crew that attended, it fell onto my shoulders to get her to the hospital for a mental health assessment and the help she needed. It was winter, and snow and ice had built up on the sidewalks and roads throughout the city. When I was going to take her to the hospital, she refused to put on her boots, or any footwear for that matter, besides the socks she was wearing. She went so far as to kick the boots off as they were offered to her.

Instead, she wanted me to carry her to the car. That wasn't going to happen for a couple of reasons. First, it was icy. Second, she was an adult and quite capable of making the decision to cooperate or not, and she chose not to. I brought her boots along in case she changed her mind. She didn't. But then she complained about my actions and asserted that I had been insensitive to her request to be carried. When I was called in, my mind flooded with worst-case scenarios. Had I done something wrong? I didn't think so, but perhaps others wouldn't see it the same way. After explaining my decision, my superiors determined that my refusal to carry her was not unreasonable, and I faced no further censure.

Another instance where worry got the better of me was after I was involved in preventing a dangerous car pursuit. We had attempted to box in a suspected stolen car, but the suspect rammed our police cars to escape and eventually rolled his vehicle several blocks away, sustaining severe brain injuries. When our actions were reviewed, I remember fretting for days, even though I knew we had done nothing wrong. The subsequent investigation revealed the same. Regardless, catastrophizing robbed me of more than a few nights of sleep for something I didn't have any control over; what was done was done and could never be undone. I know we all make ripples, but I frequently have to remind myself that my actions do not determine the choices someone else makes for themselves. Each one of us has the choice and responsibility to make our own decisions.

A life of service has taught me that most of what we all get worked up about can be trivial in the big picture. When you experience the extremes of life and death, you realize that getting worked up over daily grind crap is not only pointless, but it is also detrimental because it pressurizes our body and mind often needlessly.

Perspective is a powerful antidote to worry.

Perspective helps free us from catastrophizing. So does choosing to

Cultivate a habit of appreciation.

I work in a career many would find interesting. The fact is, there are more professional hockey players living in this town than homicide detectives, and the stats say only one in every 85,000 kids playing hockey will ever get an opportunity to play a game in the pros. I live in a city of nearly a million and a half people. I work in an organization of more than two thousand. There are only eighteen of us city-wide who have the luxury to work homicide, the gig we dreamed of as kids reading Hardy Boys and Nancy Drew. The odds that I would even get this chance seem near impossible, yet here I am, and I'm grateful. Experience has taught me that fretting over every detail of every day that has troubled me takes away from what I consider to be the very enviable situation that I find myself in.

Understanding Why

Why do people do horrible things? This is the question victims' families ask homicide investigators the most. As they suffer through incredible loss, they ask, *Why*? Searching for the why in tragedy can prevent us from moving forward. Only those who commit murder know the answer to that question, and they often minimize their role in the crime, deflecting blame to others or to an addiction to drugs or alcohol. Often, families fortunate enough to hear from the offender are disappointed by an explanation that minimizes the offender's role.

A perfect case in point was one I investigated several years ago. The accused phoned a young cocaine dealer with the intention to rob, murder him, or both. He confessed to us he had planned to take the younger man's money and drugs by force if needed. According to him, he did just that, stating the victim fought the robbery attempt and left him no alternative but to kill him with a hammer. The evidence in this case overwhelmingly supported the fact that this was a planned event. The difficulty, however, was in knowing if the planned robbery included murder. The accused blamed his addiction to drugs as the catalyst for the events that ended another man's life, not his greed or his propensity for violence.

Sometimes, friends and family never have the opportunity to ask why. Over a ten-year period between 2005 and 2015, our unit solved eighty-one percent of our cases. It's a decent statistic unless you are one of the families waiting for answers that may never come. The circumstances of death might be a mystery forever if a lack of conclusive evidence thwarts a finding of suicide, accident, or homicide. It's a frustrating situation for those who investigate suspicious deaths and for those left to pick up the pieces.

Take, for instance, when a dog-walker came across a skull in a wooded area but no other bones. Search teams were sent out to find the other remains; in cases like these, animals can scatter them over a large area. The medical examiner analyzed the partial skeleton recovered and notified investigators that there was no evidence to identify the victim's cause of death. Regardless, the investigation began to determine who the victim was and the circumstances around the time she was last seen.

We learned that, prior to going missing, the victim was having domestic troubles and was in the process of leaving her husband. She also had three past hospital admissions for depression and was on medications. Lastly, the area where she was found was not one she was known to frequent. Her phone records were no longer available—the provider had purged them. In examining her home, there were no visible signs of violence, but shortly after going missing, the husband had renovated the entire main floor. The officer who originally questioned the husband noted no signs of foul play, although her vehicle was still in the driveway—which seemed odd. No suicide note had been found. In those early days, police interviewed the husband on two separate occasions, and one officer went as far as to enter into his notebook: "appeared to answer questions appropriately."

These early interviews were important because, as the investigation progressed, the husband no longer wished to cooperate with the police. The victim had no life insurance policies, and one friend said in the past, the victim had expressed thoughts of killing herself with pills. There was not enough information to provide conclusive answers to her death.

Experiences like these have taught me it is more beneficial to reframe our focus toward the memories and the legacy of our loved ones rather than focus on why they were taken from us. It helps when families focus on *what next*. I realize this is easier said than done, but from what I have seen, the families most successful at overcoming grief have put into place new traditions, foundations, and charity causes as a way of memorializing their loved ones. This choice to lift others up can be a powerful antidote to crippling grief.

In the aftermath of losing their daughter, a family

launched a challenge on Facebook for each of her friends to pull off twenty-one random acts of kindness and post them on social media. Another family fundraised to continue supporting a health-related cause that their loved one believed strongly. Another courageous family, with help from a donor, started a foundation in their son's name that now benefits a variety of children's charities in our city. These families embraced shifting horrific negative experiences into uplifting, positive action. Their examples teach us that adjusting to a supportive mindset is an incredibly powerful choice.

People can get stuck when they fixate on finding answers. We have a strong human need to understand why bad things happen. Staying focused on the why can keep people trapped in misery and cause their anger and grief to rob them of the memories of loved ones. This is something I have seen happen to family members of homicide victims. On several occasions, I have also seen this change the family dynamic. By the end of the trial process—often years later—they are angry, fractured, and broken. The tally of victims grows.

After the violent loss of a loved one, family members can understandably fall into an overwhelming need for vengeance, and they look to the justice system for satisfaction to know the perpetrator will suffer. For some, the length of the sentence becomes a measure of how much the loved one's life was worth, but that is not the intention of the system. There is no sentence a court could impose that could turn back time. If a judge was to hand down a sentence of life in prison with no eligibility for parole for ten years, understandably, the family would want at least twenty-five years. If we had the death penalty in Canada, twenty-five years wouldn't be enough. If a court imposed death by lethal injection, the victim's family might want the perpetrator killed more brutally, but where does it stop? There is no punishment a civilized court could impose that will ever bring a complete sense of justice to the family of a murder victim. Resilient, forgiving families can move past this very normal—but very debilitating—desire for vengeance.

My father died of cancer at seventy-four, still a young man in this day and age. He was a fantastic grandpa. He adored all his grandchildren, and they adored him. He was also a brilliant man who had committed his life to science. This is why his decline seemed so cruel; whether it was the drugs or the cancer, his mind deteriorated.

Several weeks before he died, my daughter asked me, "What will happen to Grandpa when he dies? Do you think he will come back to visit or send us messages?" To answer her questions, I first had to adjust to the sorrow of my father's impending passing and make a space for optimism.

I shared my re-framed philosophy with my daughter, who was eleven at the time.

"Yes, I believe your grandpa could come back to us

in spirit, but definitely in memory. All you have to do is quiet your mind to see him, remember him, or feel his presence. Close your eyes, and I will explain. Two parts make up every person: body and soul. When the body dies, the soul or the memory of a person will live on. I can prove to you what I mean. Keep your eyes closed and quiet your mind, and tell me if you can feel where my hand is."

I moved my hand up and down my daughter's arm, shoulder, and back without touching her. At each point along the way, I would ask her to tell me where my hand was.

"Do you see? I didn't touch you, yet you knew I was near. For you to do this, your eyes needed to be closed and your mind quiet. After Grandpa dies, if you close your eyes and quiet your mind, you will still be able to see him in memory and maybe even feel his presence around you."

The lesson to my daughter on this day was simple and lasting:

The easiest way to enjoy memories, honor legacy, or feel a presence is with a clear mind, absent of anger or other emotions.

Getting trapped in why can steal the closeness we had with the person we so desperately miss. It can prevent us from moving forward, from healing, from rediscovering our optimism.

Mental Maturity

There are times in life when we experience challenging situations that can be tough to process, but some can be avoided. I now realize how easy it is to put garbage into the human brain and how hard it is to remove it. Of course, this revelation came *after* I viewed video footage taped by a young woman's killer after he shot her in the chest. Her murderer, off-camera, cruelly mocked her as she lay convulsing on the kitchen floor, taking her final gasps of air. It was not imperative I view the video—it wasn't my case—but I watched it, and now I have very disturbing images that get stuck on replay. Since that time, I have developed the mental maturity to know:

Only look when you need to, and avoid peeking when it isn't prudent to do so.

Curiosity can be damaging to the mind. What about people who consume violent entertainment? Don't the same defense mechanisms work in their brains, too? Of course, they do. But the mechanisms that help me get through the day are the same ones that desensitize us all to the violence we consume. As a society, I can't help but wonder if we are peeking a little too often at violence and predator behavior in video games, TV series, and movies.

Is a symptom of this steady diet of violent narrative and image the anesthetization and acclimation of society to brutality? Maybe. I am not saying that there should be boycotts and bans on entertainment—I, too, enjoy all the biggest hit series and movies with swearing, sex, and violence—but I can't help but question how these things are affecting us today. Is the price of violent entertainment a more dangerous culture for us all?

Take guns, for example, and the surrounding attitudes. Guns are lethal-force weapons. They are designed and built to take life, not to wound, not to miss. There is no other purpose for a gun. Any other conception of them demonstrates a misunderstanding of the purpose of guns. It is not a deterrent; it is a lethal weapon. My dad used to say the most dangerous gun is an unloaded one, and I agree. When people are "accidentally" killed, the first words out of the mouth of the person who pulled the trigger is, "I didn't know the gun was loaded." When a gun is pointed at someone and the trigger is pulled, the only reasonable, expected outcome is death. Believing a gun can fire without lethal consequences (even if it's aimed at an arm or a leg) is an unrealistic expectation supported by violent games and movies. When a round is discharged from the weapon, and it penetrates a body, it creates a wound cavity that shreds organs and causes purposeful, specific bleeding. Believing guns can be used in any other way is not grasping the gun's designed ability to take life.

Knife attacks are similarly misconstrued. Most "stabbers," think plunging a knife into someone a couple of times isn't enough to kill them; they're shocked when the person dies and they're charged with murder. Even in courtrooms, the number of stab wounds inflicted on a victim is used to gauge the degree of the intent to kill. In my view, thrusting a sharp, pointy weapon into the body of someone else, even just once, is a lethal action, and death is the expected outcome. I have heard this argument repeated in courtrooms, and I believe this example illustrates our growing apathy toward violence and the slow acclimatization of our society toward unnatural, violent death.

I'll cite two more cases to make my point. The first comes out of Edmonton, Alberta. In this case, the victim was lured from a dating site to the home of the offender, who was allegedly obsessed with the TV series *Dexter*, a show about a vengeful serial killer who worked for the police as a blood pattern expert. In his spare time, he hunted and killed people he believed to have committed atrocious crimes. In the Edmonton case, the offender mimicked the signature of the Dexter character: he murdered and then dismembered his victim in his garage, tarps and all.

The second case is one that my colleagues worked on. The guy confessed to murder as if he was in a video game, telling his friend he had been playing the game, and now the cops were looking at him for first-degree murder. This confession gave me pause. What was this offender's concept of reality or fantasy the moment he took life? These are extreme cases, for sure, but where do our views about violence come from if our natural inclination is to avoid or dismiss violence?

Rather than filling our minds with violent imagery and narrative, we can train our brains to focus on the good, the positive, the solution, and the compromise rather than the bad, the negative, the problem, and the catastrophe. This is the foundation of thinking from a different box.

Having the mental maturity to know you don't have to peek and to know it is not only okay to make decisions that keep you mentally safe, it is responsible. I didn't walk on the job really understanding how important this was. I learned the hard way. I share now, so you don't have to.

Knowing to ask for help takes a while for some of us, too. *Support systems are our parachute, our sanity check, and the warm blanket when we've gotten too cold.* Thinking outside the box, changing your perspective, and shifting to healthier paradigms can be hard. Having people you can count on is important, and in some cases vital, to our success in these endeavors. Our relationships matter. Your friends, family, or professional care providers giving that place of respite all help us work through life's hurdles. It makes a difference. Knowing what you need or asking the right questions to figure it out, and then, of course, taking action, all goes a long way to living in that place of optimism.

Our Path to Thriving

I am acutely aware that my boundaries and inability to feel offended have stretched beyond what most people's norms could ever be. It has become difficult to shock me. This is not a beneficial consequence of working a career that has stretched my center of normal somewhere off the scale. It is also one of the reasons I realized I needed Sarah for this project as my social filter. The truth is, I am neck-deep in a twisted world where inappropriate commentary is used to lighten the darkness of the day, and sometimes it is a challenge to censor myself in the real world. However, instead of dwelling on this as a negative, I see this glass as half full, too. I suspect no one at a kids' showcase or sporting activity grooves more on the positive energies these events bring than I do. I relish seeing people happy and having a good time, and that *is* a direct benefit of being around negativity all the time. That's what we do to thrive. We find what we need to live our lives with meaning and happiness. Optimism helps me. So does witnessing others walking bravely into new perspectives.

As a rookie homicide detective, I had a case where two friends got into a heated argument that led one to stab the other a dozen or so times. When the case went to the preliminary hearing, I watched as the victim's father experienced a profound change sitting in the courtroom. Still grieving the loss of his son, he saw the accused's father across the gallery, there to support his own. At that moment, the victim's father realized that as tragic a place he was in, the other father was in a worse one. "A greater hell is what that father is going through," he said to me. "At least I know my son did not kill another man's son."

This is a powerful example of someone accepting loss with grace and recognizing another's significant pain. The wisdom in that grieving father's words has stayed with me ever since.

Remembering that things can always be worse somehow helps when we are trying to overcome our own challenges and pain.

Life can present challenges, some unimaginable, until we are going through them. It helps to remember we choose how we frame our experiences, and thinking from a different box can help us get there.

Unleashing Your Inner Jedi

*"Power is a tool, influence is a skill;
one is a fist, the other a fingertip."*
- Nancy Gibbs

Our lives and behaviors are influenced by our compulsions to adhere to our cultural norms. We can unleash our inner Jedi by knowing our actions create ripples, knowing what we are setting into motion, and being cognizant of what others have set in motion that may affect us. When used responsibly, influence is a supportive tool to pave forward positive outcomes. If used irresponsibly, it dissolves trust, credibility, or worse. We are approaching influence from a place of positive intention where it can create preferable outcomes for all. To achieve this, we will need to understand how we have seen influence work.

Understanding how these social triggers affect behavior is invaluable for investigators trying to apprehend bad guys or resolve conflicts. The most prevalent of these influences—reciprocity, commitment, likability, authority, conformity or groupthink, and scarcity—are rarely discussed openly in law enforcement. I certainly didn't learn about them through any textbook or course on the subject. I learned by observing police officers deal with difficult situations successfully and unsuccessfully. Successful officers know how to handle and deploy persuasion. They use their knowledge to encourage positive, cooperative behavior in others.

It wasn't until I watched the video *The Science of Persuasion* by professor, author, and psychologist Robert Cialdini,[1] that I realized my musings were an actual thing psychologists were studying. Cialdini made sense of what I had been noticing for years.

There are unspoken and unwritten "rules" compelling us to act a certain way at any given moment. That means we have the ability to activate those rules to influence others as well. Persuasion can be used to lift people up or put people down. Learning how to use persuasion responsibly is like unleashing our inner Jedi.

Reciprocity and Commitment

People we help today are more likely to want to help us tomorrow.

Reciprocity is our social obligation to give back when we have received it, whether it is a service, a gift, or a compliment. Most of us don't like the feeling of owing another person, so we respond in kind immediately. Imagine you and your colleague go for coffee, and when it's time to pay, they pick up the tab. Will you pay the next time? What if next time, your co-worker also orders a muffin or bagel with your coffees? Do you still feel compelled to pay? For most of us, the answer is "yes."

During the holiday season, did you feel anxiety if you received a gift and had nothing to give in return? What if the gift you gave paled in comparison to the one you received? That anxiety comes from our inherent compulsion to want to reciprocate, and our failure to do so leaves an unspoken social contract unfulfilled.

Ask your mom if she remembers attending kitchenware parties. She'll remember that the first thing you received when you joined the party was a free piece of kitchenware. By giving you a free piece, the hostess wanted to persuade you—through a strong social compulsion to reciprocate—to buy more at the party.

Reciprocity can also be created through positive interactions between two strangers, like holding the door open for someone. If they have held it for us, we will go out of our way, sometimes awkwardly, to open the inside door for them.

Reciprocity is also at work when friends share a personal story or a dark secret; we will be more apt to disclose something, too. This is part of how undercover operations work: I'll share my secrets with you if you share yours with me—and people do.

Homicide cases across Canada have been solved using this legal and valid technique. However, the use of undercover police to obtain covert confessions from persons who have committed serious crimes is controversial, and recent changes in the law that govern the admissibility of these types of statements now place the onus on the prosecutor to prove reasonableness. In chapter four, we discussed the ethical considerations of undercover operations and the betrayal some suspects feel, but there can be more pressing practical questions.

Given human nature, isn't it possible that so-called confessions to undercover cops are actually false boasts and brags petty criminals use to look tougher?

Yes.

Could someone really be *that stupid* to tell their secret?

Yes.

It is entirely reasonable that a person may say something self-incriminating to impress another. To protect against this possibility, investigators and courts are cautious to accept a covert confession without specific details that could only be known by the person who committed the crime. This is known as holdback evidence—information known by only a small group of investigators and, of course, the perpetrator. It is the evidence that assures investigators they have not elicited a false confession through the social influences of reciprocity and likability (which will be discussed shortly). So pervasive are false confessions that identifying holdback evidence for later corroboration is considered standard operating procedure in homicide cases.

A good example of holdback evidence is the caliber of gun or the type of weapon used. At one autopsy I attended, the seriousness of the visible injuries indicated the victim had been bludgeoned to death by a bat, a fact difficult to hide from anyone who had even glancing contact with the body, including the funeral home staff and family members. As a result, the victim's cause of death was never considered strong holdback evidence. However, unbeknownst to all but the killer and a small number of investigators, the victim had also been asphyxiated. Months later, this detail and others came out in a suspect's confession to an undercover police officer. We knew the confession wasn't just two people boasting to one another, and we had the right guy.

In another case, the accused confessed to an undercover police officer his involvement in a vicious stomping death of an innocent man. In his statement to the officer, the accused spoke in accurate, five-sensory detail of the sensations he experienced during the attack. He also provided additional details not known to us but which were later corroborated. For example, in his confession, he said he contemplated using a nearby shopping cart to transport and dump the body into a garbage bin after the attack. His statement was substantiated when we looked back at scene photographs and realized there was indeed a shopping cart close to where the victim's body had lain.

Perhaps the most compelling of covert confessions are in cases where a suspect leads the undercover operator to real physical evidence. One such case occurred a few years back. The suspect and victim knew each other and had an argument that quickly escalated out of control—the victim sustained thirty-plus stab wounds in the knife attack against him. The suspect was arrested soon after.

Following his arrest, the suspect was interviewed by investigators but said little to incriminate himself further in the offense under investigation. Without a statement from him, investigators knew they would be forced to release him from their custody and continue to collect the evidence they needed to bring the case to court.

It didn't take long. Skillfully, undercover operators were able to infiltrate the suspect soon after his release, and this strategy ultimately led to the suspect showing his *new friends* the location where he had discarded the knife and his bloody clothing (real evidence), eliminating any argument that he was "just boasting and bragging" to his new buddies to impress them and giving us the final pieces of evidence we needed to lay charges against the suspect for actions in the deadly confrontation.

Courts and investigators alike know how important

it is to have evidence held back to protect a statement made to an undercover operator. However, this is not the only instance where it could be required. A false boast or brag can also come in the form of an overt confession, and although rare, I have seen it happen several times throughout my career.

In one such instance, a young man who had just finished dinner at a fancy restaurant in a trendy part of town got up to use the bathroom. Once into the washroom, the young man saddled up to a free urinal when the unbelievable happened. A stranger relieving himself at the next urinal declared, "A few years back, I killed two people right over there."

Startled, the young man murmured an "Oh, yay," and at his earliest opportunity, exited the bathroom as quickly as he could. Once out of earshot of the confessed killer, he called 911 to report what he had heard. Minutes later, police arrived and took the suspect into custody. "I killed two people just over there," the suspect declared to the arresting officer. "Take me to jail." Obliging the request, the suspect was transported to our office minutes later and settled into an interview suite. The seasoned detective assigned to interview him reviewed the case file, including the holdback evidence.

As you can imagine, the interview did not begin like most do, with the suspect clammed up and his head down. Instead, the now-arrested man greeted the seasoned investigator cordially, declaring right from the outset that "I did it, now take me to jail."

"Hold on a second, sparky, it is not that simple," the interviewer said. "We need to chat about what you did and discuss the details."

It was at this moment that things began to fall apart.

"I did it. Just take me to jail," the suspect repeated with his hands presented in a handcuff gesture.

"I hear you," the interviewer acknowledged. "But we need to hear the how and why before we can just take you to jail. What type of gun did you use?"

The suspect guessed wrong.

"Which of the victims did you shoot first?"

Again, the suspect's answer did not align with multiple witnesses' accounts from that night.

"What did you do with the gun?"

"I gave it to my friend."

Wrong. The gun had been recovered a short distance away from the scene in a recycling bin.

The suspect's criminal details were 0-3. The confession was bunk. Now, it was the interviewer's job to provide the space for the suspect to acknowledge that he was lying and to also explain why.

It turned out the non-murderer simply missed his brother, who had recently been arrested. His plan had been to be arrested with the hope of being able to spend some time with the brother he missed while the whole mess of the false confession got sorted out. It sounds strange, though true. To protect the no-longer-a-suspect from further attempts of self-harm, we felt the best option for him was to be assessed by a mental health professional in the hospital instead of any charges being brought against him.

Reciprocity compels most of us to take action, but typically, we only feel the effects of reciprocity. We don't often think about it consciously. Used responsibly, it can be a positive influence benefiting whole communities. Think of the pay-it-forward concept, where random acts of kindness are passed from one to another in an often anonymously reciprocating narrative (like a drive-thru coffee line). All it requires is a commitment from participants.

A friend once defined contribution and commitment this way, "Look at the breakfast table to see the difference between contributing and committing: the hen made a contribution, the pig made a commitment." Now, that's an extreme illustration, but the difference between the two is clear.

Commitments are strong, driving influences on our behavior. Something happens in our psyche when we make a commitment to another person. For most of us, that becomes binding, and we must see it through to the end.

For instance, I suspect more potential brides- or grooms-to-be who say "no" do so at the proposal or during the engagement rather than running from the altar on the big day. Turns out, *yes*. According to the travel research firm *SuperBreak*,[2] twenty-five percent of women admitted to turning down a wedding proposal, and in a study by the *Wedding Report*,[3] only thirteen percent of engagements end before marriage. Those numbers drop after paperwork has been filed, according to the *New York Times*.[4] Only five percent of marriage license applications in New York never get exchanged for a marriage certificate, suggesting once the paperwork is filed and the invitations are sent, there will probably be a wedding. The couple has made a public commitment, and there is a powerful obligation to fulfill it, cold feet and all.

If you have ever bought a new car, you've experienced the power of commitment. You may recall that after you committed to the dealer to purchase the vehicle for the negotiated price, you were sent to the business manager to complete the paperwork and arrange financing. This is when they likely tried to upsell you on a variety of extras like paint and rust protection. Why? Because the business manager knows a customer can be pushed harder to buy the extras after they've already made a commitment (even if only verbally with the salesman), the customer will no longer back out of the original deal.

When I interview a suspect, if I start by making a commitment that he will be treated fairly and with respect, and then I shake his hand, very few suspects will turn volatile in the interview suite. This is because they have also committed, by that handshake or promise, to treat me fairly and with respect, too.

In any interview, the investigator's mission is to get the subject talking—to get them to commit to a story of their involvement or to a story that eliminates them as a suspect. The subject's story can either be proven or disproven through the analysis of physical and circumstantial evidence. Commitment is a strong, fascinating influence. Even when suspects are shown hard evidence *refuting* their claims, very few backtrack completely from their original statements. Perhaps they assume they will look worse for reneging on their original story. This is when the commitment influence competes with the truth. The first statement becomes a hurdle, and the interviewer must show the accused significant evidence to help them get beyond that initial false statement. Outlandish, over-the-top statements have come out of suspects when they are compelled to keep up the lie, to stay firmly committed to their original story. As you can imagine, when this happens, they look pretty foolish and exemplify the truth that

Sometimes, the easiest person to lie to is yourself.

I investigated a case a few years ago where the suspect, after realizing his earlier interviews with police had painted him into a corner, claimed evidence had been planted at the crime scene by the real killer to frame him. *Really buddy?* The circumstances, facts, and evidence that implicated him in the murder were *overwhelming*: an unexplainable amount of the victim's blood was found in his vehicle, surveillance video and phone records confirmed he was the last person with the victim on the night she was murdered, and his post-offense behavior, which included destroying evidence of his crime, was discovered in the investigation that followed. In the end, the story he first told was the one he stuck with, but I felt it spoke more to his lack of remorse than his improbable innocence. The jury and judge believed so, too.

In another case, a person suspected of killing a man found dead in a parking lot maintained that he was acting in self-defense when he took the victim's life. The story carried some weight until a video of the murder was collected from a surveillance camera in the area. The video showed the victim, after accidentally bumping the suspect in a grocery store checkout line, walking away from the offender just prior to being charged from behind and then blindsided with strikes. Despite this evidence showing it was not self-defense, the accused maintained his claims. Again, he likely felt compelled because he had already committed to his earlier statements on tape.

Commitments made on video recordings are similar to those made in writing and, for most people, are more binding than verbal agreements. Robert Cialdini also spoke to this point in his video *The Science of Persuasion,* where he cited a study done at a health clinic that reduced missed appointments by eighteen percent by asking patients to write their next appointment details on the provided card. Putting pen to paper produced a stronger commitment that influenced behavior.

Cialdini's study parallels my experience with people who confess to crimes. Suspects who make incriminating statements in an interview suite are more likely to resolve their cases with a guilty plea than those who don't, suggesting that this influence can have long-term results.

A good friend of mine is a crisis negotiator, and we talk a lot about the use of commitment and reciprocity in his work. He shared two stories. In the first, a young man choked his mom and assaulted her with a pair of scissors before she was able to flee her residence and call the police. The young man anticipated the arrival of officers and, while still in full-crisis mode, barricaded himself inside the home. Three long hours passed, with the young man holding firm. Finally, he agreed to give up if the negotiators would get him a root beer. As you can expect, the negotiator agreed to his terms. He made a commitment, small as it was, and delivered on it. The young man surrendered when his terms were met. This may sound anti-climactic. I mean, it all ended with a soft drink? Yes. The commitment was honored, and the gesture returned.

The second story is about a mentally distraught man who climbed up thirty stories, commandeered a crane, and refused to leave. While the crisis negotiator attempted to persuade him down, the man became increasingly agitated. The scene was unfolding in the downtown core and bustling with people. The dramatic situation garnered attention from the public and media, who had sent cameras to the scene. The man expressed distress at the cameras and declared he would not continue dialog until they backed off. Police asked the camera operators to move back from the sidewalk, which they did. This good faith gesture calmed the man (positive presence), but he was still not convinced it was time to come down. The man remained in the crane while negotiators climbed the thirty stories to help him. At the top, overlooking the city, the dialog continued between the negotiator and suspect, with the suspect repeating over and over, "You guys don't care about me." Each time, the negotiators replied, "If that were true, why would we have climbed thirty stories to meet you?" The rhetorical question reinforced the negotiators' positive action, which persuaded a positive reaction from the distraught man. Eventually, they descended safely back down the crane's tower to solid ground below.

Commitment teaches us that the agreements and promises we make create the framework of our obligations.

If you wish to keep your relationships in proper balance, remain true to your word.

Likability and Authority

Being likable creates positive outcomes. Have you ever tried to listen to someone you didn't like? What were the chances they would persuade or influence you?

According to Cialdini, there are three important

factors that increase likability: people similar to us, people who pay us compliments, and people who cooperate with us. Cialdini cited a study that found business persons who met with prospective business associates were ninety percent more likely to close the deal if both sides spent time getting to know the other side on a personal level through connection and communication. Those who approached the same scenario with the attitude that time was money and were impatient to get down to business were only fifty percent likely to close the deal.

From my own experience as an investigator, these three factors absolutely increase likability, but I will add another—the ability to laugh at oneself and use self-deprecating humor. These four elements are keys to increasing our likability to others and contributing to the success of all our interactions. In TV shows and movies, a common interview technique is the *good cop/bad cop* routine. The idea is that a suspect will draw away from the unlikable bad cop and draw closer to the likable good cop and cooperate. It can work, but most investigators stay away from it, with good reason. Statement admissibility is judged in part on the treatment of the accused by *all* police officers the suspect came in contact with prior to making admissions or statements in an interview. If the bad cop is too bad, too overbearing, or threatening, statements made by the suspect could be in jeopardy. If the court identifies threats, coercion, or inducements from the bad cop, the statements made to the good cop may be dismissed. Most interviewers take a different approach. They work on proper rapport building, including empathy for the accused's plight, seeking common ground, and focusing on building a connection to the suspect.

I once watched a real-life cop TV show that followed a group of homicide investigators in several large metropolitan US cities. (Yes, sometimes we watch cop shows.) The suspect in this show had been arrested for a homicide, and as he sat in the room waiting for the interviewer, you could tell he was agitated. When the interviewer walked into the room, the first words out of her mouth were, "Oh my God, Tyrone, I can't imagine how scared and confused you must be. I'm here to talk to you and help explain why you've been arrested and clear up some of that confusion." This interaction immediately built a connection between the suspect and the investigator because she was empathetic.

The American professor, scholar, author, and public speaker Brené Brown,[5] says, "empathy builds connection, sympathy creates disconnection," and she provides the following analogy to demonstrate the difference. When someone's fallen into a hole, the empathetic person climbs into the hole with that person. The sympathetic reaction is standing at the opening, looking down into the hole, and acknowledging the person has fallen. This would be tantamount to the interviewer entering the room and instead saying, "I'm sorry you've been arrested today, but at least I'm going to give you an opportunity to talk to me about it." Interviewers who can create an empathetic connection by getting into the hole with the accused will probably have more successful outcomes than those who stop at sympathy.

Encouraged by an empathetic interviewer, subjects can be further disarmed with the strategic use of humor. I am grateful to be surrounded by a team of talented investigators who approach interviewing this way; I have watched many of my colleagues joke with suspects throughout an interview up and until a confession. The most effective investigators are the ones who use self-deprecating humor to bring levity to the room. I know an officer who is an expert at this. Through his actions and tone, he impresses upon all of us daily,

Don't take yourself too seriously.

His riffs on his receding hairline and his commentary on not missing too many meals build a rapport. After being given an empathetic ear by a funny, likable cop, even the most seasoned of criminals are persuaded to at least listen to him in the interview suite.

Having a simple shtick to make others smile is a way I create a positive presence in the lives of people I come to know through often tragic and sad circumstances. I wear bold, sometimes obscenely colorful socks. Why? Because producing unexpected humor helps me connect with people. I have watched individuals go from crying to smiling and sometimes even laughing out loud when they get a glimpse of my vibrant rainbow stripes or pink pigs peeking out from the bottom of my suit pants. The socks become a jump-off point: they introduce that bit of levity and respite. Discussing why I wear this often-embarrassing apparel sometimes helps people get through really bad days, and for some, the socks become strangely meaningful. I have gotten frequent requests over the years to roll up my pant leg and reveal that day's fashion blasphemy. In turn, my efforts at gentle humor are welcome for the smiles and laughs the socks generate, and I have been rewarded with a steady stream of new pairs for my collection. It's a reciprocal gesture for creating this positive, unexpected, light-hearted moment in a day of grief and their way of ensuring my tradition carries on for others.

Likability builds on lessons from chapter four: first impressions do count, and if we are to control how we wish others to view us, then we must match our actions to our intentions. The likability influence also teaches that it is important to be genuine and take the time to ask people about their lives, their days, and basically how they are doing—and mean it.

Authority—a person's credibility and knowledge of a subject, not any perceived police "power"—is another strong social influence and speaks to the persuasive power that expertise or credible knowledge can afford a person. Many years ago, while I was still working in my district as a regular patrol officer, I learned about the art of drafting search warrants. These can be complicated documents to write. At that time, the thinking was it was best left to a detective to craft, not a less-seasoned officer like me. Despite this sentiment, learning the warrant-writing process was important to me, and I wanted to be good at it. I had seen others either avoid them or get anxious when they had to write one. I didn't want to fall into the same trap and took it upon myself to write and execute several warrants while I was still a uniformed constable, something other officers of my rank were not doing. It had a strange effect: colleagues came to me with questions about the process. They believed I was becoming a subject matter expert on the topic (which was crazy because, at that point, I had only drafted a handful of them). Regardless, it was the experience of doing a few versus doing none that elevated my authority with my peers. It also led to recognition and the opening of new doors—like a posting in the Drug Unit—which I jumped at when the time was right.

Another example of the authority influence at play occurred when my partner and I were granted dedicated surveillance resources for a series of break-and-enters we were investigating. Early in 2000, we had been examining break-and-enter trends in our district and identified several groups we believed might be responsible. Their methods of operation, among other things, suggested a connection.

I still remember the Monday morning we pitched

our suspicions thoroughly and concretely to our boss. He agreed that our best course of action would be to secure surveillance resources to help catch the culprits in the act. This likely sounds like no big deal, but even though I was part of a large policing organization, resources were not unlimited, and surveillance teams were at a premium. Homicide files and other major crimes got first crack at those teams; it took a compelling argument to even sit down at the table to talk with these guys about a series of break-and-enters. The authority influence first kicked in when we got our boss to recognize and agree to employ these resources. We did this by presenting what we had on the suspects and the basis for believing they were involved.

I'll talk more about the importance of presentation in chapter ten, but how you present something really does make a difference. We must have given a compelling case because, once it was done, the phone call was made, and we got the Surveillance Unit for one half-day that week.

Excited, we went quickly to the surveillance office, where we presented our first suspect target to them. It was only about an hour after leaving their office when we got a call from the team's lead hand. They had our suspect casing houses and were preparing for arrest.

It had worked.

The surveillance team watched the target move to the back of a residence and kick in the door, after which they moved in and made the dynamic arrest. Kudos all around, and right then, our influence grew stronger.

Before the dust settled, the surveillance team was reaching into our pile of targets to go out and work the following day. Unbelievably, the same thing happened again. Who doesn't like catching bad guys red-handed? Everyone was ecstatic. Well, almost everyone. An additional two suspect groups were rounded up in the act later that week, catching the attention of the highest ranks of the organization. From that day forward, we never got another "no" when we made a request for this resource.

We all use the authority influence in our interactions with people without even knowing we are doing it. Before a public speaker takes the podium, they are often introduced with their list of credentials before any presentation begins. When a realtor is trying to sell you a house, they will speak about their experiences and other houses they have sold in the area. When I meet with a victim's family, I tell them about my background and years of experience investigating homicides. When we suspect someone may be lying to us, we remind them that *this isn't our first rodeo* and we are trained to recognize deception.

Find your passion and master it.

Knowledge matters. As this influence suggests, our expertise and our know-how have the power to bring comfort, create positive influence, and lead people to positive places. The combination of likability and authority, when we like the person who is an authority on whatever we need them to be, is huge.

Conformity or Groupthink

When otherwise independent, rational people make out-of-character or questionable decisions to conform to the flow or sway of the group they find themselves in, odds are, they're being influenced by groupthink. Groupthink stems from the idea that people look to the actions and behaviors of others to form their own. This can affect everything from religious tolerance to consumer behavior. Have you ever noticed lines of people standing for hours believing, like those around them, that something great (or at least worth the wait) awaits them at the end? This herd mentality is easy to scoff at until you notice your own soft spots of *belonging*.

Groupthink can happen wherever there is a group of people. Back in the early 2000s, our police association and membership contract negotiations with the city were not going so well. Police are legislatively exempt from striking, which makes sense, but also means that the influence strike action can bring is not available to us. What is available is job action like work-to-rule campaigns and what I got caught up in as a rookie police officer.

The thought of wearing baseball caps, not shaving, or not writing traffic summonses would not have been something I would have dreamed of doing on my own, especially considering my lack of vintage. Because everyone else was doing it, I felt compelled to support the cause, so I did. Eventually, those that may not have initially believed it was a good thing fell in line. In the end, no one wants to be *that guy*, and this influence won over any risk of reprimand or discipline.

Riots can be an example of groupthink. What might have started out as a small number of upset—but non-violent—individuals can quickly turn into a large, angry mob. Although I have never been in a large-scale riotous situation myself, I have been close. I have also studied them (as well as you can without first-person experience) when I trained in crowd management techniques. The best way to quell a riot from starting is to identify the potential provocateurs before they can negatively sway a group. It is true that once the first rock is thrown, many more are to come if the aggressors are not immediately identified and stopped.

A good example of this comes from the 1992 L.A. riots. Following the acquittals of four policemen for the brutal, videotaped beating of Rodney King, a small group of individuals soon recruited dozens more to join the riot that lasted six days, leaving over fifty dead, 2,300 people injured, and millions of dollars in property damage. Conversely, it was also groupthink, or a mob mentality, by the original four police officers who grievously assaulted Rodney King after he had led them on a high-speed chase, with speeds exceeding

110 miles per hour, out of fear of his parole being revoked.

We have all seen the looting scenarios on the evening news where a small trickle of people enter a store through a broken window, only to be joined within minutes by a swarm of others after seeing the success the first group had lifting merchandise with no repercussions. They join en masse and quickly empty the store of stock.

Cult leaders use the power of groupthink to influence entire congregations to do unimaginable things—like drink poisoned Kool-Aid. In November 1978, cult leader Jim Jones did exactly that on his Jonestown commune in Guyana, convincing his 900-plus followers to participate in mass suicide.

An aberration of groupthink is bystander apathy. There are many reasons people decide not to come forward to help in a situation (like fear), but bystander apathy can influence people to not act when they might have in a different set of circumstances.

In March 1964, an assailant stabbed Susan "Kitty" Genovese to death outside her Queens, New York apartment. In the investigation that followed, police located and spoke with approximately thirty-eight witnesses, who reported either seeing or hearing parts of the attack and screams from the victim. None of these people called the police because they thought someone else would. Tragically, no one did, and Kitty died before help came.

Twenty years ago, in our community, a sex trade

worker was attacked on a hillside in a local residential community and murdered. As in the Genovese case, several people heard the screams of the victim but believed that someone else would call the police, and so they didn't. Sadly, this case remained unsolved for more than a decade until advancements in DNA and genealogy identified a sixteen-year-old youth as being the person responsible seventeen years later.

This apathetic view that someone else will do the right thing, so "Why should I?" is more common than I would have ever thought.

One of the most alarming trends in recent years, which really highlights the "someone else will report it, so why should I?" concerns the opioid crisis gripping our city.

Over the last couple of years, our unit has seen a significant rise in incidents where a victim has overdosed and died inside a residence, and the people inside the home make the decision not to call anyone for help or to have the body removed. In instances like these, the body can remain for extended periods (weeks, even months) before the process of decomposition makes it so uncomfortable for the others inside the home that someone finally removes the victim from the house, dumping their remains under a tree or in an alley where it is found by a passerby who does call the police. Seem far-fetched? In the first six months of this past year alone, our unit has investigated five of these cases.

This type of apathy is also alive and well every time

our unit attends a homicide at a house party or a bar, and we learn that three-quarters of our witnesses have already left the scene, never to be found again. Those who don't come forward either don't want to get involved out of fear, or they believe someone else will, letting them off the hook. Regardless of the reason, non-action can derail police investigations that require witnesses to carry them forward. What can look like a random or mundane observation is potentially crucial information that could break a case wide open for the investigator.

A couple of years ago, an aspiring basketball star was gunned down outside a nightclub. Early in the investigation, CCTV collected from around the area captured some fantastic pictures of our suspect fleeing from the scene shortly after the shooting, but despite the quality of these images, we could not identify the individual depicted. Facial recognition did not work. Media releases did not work. However, when an anonymous tip was received, which provided the nickname of our man and his social media handle, this information was all we needed to be off to the races. This seemingly little bit of info led us to identify, arrest, and convict the offender for this sad and unnecessary event.

Groupthink is not always negative. By understanding this influence, strong leaders can harness conformity's power to motivate people within their teams, social circles, and groups toward positive outcomes in the projects and goals they collectively take on. In chapter three, I discussed being part of several large events our city hosted that attracted a protest and mentioned the officers on bicycles who policed the crowds, not officers armed with "hats and bats." Uniformed officers pedaling alongside the crowds sent a different, peaceful message to those gathered than the presence of officers with hats and bats ever could have.

I will explain more about this in chapter seven when I discuss the effect of infusing belief into groups while working toward a positive common goal.

Our desire to conform to a group, as this influence demonstrates, identifies the danger of letting others dictate our actions and feelings. However, it is important to remember we all have a choice, and our:

Free choice is not forfeited by an influencer.

Scarcity

At one time or another, most of us have experienced the feeling that *if I don't act now, the opportunity will be lost forever.* When we let this influence drive our actions, we act immediately and commit without thinking the transaction through. In social relationships, scarcity is often introduced as an ultimatum: "If you can't commit to this relationship, then I'm leaving it."

Scarcity can be a very potent tool in business because it pressures the consumer to buy the goods or services for sale. Recently, a young salesman came to my door selling alarm systems and dropped the names of my neighbors (groupthink) who had already bought into this "limited-time" offer. Attaching a limited-time offer to the deal was his attempt to influence my buying decisions. He wanted me to get his alarm system before the price increased.

Limited-time offers are one example of how businesses use the principle of scarcity to get customers to act faster than they would normally. Cialdini identifies three factors that are required to persuade others to act under the influence of scarcity. People must be told of the benefits they will gain if they take you up on the offer. People must be told what is unique about your offer. People must be told what they stand to lose if they opt out of what is being offered.

Police use the influence of scarcity in interviews, where it is usually introduced to remind suspects that early cooperation is key and that the time is now for their story to be heard. There are also other uses.

I once went to a serious domestic assault where we suspected that the female victim had been her husband's punching bag for some time. After another night of overhearing, arguing, and fighting through the thin walls, a neighbor called us to the home, concerned about the wife's welfare. I watched as my senior officer laid it out to her at her kitchen table.

One. She needed help, and we were the opportunity to get her that help (the benefit).

Two. The time to leave was now when her husband was going to jail for the night (uniqueness of the situation).

Three. If she didn't take this opportunity, my partner lamented, "Things are only going to get worse for you. You are far too young to be found in a ditch" (what she stood to lose).

Those words had the desired effect. Hubby got carted off to jail, and we stayed behind with the young woman to help gather her personal things.

If there is a lesson scarcity teaches, perhaps it is:

When we feel pressured, we hasten our decision-making process, and that can lead to errors in judgment.

Sometimes, this works out and is a good thing, like in the case of the abused woman who took her opportunity that night to get out. Sometimes, it can be a bad thing, like when we invest in something too quickly only to realize we bought a lemon. We can mitigate the anxiety this influence is designed to create if we,

Take a moment and think, Whose best interest does this really serve?

Fear

Fear doesn't have a lot of upsides because it is more like a fist than a fingertip—but it is an influence. If I received a quarter for every time I have heard a parent say, "If you don't behave, he is going to take you to jail," I would have been able to retire long ago. Adults embroiled in a disagreement say the same thing: "I'm calling the cops." Fear is used to try to control the behavior of another through the threat of an undesirable consequence. Unfortunately, with examples like the ones above it is likely to reinforce a view that the police are "the heavy" rather than protection against the heavy. Fear can stop people from doing the right thing, inhibit their ability to think for themselves, and can stop action.

Fearmongering is prevalent in many facets of our society. Governments use this tactic to incite fear into the populace. By identifying threats (real or imaginary), a government can justify actions that, under normal circumstances, would be met with firm opposition. A scared public is more easily swayed, and increases in defense spending, military budgets, or border controls get top priority instead of building or maintaining infrastructure, supporting social programs, or expanding knowledge bases or idea discussions. Fear constricts societies, but peace expands them. That's scary for some. Promoting fear strengthens their position, and those scary changes that peace allows for and inspires can be put off another day.

Terrorist organizations use it to instill fear globally when they foreshadow future attacks on videos and carry out dramatic attacks against civilian populations.

In criminal organizations, members agree that snitches get stitches if they talk out of turn, thus keeping the group's secrets intact and everyone in line, as discussed in chapter four. Some gangs wear "colors" (specific clothing or tattoos that denote membership) to be able to be identified as members and create a sense of fear and control. In some communities, gangs draw up boundaries and areas of control. The ordinary people living in these districts must be careful not to unknowingly "represent" other groups' colors. In other communities like my own, there is limited open displaying of boundary settings. Most gangsters instead choose to avoid the use of "colors" so as not to attract unnecessary attention or become targets for retaliatory strikes. In my city, if you have a cell phone and a car, there is no boundary. That also means no area of the city is immune to the violence gangs may have.

Not unlike gangsters, sex traffickers also use the constant threat of violent repercussions as one way of controlling the women enslaved to them. Young girls and women inexperienced in dealing with the initial false charms are no match for these predators. To create vulnerability, pimps begin by wining and dining before manipulating their prey into vulnerable positions. They often introduce drugs or special gifts like free rent or new clothes to the targeted girl. As the "tab" grows, his talons sink deeper until one day, she is trapped and forced to sell her body for sex so she can pay back what she owes and/or maintain her now-blooming addiction.

Years ago, from his perch behind the counter of a fast-food restaurant, one predator would look out into the mall's food court every day, scoping for the next girl. Like a lion on the Serengeti hunting zebras, he knew what he was looking for in a victim: the girl who was isolated, the one that sat at a table with her head hung a little lower, the one who didn't easily smile, the one who held resignation and pain in her eyes. When he spotted her, he would make his move. It would begin with a seemingly innocent courtship. Then, one day, he would remind her of all the nice things he had done and how she now owed him. With his urging, she reluctantly agreed that, yes, she would sleep with that stranger if the predator kept his promise to never hurt a member of her family, particularly her younger sister—whom he had already threatened to harm.

The girl in this story was fourteen and one of almost a dozen young girls he had manipulated, coerced, and threatened over almost a year to have sex with men, sometimes four times their age, out of fear that if they didn't, he would do something terrible to them or to someone they loved. Thankfully, this predator's misdeeds were discovered, and he went to prison for a very long time.

Fear is a powerful influence, and the young are

especially vulnerable. Another case of sex trafficking occurred years ago. It began as a report of suspicious activity at a local hotel. Responding to the complaint, my partner and I arrived on the scene to find two nineteen-year-old girls in a hotel room with a male who had a long history of pimping. The girls were living out of two suitcases. One had been crying, as evidenced by mascara smears around her eyes. The other had been reported missing by her concerned family. In the room, a garbage can brimmed with used condoms and wrappers, the air smelled like latex and sex, and the floor was littered with "trashy-looking" garments. The room was being used for prostitution despite the denials of all three. The male suspect had warrants and would be taken to jail. Despite this, neither girl would decide to leave that day. Sadly, no offer of resources or support would change their minds. As I left that afternoon, I couldn't help but feel bad that fear was triumphing over freedom, not unlike the women in the following story.

Some people with dreams of immigrating to our country have instead found themselves inadvertently in the grasp of a human trafficker who will use the threat of deportation as the reason they must stay enslaved to him.

About five years ago, I was involved in an investigation that led to the discovery of a trick pad after a customer had unexpectedly dropped dead in one. As police assessed the scene, looking for clues to explain what had happened, my partner came across a date book filled with names—women who had been trafficked into Canada for sex slavery. As we read down the ledger, I was shocked and saddened to see the name of the first girl written in the book. All her activities for the day were accounted for in black and white on the page. Between eight a.m. and seven p.m., she had been with fourteen different men—this included her "scheduled" break from two-three p.m. Unfortunately, for her and the other two women represented in the book, any chance of interdicting them was out of the question as none were present by the time police arrived at the apartment.

In relationships, one spouse may use fear to control their partner through expressions such as, "No one would ever tolerate you like I do," or "If you leave, I will kill myself," or worse, "I will kill you." Threats such as these are meant to control the other partner, with the consequence being that people stay in unhealthy, unhappy relationships for long periods of time. Don't ignore statements like these.

When a person acts like they don't care, believe them.

Only a few months ago, my phone rang in the early morning hours. My boss started the conversation like he always does.

"We have a homicide. See you at the office."

Click.

It took me a few moments to un-blur from the

abrupt wakeup. I have developed strategies to overcome the desire to immediately fall back to sleep. My phone is never within reach of my bedside table, so I must get out from under the warm covers to answer it, giving my foggy mind a chance to clear. I keep a clean suit and pressed shirt hanging ready in the bathroom so I don't disturb the house while I scramble around to get ready in the dead of night.

Out of the shower and on my way to the office, I slurped back a caffeinated beverage and wondered what it would be this time. In this case, it was a barely twenty-year-old girl gunned down in a gravel car park behind a residence. It would later be identified as our suspect's home. A barely twenty-something boy himself, jealous after his break-up with the victim, had killed her. If he couldn't have her, nobody else would either.

When the intricacies of love, jealousy, and hate intertwine, they can produce appalling brutality when the fear-monger becomes a killer. How did this young man come to see love as something demanded and subject to lethal reprimand? How would his and his victim's lives be different if he had seen love beyond possession and control? It got me thinking—

> *Love requires freedom to trust a person will stay, and if they don't, freedom to trust a relationship has run its course.*

It seems like such a simple thing, but so often, this

concept gets distorted, especially by those who resort to fear tactics to "manage" their relationships. This may sound over-simplified, but trusting the ebb and flow of life and relationships could save so many of us from a lot of avoidable hurt.

In this case, if the young man who had proclaimed his love for the innocent victim mere days earlier could have mustered the courage to hit the release button, it would have been the most loving gift he could have given her. I can't help but imagine that had he chosen unconditional release. It is likely a part of him would have remained in her heart forever.

Earlier, I identified that the threat of police is often utilized by fearmongers, but it is also used by police to stop poor behavior. Statements like, "You are one step away from going to jail," are used by some officers to attempt to send a clear warning that things could escalate if the behavior continues. It's not a problem if the officer has the authority to action the promise of jail time, but it's not a wise option if the statements made are idle threats and not lawful remedies. When it's not a lawful remedy, this type of persuasion can quickly turn public sentiment against us.

People must be mindful that when they use fear to influence another, they are exerting a domineering force (and catastrophizing) that removes the feeling of choice from the table.

Human behavior appears more predictable when we understand the laws of social influence. In an officer's life, these influences can be tapped to help navigate more positive outcomes in chaos and crisis. In our own lives, they can do the same.

Ripples

"Everything we do, even the slightest thing we do, can have a ripple effect and repercussions that emanate. If you throw a pebble into the water on one side of the ocean, it can create a tidal wave on the other side."

—Victor Webster

By understanding the social influences discussed in chapter six, we can better predict the positive or negative consequences of our actions. Most people can't, or don't, see four steps ahead of themselves. They don't understand their actions (and persuasions) have tangible consequences, not only for themselves but also for other people. The most effective police officers I know understand this:

Our actions create ripples (or tsunamis) in the world around us.

I have also come to learn,

Challenges create opportunities for wisdom.

The Law of Cause and Effect

Early in my career, I figured out I could produce predictable behavior in people simply with the presence of my uniform or marked police car. A benign example of this occurs when motorists see a police cruiser. The reaction is the immediate flash of brake lights even if the driver is not speeding. This compulsion to slow down is a positive consequence of traffic enforcement in municipalities. I've certainly learned where the popular speed traps are in my city. When I am nearing these areas, like everyone else, I'm aware of the pending trap and know to check my speedometer to ensure I'm within the posted limit. I do this at these locations even when the speed traps are not set up. Anticipating the potential is enough for me to take my foot off the gas. Consistent enforcement of posted speed limits in specific places (the cause) conditions local drivers to slow down, even when no officer is present (the effect).

Years ago, when I was on patrol on quiet nights, we would set up what appeared to be a check-stop or roadblock. There was a particular thoroughfare we suspected was used by drunk drivers and operators of stolen vehicles, and another street running parallel that was used by those wanting to stay off the beaten path. We selected our location for its visibility; anyone driving toward us would see the emergency lights from a distance away (cause). The theory was if someone was up to no good, they would reveal their concern in advance by avoiding our location with a U-turn (effect). They did not know that we had another vehicle positioned away from the main check-stop to intercept those U-turn drivers trying to evade us. For several years, this became an easy way to identify people with something to hide. It was like shooting fish in a barrel; we recovered stolen cars and took many impaired drivers off the street. This approach made us more efficient and effective at culling the criminal drivers from the law-abiding ones.

Back in chapter two, we discussed the importance of closing the loop and the effect it has when officers call back complainants to report on their progress. Even if the crime hasn't been solved, trust and confidence are built, and those complainants will be more likely to call again if they see anything else untoward (cause). Armed with a consistent and steady flow of information from the public, the police will solve more crimes in those communities, improving the safety of all (effect). Again, an active, engaged public is required to keep our communities safe.

Cause and effect are powerful, but it's important to understand it has the potential to create unforeseen and sometimes lethal consequences, especially when those involved don't realize they are creating a cause for a deadly effect. Hindsight helps. Understanding the relationship between cause and effect and the chain reactions it can generate is important.

A few years before my time, a police officer observed a vehicle driving at a high rate of speed down a roadway. Unbeknownst to the officer, the vehicle's driver had just committed a robbery with a firearm and was fleeing the crime scene. After the police officer activated his lights and siren, the speeding driver pulled to the side of the road, and the lone officer approached. The driver, likely thinking he was going to jail for the robbery, and the police officer, believing he was about to issue a traffic summons, created the perfect storm for the deadly encounter that followed. The driver of the vehicle shot and killed the unsuspecting officer on the side of the road.

Ten years ago, I worked on a case where a husband killed his wife and fled the city before her body could be discovered. Bank records confirmed he spent the following night in a small-town hotel before continuing east, presumably toward family in Ontario, a three-day drive from Alberta if you're pushing hard. While he traveled through Saskatchewan, a Royal Canadian Mounted Police (RCMP) officer stopped him and issued a ticket for speeding. His wife's body had not yet been discovered, and the officer had no idea the speeding driver had killed her and was on the run. Fortunately, in this case, the suspect took the ticket and did not attempt to harm the officer.

The unintended consequence of this action was surprising. After receiving the ticket, the husband turned his vehicle around and returned to the crime scene. He took his own life in a room adjacent to where his wife's body still lay. Perhaps the anxiety of the traffic stop, the feeling of forever looking over his shoulder and not knowing when he would get caught, was too much and enough to compel him to take his own life. Maybe he wanted to be with his wife when he did it. He was more likely surprised that he was not arrested and wondered if his wife was still alive. We will never know what was going through his head. What is certain is that the traffic stop was the catalyst for the husband to return to the crime scene, whatever his reasons.

It's widely known within law enforcement a person's curiosity can get the better of them. Arsonists, particularly those who light fires to feed an obsession, have stayed behind to watch their work while emergency crews battle the blaze. Killers sometimes do the same, returning to the crime scene, curious to look upon the mayhem of their deadly deed or curious to know if the body has been discovered. This was the exact scenario that led to the identification of the heinous offender mentioned in chapter two, who murdered three family members and was caught on residential cameras driving past the victim's residence the following morning.

Mindful of this compulsion, an investigator may set up a scenario to entice a curious suspect back. Years ago, I was involved in a case where the investigator did just this and used a trick (cause) to create an effect. It was springtime in the city, and months had passed since the victim had been last seen. Growing desperate to find her remains, a plan was hatched to try and lure the suspect to the location of her remains, wherever that was. We had no idea. Picking up the phone, our charismatic detective with a soft British accent simply asked him, "What exactly was she wearing again after you dropped her off?" Following up with the comment, "The reason we ask is late this afternoon, the body of a female was discovered, and we want to confirm if the clothing this female is wearing is consistent with the clothing you remember your girlfriend was wearing on the night she disappeared."

Silence followed. After several seconds and a few audible gulps of breath, the suspect responded with the description of the girl he once called mother to his son. "A pretty little white and black dress and running shoes."

"Okay, thanks. I'll let you know when I know if this is her," the investigator responded. Plainclothes officers were outside the suspect's home. Everyone waited to see what he would do next. Would curiosity get the best of him? Would he breeze by the scene of his crime and reveal her location to our surveillance team?

It took about fifteen minutes to find the answer. Emerging from his house, the suspect walked out his front door and a few blocks down to the local pub, where he drank the stress away.

Not the result we wished. Though he was later charged and convicted—curiosity did not get the better of him that day. The same could not be said in the next case where it got the better of me.

In my first year of homicide, I was involved in a case

where the body of a young woman was found hidden in brush behind a large berm. She had been sexually assaulted and murdered. After her discovery, I pitched to members of my team the idea of placing cameras in the area of her remains to catch her killer returning to the area, which was in a remote area of a large city park. Agreeably, the lead investigator tasked me to get the cameras into place.

For ten days, I waited, wondering if he would return. Had he seen the media attention following the discovery of her body? Had the cameras caught him? Surely ten days must be long enough to wait?

Anxious, I collected the hidden equipment, drove quickly back to the office, and began viewing the footage. There was nothing except a few curious coyotes and deer. Deflated, it took some time to puff myself back up again—there was foreseeably nothing else to go on that could assist us in identifying her killer, or so it seemed. The break we needed came by surprise when a witness observed a suspicious man go down behind the berm twenty-four hours after I had removed the cameras. She recorded the license plate of the vehicle he arrived in. Unbelievably, we were full steam ahead. He was identified as a suspect and convicted of his crime a few years later. Although the case was solved, my impatience and curiosity got the better of me. When I first placed the cameras, I planned to give it fourteen days. If I had stuck to my original plan, I would have got him doing exactly what I had learned from old FBI manuals and criminology textbooks—sometimes killers do return to the scene of their crime.

Despite my impatience, curiosity remains a strange and strong compulsion that investigators often count on to find evidence. If we consider an offender's curiosity, we can follow that trail and see where it leads. Think about your internet browser history. When we're curious about something, we can do a quick search and have a plethora of answers at our fingertips. In a second, I can have thousands of chocolate chip cookie recipes to choose from—or darker things.

In the case above, my curiosity (and impatience) did not catch the killer that day. In the end, it was his own internet browsing history that did. Following his arrest, an analysis of his computer revealed that on the morning after the victim had disappeared, the following searches were conducted: fingerprints on a dead body, how long does semen stay on a body, and decomposition of a dead body in grass.

Curiosity (cause) can lead to interesting effects, be that your new favorite cookie recipe or compelling evidence of how a murderer researched the FAQs of his particular crimes post-mortem.

Curiosity is also behind many bad decisions, some so tragic it's hard to talk about, even when the lesson needs to be shared. Several years ago, two twelve-year-olds on a sleepover pushed a chair up to the basement window, hoisted themselves up, pulled off the screen, and were off like shots in the night while the adults inside the home slept peacefully, completely unaware of the nightmare they would wake up to the next afternoon.

The pair walked kilometers into our downtown district, an area of town where nothing good happens at three a.m., especially when you are twelve-year-old girls simply wanting to "hang out." For the next few hours, this is exactly what they did. Their plan from the outset had been to sneak out at two a.m., walk downtown, hang out, catch the first bus back home at five a.m., sneak back into the house, and be snuggled in their sleeping bags before their absence was ever detected.

The execution of the first part of the plan went off without a hitch. They made it downtown no worse for wear and gained a few stories to tell their friends about later. After wandering the streets for a couple of hours, the girls finally made their way to a bus shelter, where they planned to hunker down before they caught their bus home. As they sat on the bench inside the shelter, they noticed a small vial of powder lying on the ground under their seats. Curious about what it could be, one of the two youngsters pocketed it until they could get home and look more closely at it in the light.

Arriving back to their basement window at half past five, the giggling tweens re-entered the basement in the same way they left. Once safely inside, the two lamented about their experiences and the things they had seen in the wee hours of the morning in an area known for several addiction and homeless centers.

Then they remembered the vial.

Digging into her pocket, one of the girls presented their find. The vile contained a fine pinkish powder and had a black top. Not certain what it was, but suspecting it could be a drug, one of the girls told us later that the curiosity to try it was so overwhelming that there was little contemplation between the two before the black cap came off, and each gave it a snort.

Almost instantly, the effects of the fentanyl took hold of one of the girls more than the other, and not wanting to be left out, a second snort was inhaled.

Tired but euphoric, the pair fell asleep quickly. Hours passed, and it was now one o'clock in the afternoon. Not hearing anything from the basement for hours, one of the adults inside the home went to check on the girls. Descending the stairs, he was shocked to find one of the two dead. Dead at twelve years old. Dead from a fentanyl overdose. His daughter would survive, but the gravity of the unfixable moment set in instantly. Their overwhelming curiosity had muted both girls' abilities to see past the temptation.

This was not the only time in my career that I had investigated a young person's death, where youthful exuberance and curiosity led to an unthinkable ending. Only six months after dealing with the two twelve-year-olds, I investigated the death of another minor. This time, a nine-year-old was found hanging from the top bunk with a bed sheet. Days before this crisis occurred, the mother was doing all the things a mom should do: she was staying on top of the kids and their activities, and she paid attention to what they watched on television and what they consumed over the internet. In doing so, she found that her youngest had begun to watch videos online of kids asphyxiating themselves until they passed out. Known as the "choking game," this idea has been around since I was a kid. Still, now, in 2021, it was no longer just a schoolyard trick that left us lightheaded but a social media challenge that had children and young adults tempting fate by timing how long they could actually mechanically asphyxiate themselves for, using a bed sheet or a towel, before they became unconscious and passed out.

Recognizing the dangers of such a ridiculous and irresponsible "challenge," the mother, in this case, acted quickly and prudently, knowing how susceptible her son was to the ideas of others, even the bad ones. Removing the tablet from her son's possession and following it up with a conversation about why putting pressure on the neck until he went faint was dangerous and not a good idea. She believed she had nipped this issue in the bud until a week later, she found her son dead.

No words could ever express the utter devastation and grief which followed.

Be mindful of your curiosity. It informs our actions and can lead us to great discoveries or dark places.

Media

Professional media outlets remain a valuable resource in keeping the community informed and bringing about change, and for the police, they are vital for disseminating information to the public. I do not have enough fingers and toes to count the number of times news reports have led to tips and information that captured some of our city's most dangerous offenders or solved some of our most upsetting crimes.

In police investigations, the media plays a huge role in putting cause and effect into motion. For example, a young couple reeling from losing their baby was in town for a ceremony to honor the baby's memory at our local children's hospital. Afterward, the couple went to a nearby hotel bar to have a drink and something to eat. At some point in the evening, the couple got up from their seats and left a purse unattended at the table. The purse contained the ashes of their deceased child. A duo inside the bar noticed the unattended purse and stole it, likely believing it contained cash and credit cards. Upon catching wind of this story, well-intentioned journalists reported the couples' plight on television and provided video and descriptions of the culprits (cause). Within days, tips from the public led police to identify both offenders, lay charges, and recover and return the ashes to the grieving parents (effect).

Both the media and law enforcement play vital service roles within our society, but they are different.

The media's decisions are not always the same as law enforcement, nor should they be. Sometimes, the media's role can be to our advantage, sometimes not. It turned out in our favor in the following case, but it could have easily gone the other way.

Several years ago, a gangster fired a single bullet into a crowd of people—just because—and struck dead a woman enjoying a night out with friends. The victim's fate seemed almost eerily predetermined. It was like that bullet had eyes when it struck her in the chest with such lethal precision. She was likely dead before knowing she had even been shot, and her tragic story is a haunting reminder:

Embrace life today.

Early in the investigation, we garnered a description of the getaway vehicle from surveillance cameras and eyewitnesses. We made efforts to identify the driver and the vehicle's location before it could jeopardize evidence or the players involved could go dark. We considered releasing the vehicle's description to the media to elicit help from the public, but we deemed the risk too high. Cause and effect is one of those things that can help or hurt, and, in this case, we were concerned that making the vehicle's description known to the public before our attempts to locate it were exhausted could lead to the vehicle being altered or hidden or evidence destroyed.

Ultimately, our risk-management decision did not matter; a media outlet got hold of the same information and released it. This caused a real scramble and race against the clock before the suspects saw the news. Fortunately for us and the victim's family, our concerns were moot. After watching the evening news, a person in the getaway vehicle blew the case wide open when he came forward to tell his side of the story. This was one of the only times I have seen that happen in a murder investigation, but I was thankful it had.

Law enforcement will solicit the media's help, for example, to release the composite sketch of a suspect or a detailed description of a person of interest. It's important to understand an action like this sets many dominoes in motion, and police must have a plan in place to handle the inundation of calls and tips, as well as an efficient process to prioritize the volume of information for the pertinent and applicable tips in relatively short amounts of time. Everyone who has ever seen a composite sketch knows the resemblance to someone they know can be uncanny.

There is more than volume involved, though. We must,

Be mindful of what we are setting into motion—and mitigate the risks—before they become problems we can't easily fix.

I was involved in several cases where a suspect was identified but could not be located. In cases like these, before going to the media with information about the suspect, we put into place processes that help ensure the soon-to-be-accused person won't flee the jurisdiction or country once we tip our hand and release their name. This includes contacting international border officials, looping them in, and entering our suspects into national police databases—important first steps to avoid a suspect trying to elude an investigator's dragnet. However, despite these best efforts, sometimes they do. When that happens, the costs associated with getting them back can be astronomical—including the cost to justice when they cannot be tried for their crimes committed here.

I will always remember one case where the suspect had been involved in a lethal swarming attack on a young man outside a nightclub. The primary investigator moved quickly to identify all five men involved in the murder, and in short order, they were rounded up and remanded for their various roles. However, in the months following their arrests, several suspects made applications for bail and were released pending their trial. Upon his release, one of the suspects crafted fake identification, including a fake passport. He boarded a plane and was off to Vietnam before anyone—including his father—knew he was even gone.

Over the next year, the lead detective worked tirelessly to bring him back to Canada to stand trial.

She negotiated with Vietnam officials and asked for their assistance in finding him. Dogged determination was what ultimately led to her success. After he was finally in custody, she and her partner hopped on a plane to Vietnam, unsure if he would even be released into their custody.

After spending several weeks in a Vietnamese jail, I am not sure who was happier to see who when she finally got permission to bring him back to Canada. He was convicted a year later for his involvement in the murder.

Game of Chess

I have often thought of homicide investigations like a game of chess—our next move depends on the last move of the perpetrator, and we need to employ multiple strategies to find the truth. These strategies are scripted, and the steps are a sequence. As we roll out each new strategy, we anticipate there will be a measurable effect.

An example of this occurred five years ago when I was investigating a person who was believed to have killed his friend. As the evidence began to mount, I prepared for an arrest, including a campaign to "soften" our bad guy for the interview room.

At my request, the family stepped forward to give several different interviews to local media and were asked to share that they were looking for an apology more than anything else. We also had uniformed police officers become more visible around the area of the suspect's home, not to harass him but to remind him that without dealing with what he had done (murder his friend), he would always be looking over his shoulder. Both were powerful themes the interviewer could use later.

It worked. In the days following, the subject was arrested, and the interviewer secured several important admissions from him from the themes we had begun building earlier in the week.

Another case I worked on started as a *who-done-it* homicide that quickly morphed into something more. The victim was a person who tended to live in dark places, drugs in this instance, and one summer evening was gunned down in front of his house. Information obtained from the street, phone records, and video surveillance focused our investigation on a small group of suspects associated with the victim and ultimately led us to follow them around the city.

You can learn a lot about the people you're investigating through surveillance. In this case, we learned our homicide suspects were also prolific home invaders who spent hours each day planning their next drug rips or scores on unsuspecting victims. Remember, as police, our primary function is maintaining public safety. As we watched, we were duty-bound to prevent these robberies before someone got hurt or killed. To thwart the criminal behavior of this small group, we looked to different strategies (causes) to get the job done, which included creating a high-profile police presence around identified residences they were planning to rob. These strategies worked long enough to scare off the group (effect) and gave us enough time to gather the evidence that landed all five men in jail.

Years ago, I was asked to assist an outside agency investigating the murder of an elderly woman who had been brutally killed in her home. The evidence pointed toward one person—the woman's daughter. Investigators theorized that their suspect had savagely killed her mother for financial gain to feed her out-of-control gambling addiction.

The dilemma the investigators faced was that, based on the evidence collected to that point, the victim's daughter was their primary suspect. Yet, they suspected there was more evidence still outstanding that could make their case rock solid. Their concern, and rightly so, was that by speaking with more people who may have additional information or may have seen something, there was the potential that the suspect would catch wind of these inquiries and realize she was their primary suspect. The investigators did not want this. They wanted her to continue to leave little breadcrumbs of evidence, none the wiser. Something needed to be done to allow investigators to ask more direct questions about the woman.

A plan was hatched. Investigators would put the suspect in front of the media cameras and have her plea to the public for help solving her mom's murder case. In doing so, community members who recognized the woman could call with information about what they may have seen that they now found suspicious.

On a Thursday morning, our team members met with the suspect, who agreed to go on camera. Crocodile tears streamed from her eyes as she delivered her plea to the world (cause). By doing so, two critical witnesses came forward (effect). One saw the woman around her mother's home on the day of the murder, and the other was a store clerk who recognized the woman as a customer who had bought the same jacket on two different days and afterward had asked that the store video be destroyed.

Investigators were now able to ask the woman more direct questions to see what she would do.

"Hey there, something weird came up after talking to the media. A tip came in from someone who said they saw you around your mother's house on the day of the murder. Could this be true?"

"Hi, me again. Another tip came in that you purchased two of the same jacket from a local store and then asked the clerk if you could destroy the video of yourself making the purchases. Could this be true?"

Slowly, she was placed on the proverbial hot seat. Not long after, she confessed her sins to a skillful interviewer.

Juries

I once had to explain cause and effect to a jury I was giving evidence to on a murder trial. One of the accused had read about the case in the paper (cause) and confessed his involvement in the crime to a friend (effect). I explained the phenomenon this way. "Imagine if I told you on my way to the courthouse this morning, I saw a fatal car accident involving a black minivan. For any of you with loved ones who drive black minivans, it is reasonable to predict that you would act. You may call them to make sure they are okay, maybe you check the news or go online for details of the accident, confirm it wasn't them. Perhaps you would drive past the accident scene. In any case, hearing about an accident involving your loved one would prompt some sort of action. In most cases, the police could measure your reaction to this news through surveillance."

Juries provide a valuable function within the criminal justice system but can introduce challenging dynamics. Most jurors have had very limited exposure to the courts before sitting in a juror's chair and benefit from clear, strong explanations from professional witnesses presenting evidence on the stand. For many jurors, the only exposure they have had to police or court proceedings is what they have watched on TV, in movies, or in the media. There can be hefty gaps between what the entertainment-based versions and a real police investigation and the justice system look like. The term "CSI effect" was coined a few years ago to explain these preconceived notions and erroneous, damaging expectations. Jurors ask why a certain technique (often improbable or impossible with current technology and science applications) wasn't applied to a particular piece of evidence, or they come in with a misunderstanding of what forensics can and can't do.

Investigators can also get caught up in this effect. I once searched for a cigarette expert because I wanted to show that the burn time of a cigarette could help explain when it was discarded, important evidence if it could be proven. I was trying to narrow a timeframe and pinpoint when my suspect had dropped his cigarette butt. Turns out my inquiry was bunk science. *Burn.*

Another example is the dating of bruises. Now I know it can't be done, not as specifically as I was looking for, anyway. Neither can establishing a proof-positive, exact time of death when a death has not been witnessed or captured on video. The best is a ballpark timeframe, and even that depends on many variables, including environmental temperature, physical exertion prior to death, sepsis or infections in the body, and the list goes on and on.

The CSI effect can be damaging when a jury doesn't understand what they saw on their favorite cop show just can't be done, and these preconceived notions affect court cases. I remember watching one show where the forensic video technician zoomed in on the reflection of the fictional victim's eye caught on video and saw the reflected image of the killer. This totally ruined the episode for me and seemed more like a gaping plot hole plugged with fertilizer than a creative twist. But for others, the concept makes sense.

Perhaps one of the most famous cases where the CSI effect has been identified as influencing an outcome is the case of two-year-old Caylee Marie Anthony, who lived in Orlando, Florida, with her mother, Casey Marie Anthony, and her maternal grandparents. After her grandmother reported her missing, the toddler's skeletal remains, with duct tape at her mouth, were found with a blanket inside a trash bag in a wooded area near the family home. The grandmother had become suspicious about her daughter's behavior, as did detectives when the woman gave them odd and conflicting information. She was charged with first-degree murder and pleaded not guilty. The prosecutors alleged Casey murdered her daughter. The defense countered the child had accidentally drowned. The jury found Casey not guilty of murder or child abuse but guilty of providing false information to a law enforcement officer.

In murder cases, the medical examiner determines both the manner and cause of death. During this trial, the medical examiner mentioned duct tape as one reason why she ruled the death a homicide (manner) but officially listed it as "death by undetermined means" (cause). This seemed to be an insurmountable snag for the jury; even with the significant circumstantial evidence and post-offense behavior by the accused, there was no forensic evidence that could say definitively how little Caylee died.

In my experience, when human remains are found in poor condition, it's common for an undetermined finding to be recorded for the cause of death. Suppose there are not enough of the remains intact. In that case, it's difficult for a medical examiner to determine why someone has died as the evidence has long since gone through the process of decomposition and predation by animals and insects. Sometimes, there are markings on the bones if there was a weapon or tool used or post-mortem damage to the skeleton that can be identified. If the cause of death is from something like choking or smothering, it's less likely that bone analysis (without tissue to examine) could make that determination. Sometimes, remains are found scattered by nefarious means (dismembered) or something more innocuous like animal distribution, and a complete body is not recovered. Potential clues to the cause of death could then be missing. Investigators must use sound logic and circumstances to fill in the missing pieces when this occurs.

In the Caylee Anthony investigation, three out of the four manners of death (accident, natural causes, suicide) can be ruled out very quickly. The investigators and medical examiner came to that conclusion. The discovery of duct tape over Caylee's young face, the persistent denials and inconsistent statements made by her mother, Casey, to investigators, and the discovery of her body in a bag in the woods leave only one conclusion. This was a homicide. That the jury couldn't get there speaks to the influence of the CSI effect.

This case is troubling. When expectations of what actual forensic science can do are dictated by fictional examples on television and movies created to entertain us, not advise juries, the chance for justice is significantly jeopardized. I'd love a gadget that burped out an admissible report of precisely how and when a person died or an app that beeped when I was standing next to the guy who did it. There are powerful technologies available to law enforcement, but it's important to remember not everything we see in a show or movie is real.

What does this insight into expectations and possible preconceived notions mean for investigators? We must effectively explain why evidence may be absent from a scene and why there may not be a "smoking gun" for every murder. Why wasn't the suspect's DNA found under the victim's fingernails? Perhaps the victim never had a chance to fight back from the attack. Why didn't the suspect leave any footwear impressions at the scene? Perhaps they removed their shoes at the door. Why couldn't the medical examiner determine an exact cause of death? Because the victim's remains were significantly compromised from animal and insect activity and decomposition. Why couldn't the police get the plate number of the getaway vehicle if it was captured on video? Because the pixel quality of the video was such that, even with enhancement, the numbers were illegible.

And so on.

Sometimes, the absence of information is a clue in itself.

Living the Lessons of Cause and Effect

Understanding cause and effect means understanding that we face choices that impact ourselves and others every day. The question is, are we cognizant of what our actions create? For instance, a parent finds out their child did something wrong, asks them about it, and the child admits the wrongdoing — if the response is a punishment for the unacceptable behavior, instead of acknowledging that the child has told the truth, the effect will be that the parent is conditioning the child to lie. Obviously, this is not the intention, but it's the outcome their actions create.

Several years ago, I was involved in an investigation where we arrested a suspect for the murder of his girlfriend. After a few months in jail, the alleged killer pleaded to the court for bail.

In preparation for the hearing, the senior crown prosecutor on the case worked diligently to ensure that the court had all the available facts. He knew the evidence against the accused was strong and that this diligence would help ensure that the offender remained in custody while awaiting trial.

On the day of the bail hearing, I sat with the murdered young woman's family. I watched as the prosecutor masterfully laid out the police theory of what had happened and the evidence that led to the arrest of the accused (cause).

Across the room, the family and friends of the offender sat, also listening intently to the presentation of the evidence. In the end, the judge was swayed by the crown's case and dismissed the bail application.

Relieved by the court's decision, I continued my work and moved on to other pressing matters until, one day, a letter from the mail room was dropped off on my boss's desk (effect). The envelope, which contained no return address, immediately caught both our attention and piqued our curiosity. As we opened it carefully, several grains of white powder spilled out, prompting a call to our local fire department for assistance.

Clearing the office of any would-be hazardous materials, fire officials determined that the powder was not something toxic and likely nothing more than a scare tactic.

With the threat of inhaling a noxious substance over, we delved deeper into the letter's content, which was a boastful and exuberant account of the crime against the victim as told through the eyes of the "real killer."

The letter contained several erroneous pieces of information. It also lacked any holdback evidence not discussed at the hearing, though it did include truly wild assertions.

Its intent and timing raised obvious questions. The motive seemed clear—create doubt and weaken the crown's case. However, the sheer volume of mistaken details did the exact opposite. Someone was desperate enough to manufacture such a letter in an attempt to get the accused to escape justice for his horrible crime.

We dug deeper to ascertain the identity of the sender and, in doing so, found more pieces of damning evidence that may not have been found if the letter had not been sent. This additional evidence further solidified that we had the right guy from the beginning. He was convicted of his heinous crimes by a jury of his peers no more than a year later.

I learned early not to pick a fight I couldn't win. There was no point threatening an action I knew I couldn't follow through. Over time, idle threats—when a person states a consequence they have no intention or authority to impose—undermine a person. Nothing they say will be treated as valid, and the subsequent threats will be ignored.

Developing a win-win or lose-win philosophy has helped me in knowing when I can and cannot push. Let me explain. The *battle* equals the short game (immediate result), and the *war* equals the long game (long-term impact on the team).

A win-win scenario is when you win the battle and

the war: the immediate result is a victory, and the long-term impact on the team is also a winning return.

A lose-win is when the battle (game) is lost, but the war is won (how the game was played and coached supports the long-term health and effectiveness of the team).

A win-lose is when the battle (game) was won but with strategies that undermine the long-term viability of the team, so the war was lost.

And a lose-lose scenario is, you guessed it, when you lose the battle and the war: you attempt to win by employing strategies that jeopardize the long-term strength of the team and still lose.

Having a grounded winning philosophy is something good to keep in mind. Accepting that losing is part of any game is not defeatist; it's understanding the big picture. I don't believe we should celebrate losses like wins, but there will be days when things don't work out the way we hope. Losing on the scoreboard should be the least of our concerns if, in doing so, we sacrifice another trying to get the win. When coaches place the best players onto the ice, court, or field in the dying minutes of the game, trying to tie or win at the expense of others (cause), it sends negative messaging to the rest of the team that they aren't as valued (effect). This destroys belief within the group for nothing more than the short-term goal of winning that single game and derails the long-term progress of the team.

Play to the long game.

Instilling belief in an individual, team, or group sends impressive, positive ripples. It's one of the ways I have used cause and effect and the positive influence of persuasion in my life—especially when I was a coach.

Hockey is a team sport that requires players to respect their coaches and teammates. That respect keeps the team harmonious and effective. Our team rules were always: respect yourself, respect your teammates, respect the opposition and officials. When things would get pushed against the team rules in practice, I would ask the dissenting player to stand at center ice with me while his teammates skated their hearts out for him. This was my way of reinforcing the message that being part of a team meant not letting down your teammates so they don't have to work harder for your mistakes. Although some may gasp, the effect was actually very positive, and the players immediately began to police each other. Of course, it is essential to closely monitor and immediately address any unintended negative effects of this type of discipline, such as the disciplined player being isolated or bullied by their peers. To mitigate this risk, having all the players share in the lesson at center ice seemed to help, and in all my years of coaching, I never had an issue.

I once heard a coach say there are a hundred ways to say "good job." He was right. I'm really impressed with how hard you're practicing right now. I really like the way you're moving your feet today. Keep doing what you're doing, and you'll master that skill. Incorporating positive phrases and messaging (the cause) into our interactions with others is the simplest way to get results (the effect) and more effective than shaming someone, whether we are teachers, business leaders, parents, coaches, or police officers trying to change a person's path.

Positive messages are the engines that inspire eople, build confidence, and create positive action.

In life, it's common to get frustrated with what we may consider a lack of effort by others. Often, people need that extra motivation to work harder and run faster or farther. The best coaches know when we revert to phrases such as, "What are you doing? Get moving!" (cause), these words demotivate a player. They kill confidence and zap all the fun out of the experience (effect). Instead, if we acknowledge the behavior we want to see, there is a better chance of producing that result through a positive presence. "You are really dribbling well today. If you can remember to keep your feet moving all the way through your next shift, I think you will see an even bigger difference the next time; give that a try." This approach creates a reciprocated uptick in effort.

Another strategy to get a group thinking and moving together is to identify the person working hardest and use their example to inspire the rest of the group. "Look how hard Ethan is working for you guys today. He hasn't stopped moving his feet. Let's have everyone do the same and see what happens." Instilling belief in individuals benefits the whole group, organization, or community. We should understand our actions speak as loud or louder than our words. If we forget this, we can lose all we have gained or tried to accomplish in one fell swoop.

We all create ripples in our world through our actions, influences, and words, and we must be mindful of what we are putting into motion.

Nine Principles

"I can do things you cannot, you can do things I cannot; together we can do great things."

- Mother Theresa

There are as many ways to organize ourselves and our decision-making processes as there are people. However, when the stakes escalate, like they do in major cases, we need more coordinated approaches to get the job done and get it right the first time. The consequences of failing can be steep. As homicide investigators, we must always remember that the integrity of our investigation is paramount; following the evidence is key to preventing miscarriages of justice and seeing justice be served. So, what are the stakes for the people we investigate for murder in Canada?

In Canada, when a person is convicted of either first- or second-degree murder, their sentence is life, which means *until their heart stops beating*. On first-degree murder, twenty-five years is the minimum time before they can apply for parole—not a firm date of release. Only thirty percent of people serving a life sentence who apply for parole receive it. A common misconception is that a life sentence in Canada equates to twenty-five years. When an inmate has served through the parole ineligibility date (the number of years set at the time of sentencing that falls between ten to twenty-five years), the inmate may apply for parole.

As with any application process, it is not a guaranteed get-out-of-jail-free card. For many inmates, the date will come and go, and they will never be granted parole. Clifford Olsen, a notorious child serial killer who died in jail despite applying to get out, is one such example. There are many more.

There are those who get out after serving up to their parole eligibility date. However, when they do, their life sentence continues to hang over them. What that means is that back in the community, if a convicted murderer breaches his parole conditions, he is returned to jail to continue serving his life sentence. Just like those who remain incarcerated, the life sentence for those placed back into society does not end until they are dead. Those consequences are steep and require everyone involved in the administration of justice to make sound, principled decisions.

When I was a young, uniformed officer, it was always my partner (if I had one) and me handling and resolving the day's calls. Our decision-making processes followed the principles of discretion and what the law and policy-and-procedure manuals guided us to do. We would also bounce ideas off one another, but typically, the decision-making process never left the car, and most often, the senior officer had the final say.

Our system to track and stay on top of our follow-ups, arrest warrants, subpoenas, and arrest paperwork was simple: the passenger-side visor was for completed tasks, and the driver-side visor was for tasks yet to be completed. It wasn't particularly fancy, but it was effective for our purposes and demonstrated a basic workflow process. We organized our briefcases to work well from the car; the required paperwork had its own specific spot, and dividers kept each in order. Our system had built-in accountability mechanisms to ensure we were staying on top of our cases.

Looking back, I realize that these were not fail-safe, but for the most part, worked well so we could do our jobs effectively and efficiently. Our simple approach worked because of the relative lack of complexity these early investigations provided. These early cases were no less important, *and* they became sound building blocks for the more complex investigations to come. Keeping what fits in a briefcase and a couple of visors organized is necessary if you ever expect to keep warehouses of paperwork organized and the contents searchable and accessible.

When I first entered the world of organized crime and later homicide, I was introduced to a policing model I was not familiar with called Major Case Management (MCM). The model came as a result of the Campbell Inquiry, the formal investigation that identified systemic issues within the legal system, which had allowed serial rapist and killer Paul Bernardo to avoid detection and commit further heinous crimes for an unconscionable amount of time. In the early 1990s, Bernardo was involved in a series of rapes in Scarborough, Ontario, and later the sadistic murders of Tammy Lyn Homolka, Leslie Mahaffy, and Kristen French, committed with his then-wife Karla Homolka.

In his 1996 report, Justice Campbell identified that the lack of coordination, cooperation, and communications among police and other parts of the justice system contributed to a dangerous serial predator falling through the cracks. In the original investigation of the Scarborough rapist, Bernardo had voluntarily provided his DNA to investigators, but it was not tested for twenty-six months because he was not a prioritized suspect. When it eventually *was* tested, he was identified as the rapist.

Justice Campbell's inquiry also found that different police agencies were not communicating effectively, if at all, and Bernardo's files were not jurisdictionally linked early enough in the murder and sexual assault cases. MCM is now used by police agencies across Canada as a means of preventing other serious offenders from falling through the cracks and is a model that supports accurate, thorough, timely, and thoughtful investigations.

The nine principles of MCM are:

- The Command Triangle
- Communication
- Accountability Mechanisms
- Investigative Strategies
- Partnerships
- Leadership and Team Building
- Management Considerations
- Ethical Considerations
- Legal Considerations

MCM works. I have been using the MCM model for almost two decades in my investigations and think of these nine principles as universal guideposts, helping us to navigate and find more successful ways to deal with everyday problems or dilemmas and producing more positive outcomes in all of our projects and tasks.

The first six principles focus on strong and cohesive teams and speak to the logistics and value of working within a team. The last three principles guide a decision-making process. Together, they create an incredibly effective way to execute projects.

Did you know that every project moves through a series of phases? So too does every successful major case.

In any major police investigation the phases are:

An **Initiation Phase**
911 call and first response

A **Research Phase**
Learning about the victim, exploring motives, researching people of interest.

An **Analysis Phase**
Reviewing the evidence

An **Execution Phase**
Arresting the suspect

A **Close Out Phase**
Court Proceedings

A **Legacy Phase**
Sharing what we learned with others - what worked, what didn't.

Present and guiding through each of these phases are the nine principles.

The Command Triangle

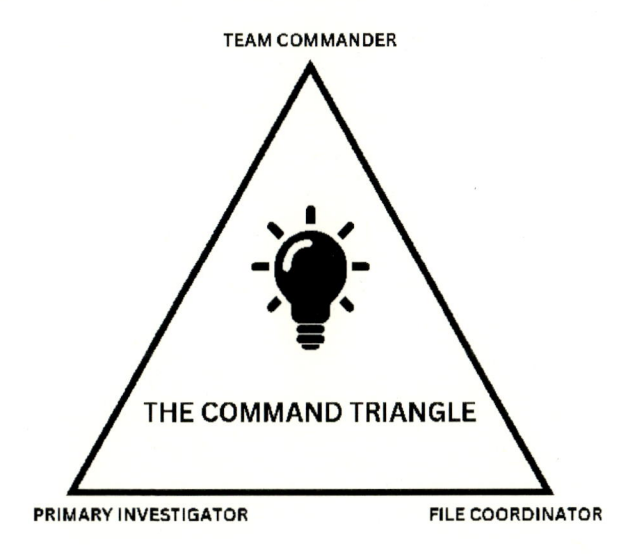

```
        TEAM COMMANDER
            /\
           /  \
          / 💡 \
         /      \
        / THE COMMAND TRIANGLE \
       /_____\
PRIMARY INVESTIGATOR    FILE COORDINATOR
```

Long gone are the days of the lone detective going to a murder scene in the dead of night, wearing a fedora and trench coat, smoking a cigar, and examining the area under the dim light of a street lamp. In Canada, serious investigations (major cases) are conducted with a team approach under the watchful eye of the Command Triangle. MCM recognizes that working with others to solve problems is more efficient and effective.

Within the Command Triangle, there are three major roles, each with its own set of responsibilities. Picking the right people to fill those points on your triangle will support a better outcome. Remember, one of the secrets to success is to surround yourself with successful people. That lesson applies here.

The Team Commander sits at the top of the triangle, and their role is to ensure the investigative team has the adequate time, tools, and training to successfully complete their objectives while being mindful of budgets and the allocation of resources. Rarely does the team commander make investigative decisions; theirs is more of a support role. This might sound boring, but without resources, whether the green light for necessary overtime, replacing smashed surveillance gear, or that extra interview training, we wouldn't be able to do what we do. They are also often the face of the investigation for media reporting and have their finger on the big-picture pulse of the investigation.

The second point in the Command Triangle is the File Coordinator, the person designated to review, collect, organize, and sort through the volumes of evidence that accompany a major case. They also set up a process to manage all that information. We have team members who positively excel at this critical role. The file coordinator is the investigator who finds those peek-a-boo holes in cases that only someone working so closely with all the evidence could find.

I was involved in a grisly case involving a lovers' triangle, where the "lover" killed the husband with a knife, believing he could then marry the love of his life—the victim's wife. The lover removed a bloodied laptop from the victim's residence, undoubtedly because it would connect him to the murder, and threw it in a recycling container a few blocks away.

The following day, a bottle picker came across the blood-soaked computer and turned it over to the police officer assigned to guard the residence while an interior search was conducted. The well-meaning officer jotted down what he had received in his notebook and entered the laptop into the property room. All good, except he told none of us of his discovery. It wasn't until the file coordinator reviewed the officer's notes that the break in communication was caught. An investigator was sent to recover the laptop, and the DNA testing conducted helped secure a conviction.

As a file coordinator, I was involved in a two-month-long investigation where over 35,000 electronic files were collected. I have been in others where it took only a few days to reach this number. With that volume of information, there is a risk of things falling through the cracks as it did in the Bernardo cases, or as was almost the case with the murderous lover. The file coordinator's role is to recognize those pieces of applicable information or evidence, "needles in a haystack," if you will, and be able to procure said information or evidence, share it with applicable parties, and keep tabs on the rest of the haystacks as the case progresses.

In a police environment, files can be anything from officer notes to statements of witnesses, to exhibit photographs, and everything in between. The file coordinator also sets the tone of an investigation's start-up by ensuring all members of the team know the expectations, workflow processes, and individual roles and responsibilities. For our purposes, I define workflow as a process that accounts for how information flows from the originator to the reviewers and end users and defines where they may find that information later.

Nothing significant can be built on shaky ground.

In this world of project-based investigations, many cases can be destined for failure if the start-up does not go smoothly. Even collaborating on this book started bumpier than it needed to. Sarah and I didn't take enough time, in the beginning, to lay out our own expectations or workflow processes. In our zest for the project, we did not keep close tabs on our chapter version controls and did not define a standard process to accommodate documents going repeatedly back and forth or a standard naming convention. The kicker is—we both knew better. This made more work for us, but we recognized it early and adjusted course before we could sink ourselves right out of the gate.

The last point in the Command Triangle, the Primary Investigator, drives the investigation. Also known as the Lead Investigator, the primary controls the direction, speed, and flow of the investigation in consultation with the team commander and file coordinator. Think of the primary as the puzzle builder, the person whose role it is to identify what tasks need to be done and assign members of the investigative team (puzzle-piece collectors) to gather the evidence and information (puzzle pieces) required to resolve the case (put the puzzle together). When I am the primary investigator and assigning tasks, I am always mindful of three things. First, how the assigned tasks will affect the overall investigation. Second, what am I setting into motion? I shared earlier how potent cause and effect is and the wisdom of being conscientious of its power. That applies here. Third, what tasks should be assigned that could identify evidence to aid in the presentation of the case in court? I will speak to this more in chapter ten, but there is a process to creating effective presentations and starting early in investigations significantly aids this process.

Let's walk through an example. A young woman is found murdered in her residence, and I am assigned as the primary investigator. I send members of the team to the scene, members to conduct a canvass of the neighborhood, members to notify the girl's family, and an investigator to attend the autopsy. Each will complete their task and report back to me, as the primary, with any new information. This, hopefully, moves the investigation forward. For instance, after conducting the canvassing, the first officer reports back that he spoke with a neighbor who saw a red car parked in the driveway of the victim's residence during the time it was believed the murder occurred.

The next officer reports that, while attending the scene, she noted there were no signs of forced entry. The third officer informs me he spoke with the family and learned the victim had an ex-boyfriend who caused problems and drove a red vehicle. Lastly, at the autopsy, it is learned the victim suffered over seventy stab wounds to her face, neck, and chest, the overkill suggesting the attack was very personal.

Based on this information, obviously, the ex-boyfriend would become a person of interest, and the next series of tasks may focus on finding and speaking with him. However, I may delay tasking anything that would alert the ex to my interest in him and instead direct new tasking that focuses on collecting more evidence, which either implicates or exonerates the ex before he is ever approached.

Keeping the law of cause and effect in mind, the element of surprise is a versatile tool in an investigator's toolbox. Showing our cards too soon, before collecting all the evidence, could make it difficult for an interviewer to refute statements made by the suspect. Tipping our hand could create a situation where the ex flees before we lay a charge. Holding off and not approaching the ex early enough could also result in the destruction of potentially valuable evidence, like bloody clothing, the weapon, and so on. Understanding the relationship between actions (cause) and results (effect) is important, especially when you're the person driving the bus or, in this case, the primary investigator in a major case.

Presenting in court is an important part of the primary's job, and I am always cognizant of assigning tasks that allow us to present the best evidence to give our court presentations the clarity and engagement we need them to provide. When I am a primary investigator, I think about tasking as if I am building an effective presentation because, ultimately, I am. Obtaining the applicable 9-1-1 calls, in-car police video, surveillance camera video, and crime-scene photos aid the prosecutor in presenting the facts of the case. It is important to find the quirky facts, unique and interesting details, or the haunting truths that every case has and that are so powerful in communicating the real story.

A haunting truth for me came several years ago. Two caregivers murdered a six-year-old girl following a week of torturous abuse and neglect. I was at the children's hospital on the day she died, and after she had passed, I was present with the doctor as he carefully examined her badly bruised body. Her hair was in a blue ribbon, originally tied in a bow to hold her ponytail, no doubt by a caring adult. This little girl must have felt so pretty then, as it would have showcased her blond locks, but on this day, as I looked closer, I saw the ends of the ribbon were frayed, the structure of the bow long gone, the hair matted and tangled. For me, the bow in this condition symbolized the reasons she was now dead—cruel neglect, and it signified the dichotomy of the moment. It was also evidence, and the case's prosecutor agreed. It would be shown to the trier of fact (judge or jury), who might come to the same conclusion.

There is another reason tasking this way is so important. When you are actively looking for things that will make your presentation more effective, you often find evidence you did not realize was there. I cannot overstate the importance of this. This approach creates opportunities to dig deeper, to find those layers you didn't realize were part of the story.

I had a case where we didn't know how the offender came to be in the area just prior to the crime, and we felt this was an important gap to close. The story started with the perpetrator and victim getting into a fight, and we wanted to figure out what happened before that. I tasked team members to look for evidence of both the victim and offender entering the area prior to the murder. We canvassed city transit and cab companies and, in doing so, collected a key piece of video of the homicide occurring; the video captured the sounds of gunfire and people screaming and running from the scene. The cab driver hadn't come forward to the police, and we never would have known about that video if we hadn't wanted to fill in those story gaps to create that lucky break.

I will discuss more about the value of effective presentation in chapter ten's *Selling Life Sentences*, but the takeaway now is to remember what makes a great presentation can inspire you to seek out—and find—previously unknown information that can help you communicate your findings, whether you're walking into a courtroom or a boardroom.

The collaboration of these three roles—the Team Commander, the File Coordinator, and the Primary Investigator—makes the Command Triangle a vital and effective principle in the MCM model. The Command Triangle recognizes that going it alone doesn't work and demonstrates that:

> *Collaboration with the right partner is key to making decisions that move us forward.*

Communication and Accountability Mechanisms

> *When we hold ourselves and others to account, we are practicing maturity and demonstrating responsibility.*

I believe communication and accountability, the second and third of the nine principles, go hand in hand. Accountability mechanisms are the processes in place that communicate and ensure tasks are completed on time and evidence or information is not overlooked. For example, in the Bernardo case, there was a flaw in the accountability mechanisms that, in part, prevented Bernardo's DNA sample from being sent and analyzed earlier. When businesses, organizations, or individuals consistently fail to deliver products, services, or themselves on time, this speaks to either a breakdown or the complete lack of accountability mechanisms.

In most major cases, I have been a part of mitigating this by using task and decision-making logs to stay on top of outstanding items or the decisions made. Many software programs exist that can help increase accountability, but it can be as simple as using a basic spreadsheet. Whichever system you choose, it is important to implement it at the start of a project. The more moving parts, the faster things can get out of hand. You will know, sometimes the hard way, if your process isn't working. It is also important that the system used is understood and accessible to everyone involved in the project. Besides the obvious consequences of off-task or chaotic projects, when everyone knows exactly what is expected of them, they know where they stand and that they are doing their job. This supports stronger and happier teams.

Accountability can be increased through the influence of commitment. In chapter six, I talk about commitment and its ability to influence people to follow through. Because commitment is a strong social influence in a project team, if accountability is an issue, implementing this influence into the group will increase performance. For our investigations, a large television monitor in our war room broadcasts our name next to our assigned tasks and decisions for all to see. This technological tweak has definitely increased our accountability.

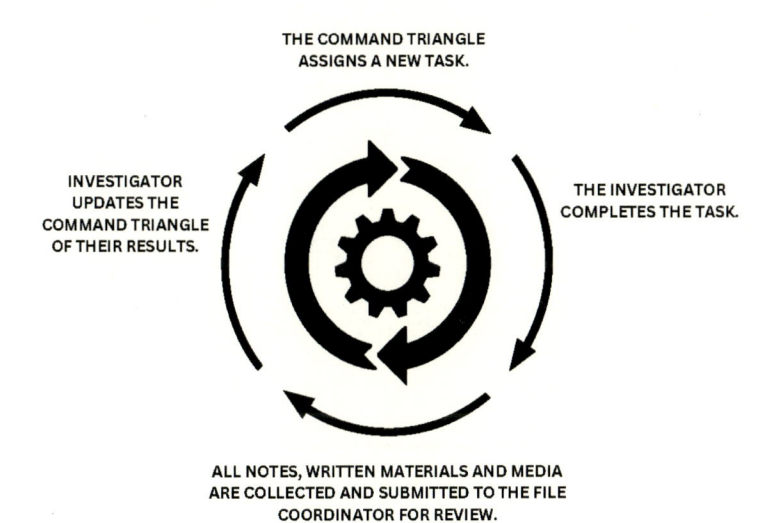

THE COMMAND TRIANGLE ASSIGNS A NEW TASK.

INVESTIGATOR UPDATES THE COMMAND TRIANGLE OF THEIR RESULTS.

THE INVESTIGATOR COMPLETES THE TASK.

ALL NOTES, WRITTEN MATERIALS AND MEDIA ARE COLLECTED AND SUBMITTED TO THE FILE COORDINATOR FOR REVIEW.

The example above demonstrates what a workflow process could look like from the assignment of a project task up until it is completed.

One of the greatest issues identified in the Bernardo case was the inability of well-meaning investigators to communicate across jurisdictional boundaries. Frequent operational briefings are a must in police investigations because these ensure everyone is on the same page and that the three persons within the Command Triangle remain open and approachable to all members of the team. An open and transparent investigation with solid communication practices will produce a sense of ownership and buy-in by the entire investigative body—but don't stop at talking. Visual aids are gold for communicating major details the team must understand, organizational charts communicate proper reporting lines, and diagrams explain expectations of workflow process (what information goes where).

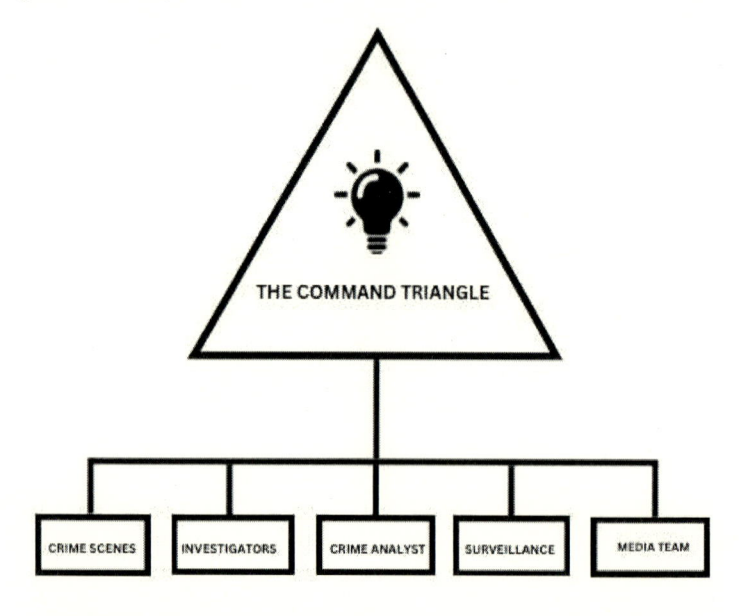

```
                    ┌─────────────┐
                    │     💡      │
                    │ THE COMMAND │
                    │  TRIANGLE   │
                    └──────┬──────┘
         ┌────────┬────────┼────────┬────────┐
    ┌────┴───┐ ┌──┴──┐ ┌───┴──┐ ┌───┴──┐ ┌───┴──┐
    │ CRIME  │ │INVES│ │CRIME │ │SURVE-│ │MEDIA │
    │ SCENES │ │TIGA-│ │ANA-  │ │ILLAN-│ │ TEAM │
    │        │ │TORS │ │LYST  │ │ CE   │ │      │
    └────────┘ └─────┘ └──────┘ └──────┘ └──────┘
```

Organizational charts such as this assist all members of the team in understanding how information is disseminated and also received within a larger project group.

As a side note, Ralph Waldo Emerson said, "What you do speaks so loud, I cannot hear what you say." We broadcast non-verbal cues that say more than our words (written or spoken) ever could. I'll expand more on this in chapter ten.

It can be infinitely embarrassing when things you should have been told get missed. I have moved among several areas within the service throughout my career. Each time, I was trained by a more senior member of the new unit and provided, *verbally*, the best practices established for that given area. Each unit has its own set of nuances to workflow processes and procedural controls. That makes sense, but sometimes, being taught the tricks of the trade by the "old dog" resulted in things getting missed. When I was a young member of the Drug Unit, one of my responsibilities was to sort through the vast array of tips the public had called in regarding suspected drug activity. Typically, a tip would read something like this:

John Smith is a cocaine trafficker. His cell number is 111-1111, and he lives at 123 Fake Street.

Based on that information, I would assess the viability of the tip to determine if there was enough to begin a drug operation. Moving through tips like these became part of our daily routine when starting our shift, and it wasn't long before I noticed a pattern regarding one particularly notorious family called the LNUs. Frequently, I would read tips referring to Bob LNU, Jimmy LNU, Rick LNU, Erin, and Stacy LNU, and recognized that disrupting this particular drug operation was clearly part of the solution to solving the growing drug epidemic in our city. Proud of this epiphany, and after receiving another tip about the LNU clan, I stood up from my desk and proclaimed to the team it was time to start a major investigation into the LNU family. Dead silence followed. Then, a volley of laughter broke out. "Dave, you're an idiot. LNU means 'last name unknown.'"

Ugh, I was a fool—and maybe a bit miffed my old dog mentor hadn't included that helpful little tidbit months earlier in my orientation. To avoid these types of little mistakes, and really this was minor, the unit could have written this information down for new members and standardized the process. Legacy knowledge is lost when it is not recorded, and old dogs retire. Establishing business rules or standard operating procedures—which are different from policies—ensures everyone on a project team is on the same page, and mistakes like the infamous LNU drug clan will be less likely to occur.

Finally, on the topic of communication, I think most of us have been on projects where we, or someone we know, have become frustrated with our role when no one has communicated how that role feeds into the greater vision of the project. When this happens, people can quickly become disengaged and even seem like they are not playing on the same team. It may not be them so much as the absent communication model that creates an uncomfortable environment. This can be easily fixed with open, honest briefings or meetings, and a willingness by the project team to encourage everyone's input, as was discussed earlier in chapter four, with successful support systems.

Often, it's the quiet guy in the corner who usually has the best ideas.

Communication is key to good collaboration, good collaboration creates cohesive teams, and cohesive teams produce successful projects.

Investigative or Crime-Solving Strategies

Investigative or crime-solving strategies, our fourth principle, are the tools used to successfully resolve a case. Surveillance, wiretaps, undercover operations, expert witnesses, composite sketches, and public assistance are a few examples we use. In our own lives, there are myriad strategies we employ to solve the problems of the day. I am reminded of the television game show *Who Wants To Be A Millionaire*, where contestants could choose one of three lifelines to help them pick an answer: they could call a friend, poll the audience, or have two of the wrong answers removed from the list of possibilities.

These are examples of strategies we use every day, like researching a problem on the internet, speaking with a trusted friend, hiring a consultant or outside expert, or simply organizing thoughts into lists to see our information more clearly—all to make more informed choices. These are practical ways people navigate their decision-making processes. But it is not just collecting more information. It is also actioning that information. In major cases, these actions are investigative or crime-solving strategies.

Ever wonder if watching paint dry could help catch

a murderer? That's a trick question. It totally can. A few years ago, two callous individuals were drinking beer and spray-painting graffiti in an alleyway. Their unsuspecting victim entered the alley, his route home, when the two violently took his life "just because." During the unprovoked, vicious attack that one of the accused later described as "like two pit bulls on a steak," they held the victim against the wall with the fresh graffiti. Some of the paint transferred onto his jacket, which he was still wearing when he was found dead the following morning.

In the investigation that followed, the two suspects were identified early on, and a can of spray paint was recovered from the scene. What could be done besides the usual fingerprinting of the can? The primary investigator surmised that if we could prove the suspects were the ones who had vandalized the wall, we could timeline them in the alley when the wet paint was transferred onto the victim's jacket. We could utilize the specific dry time of the paint—something fingerprints could never do.

Proving the graffiti tags were theirs wasn't hard. Scrap paper with the doodle sketches of those particular symbols was found in one of the suspect's garbage. The second part required a little more work. From the spray paint can seized as evidence, we knew the make and manufacturer of the paint, and a sample was sent to the lab to make sure the paint on the wall matched the paint from the can. It did.

Next came the "watching paint dry" part. We

applied the known sample of paint to the same wall on a night when the temperature was similar. Our experimentation consistently produced an eight-minute dry time, after which the paint was no longer transferable. This meant the taggers had been in the alley within eight minutes of the victim entering it. That unique evidence, coupled with other forensics and a confession, led both accused to eventually be found guilty of this heinous crime.

Brainstorming, implementing, and actioning strategies are an important part of the MCM model because they are the tools that allow investigators to gather the evidence required to solve the problem (the crime). This is really the essence behind task forces and why police services assemble them. I have been involved in several targeting drug trafficking networks, violent groups, and gangs. They typically bring together a diverse group of resources and expertise to address complex cases. The MCM model recognizes that.

Informed action is required to resolve a problem.

Doing nothing rarely works. Just like in chapter two, moving from a trying mindset to a doing one creates success. When police assemble a task force, it recognizes that a problem has grown sufficiently in size to need specific attention to resolve.

> *When we have things in our life that require a task force, assemble one.*

No one has to be dying or overdosing to bring a group of people together to accomplish a common goal.

Partnerships

Partnerships, the fifth principle, are all about relationships and how our collective and complementary efforts and skill sets are brought together to reach common goals. This is essential in my world, which means solid working relationships are a must with the Crown Prosecutor's Office, Child and Family Services, the medical examiner, and other outside police agencies.

I worked on a case where the suspect was believed to have killed his ex-girlfriend, the mother of his child. Early in the investigation, it was the Medical Examiner's Office that determined the cause and manner of the victim's death. From there, the investigative team worked closely with the RCMP Crime Lab, which analyzed the exhibits from the crime scene to confirm if the suspect's DNA was present. When the evidence pointed to the ex-boyfriend as the killer, we consulted with the Crown Prosecutor's

Office for charge approval before the arrest was made. Finally, on arrest day, Child and Family Services were brought in to the investigation to help the soon-to-be displaced baby girl land as softly as she could.

The individuals from each respective agency contributed their specific expertise to help find the best solutions in a tragic event: the medical examiner brought the science and medicine, the crime lab, the forensics, the crown's office their legal know-how, and Child and Family Services their commitment and compassion. For me,

> *All partnerships need to be nurtured if we are to have any expectation of keeping them.*

It is with our time, effort, and attention we create a positive presence and maintain our relationships, whether they be business or personal. Acknowledging the strengths and necessity of others is key to establishing and nurturing solid working relationships with the partners we have in life.

Leadership and Team Building

Leadership and team building are our sixth principle and encompass how leaders build teams up. Who would you follow through fire? Who would you trust to lead you? There is a difference between managers and leaders, and they serve two different purposes. Both can build teams up but do so in different ways. Managers exist as a function of organization; leaders exist in any group of people. Managers provide tools and support to do your job, they support the doers and the worker bees, and they make sure all the moving parts have what they need and are all going in the same direction as the goal or purpose. Teams need that.

Managers may be leaders, but they don't have to be. Leaders inspire us to be better versions of ourselves, encourage us to move forward, even if forward looks insurmountable, and get the job or task done, regardless of how challenging it is. When there is a proper leader within a team, everyone will reach extraordinary heights, and possibilities never dreamed of quickly become realities. Leaders are found in all areas, from that kid on the playground who just has *it* to the innovative CEO and everywhere in between. When the manager and leader are on the same page, then teams truly have a chance to thrive.

A decade ago, I had the pleasure of hearing Dr. James Reese lecture at a conference on leadership and customer service. He is a former Federal Bureau of Investigation agent and worked in the now-famous Behavioral Sciences Unit. He also had one of the best metaphors for grouping and understanding people that I had ever heard, which is handy when trying to understand your colleagues. He described two types of people, eagles, and ducks, in a clear, no-nonsense way.

Dr. Reese explained eagles are the leaders. They are the ones who soar high with strength and independence. Eagles find their own food, take care of themselves, and dispose of their enemies. They keep their family protected and understand their role as servants in their community. Eagles are not risk-averse, nor are they careless. They understand they could get hurt while hunting and accept the dangers. They prey on destructive animals in their ecosystem and keep everything in balance. They are decisive, direct, and have great vision. Eagles are confident in who they are and approach every challenge with tenacity and a positive attitude.

Dr. Reese explained how ducks are different. Ducks tend to be "yes-men" and need to be with other yes-men for their system to work. They keep up only with the status quo, often doing what is easiest to keep up static harmony. They can be found floating around the pond, pecking, waddling, and quacking. Dr. Reese explained this is tantamount to complaining around the water cooler or not doing something that is justified if it is against policy instead of changing the defunct policy. That helps to explain why ducks need to be with other ducks. They spend more time convincing everyone why they should not do something instead of just doing it in the first place. For me, they choose to get their feet wet over flying and have a harder time seeing the big picture because they simply are unable to, from their limited view on the pond. Ducks believe it when someone says, "It is not possible." I have seen eagles target ducks not to bully but to inspire ducks to realize their full potential. Eagles know shaking up a pond full of ducks will inspire some to take flight, to get that bigger picture and greater perspective.

I've seen a third category I call slugs. Fortunately, they do not make up a large percentage of the population. Slugs are unadaptable and lack motivation. They are slimy, spineless, impersonal, and leave behind tracks for others to clean up. Not a top pick in any organization.

I have worked with managers who have been eagles and those who have been ducks. The ducks clung tight to the rules of a process at the expense of people and projects. That view-from-the-pond thing is real and incredibly limiting. The eagle managers understood that a process is a tool, not a brick wall to break dissidence on, and when the process becomes an impediment, it's time to adjust it. They had that panoramic perspective and saw the comprehensive picture, not simply isolated components. Management is a support role, just like law enforcement is a life of service, and positions of authority are, at their core, service roles. Eagles know this, ducks suspect it, and slugs fight it.

Victims of crime want eagles, as do patients in hospitals and customers at the service desk. As discussed in chapter two about owning your path, all of this is our choice. Do we want to be eagles, ducks, or slugs, remembering that ducks can rise to meet challenges like eagles, and eagles can slide into the comforts of the pond?

What does this mean for the teams or groups of people you find yourself within? When you take the time to understand these roles, you can better understand your team and subsequently know how to work with them, regardless of whether you are the boss or the new intern. Don't stop as the duck clings to policy. Why do they? Don't dismiss, care.

> *Inspire people to rise above that tenacious grip of mediocrity.*

If you're a duck, understand why those damn eagles are constantly riding you. Find the common ground. Listen to each other. Utilize each other's strengths; don't trip over each other's weaknesses. That's what builds impenetrable teams that will move mountains.

We want eagles in our Command Triangle, those proven leaders that can lead by example and are strong, confident, and decisive. We need those who know how to focus on what should be done and can identify the right people for the jobs, leaders who will embrace the knowledge, abilities, and skills of others and are tolerant of diverse personalities and styles. They must be able to embrace change. I have been involved in cases where those put within the Command Triangle did not possess these qualities, and the entire investigation was a struggle from beginning to end. It bears repeating that leadership is not rank-specific, despite what some may believe. The MCM model recognizes this, including filling the roles within the Command Triangle.

I've talked about the difference between leaders and managers and understanding your colleagues. There is another key ingredient to strong, effective teams, and it is simple: happiness. There is much research about keeping employees happy, which keeps them engaged, both of which directly impact a company's bottom line and, in investigative circles, the ability to solve the cases.

Several years ago, I was invited to tour a software company in California that was promoting a case management package our service was interested in. On the day we arrived, I was incredibly impressed with how this company ran the employee side of their business. In the main loft-style office space, a ping pong and pool table were front and center. Every day, the employer provided the staff with lunch: healthy sandwiches, salads, and soups were on the complimentary lunch menu, and the vending machines did not require money. Every cubicle workspace had the *right for light* (windows to the outside), and employees were also provided an area in the office for sleep. The environment was one of the most positive I had seen.

While talking to the office manager, who was in shorts and a T-shirt, I learned that most employees there put in between a fifty- to sixty-hour work week but were only paid for forty—yet there was no grumbling and no turnover. The theories of reciprocity and commitment (chapter six) were alive and well here. It was a highly successful and profitable company that invested in its employees, and the payoffs were substantial. The team was treated exceptionally well and had a comfortable environment, which was also conducive to enjoying their colleagues. They were engaged and motivated about their work and were happy. They gave back to their employers with time and commitment.

Organizations that create a company culture that recognizes and actions employee needs will see happier, more engaged staff who want to give back. It doesn't have to be with game tables and free lunches. Finding creative ways to show your team you appreciate them goes a long way.

The principles of leadership and team building also apply to our personal lives. Like *happy wives make happy lives*, and *families that play together stay together*. When parents demonstrate the truest qualities of leadership, the effect it has on their children is so noticeable. My whole career exists because, in some families, the dysfunction has created the opposite of strong, independent kids willing to own their mistakes; it has generated the space for angry souls intent on doing more harm than good. Don't let this happen to your project team. Know your people, play to their strengths, treat them well, and let them know how much you respect and value them. That is the essence behind MCM's sixth principle.

Management, Legal, and Ethical Considerations

The first six principles of MCM support strong and cohesive teams, and arguably can help foster all of our relationships. The last three principles are specific to decision-making processes.

Under the principle of management considerations, budgets, liability to the organization, and adherence to policy and procedure should always be a part of any project's decision-making formula. Without these considerations, projects could easily overrun expenses or expose the organization to liability or criticism. Consider this dilemma: a police service is aware of a serious offender who is believed to be committing nighttime break-and-enters. The suspect has several minor warrants out for his arrest, and these may land him in jail for a few days. An ongoing operation has identified him and his location, and investigators are waiting to see if he trips up and gets caught in the act of the more serious offense of break-and-enter.

Should the operation targeting this individual be allowed to continue, or should the offender be arrested on the warrants, even though it would expose the ongoing investigation? Scenarios like this play out every day in police services across the globe. The management considerations that would weigh in on this decision include: What is the cost of the operation? Is there a risk to the public if this offender is not arrested immediately? Is there a risk to the service by holding back on the warrants?

MCM's principled approach also weighs legal and ethical considerations. For you, are there any circumstances when it would be acceptable for a police officer to pretend to be a lawyer to obtain a statement from a suspect? Is torturing a suspect ever reasonable? What if it would save the life of a missing child? What if it would save the lives of a whole school, everyone in a downtown core, or even the whole city? Should that change anything? These questions are hypothetical, but investigators must ask themselves:

- Will the general public be concerned about how police are tackling this problem?
- Is it legal, moral, and ethical?
- Are we placing the general public at risk?

Several years ago, I was involved in an investigation where we discovered a body in a hidden place with extremely limited accessibility. The accused had murdered his girlfriend after an argument and then cemented her body into a sarcophagus in the basement of his home, where it remained for over a year before being discovered. For the sake of the case, we wanted to continue our investigation into the boyfriend without tipping him off that we had discovered his girlfriend's remains. The concern from the investigational perspective was that without a confession from the suspect, finding out how his girlfriend was murdered could be near impossible.

We knew the degradation of her year-old remains would likely make it difficult to determine a cause of death, like the Caylee Anthony case in chapter seven. We also felt a cause of death would be required to prove murder. In assessing our best course of action, we considered two choices: leave the body where it lay and continue the investigation, or exhume the remains and risk an undetermined finding at autopsy. In the end, it was decided to leave her body in place so that the investigation could continue to the point where we could prove murder. We used cameras and other surveillance equipment to ensure the remains would not be relocated or tampered with. With our safeguards in place, we moved forward. It worked. The offender eventually led an undercover police officer to her remains. In his final confession, and using significant detail, he described how he had choked the life from her tiny frame.

Not everyone will agree that choosing to leave her remains where they lay was the most ethical decision, and I would agree if ethical considerations were the only ones to deliberate. When it comes to decision-making, an investigator must weigh the options—some of them gray—before arriving on a course of action.

When we make decisions from a place of legal and ethical principles, seldom do we make the wrong one. Good decisions consider these principles and the possible consequences, including doing nothing at all. Choosing to do something that is not lawful will land a person in jail. Choosing to do something unethical will almost always backfire.

Life is full of karmic decisions.

It has been my experience that the world has a funny way of righting wrongs, and those who misstep will end up staring at the pointy end of the stick.

Understanding the nine principles of the MCM model can help us identify where breakdowns occur if we experience less than successful outcomes. It guides us on where to adjust our course to get back on track. We can even take something like a relationship that fell apart and understand what went wrong. Was it ethical considerations? Was it a breakdown in communication or accountability? What was it that the relationship snagged on? Is there a chance to bring it back on course, or is it an experience to learn from? What about with our kids? If something is going wrong, was it with our leadership, or maybe we missed communicating in a mindful way? Although written for an investigator, these principles provide a structure that can help us better understand the dynamics of our everyday life.

MCM and its nine principles work. We are stronger, smarter, and more successful when we work together in harmony, following our legal and ethical compasses toward our common goals. MCM recognizes this, and its principles speak to this path. Whatever your project, problem, or dilemma, these guideposts can help as you move toward accomplishing your goals.

When the Devil's Advocate Wears a Halo

"A dwarf on a giant's shoulders sees farther of the two."

- George Herbert

There are times in life we need that supportive friend who will ask us honestly, "Are you sure?" We need those sober second thoughts, those positive hesitations, that person who will put a hand on our arm and stop us from making a decision that may not be in our, or others', best interests.

In the last chapter, I discussed what happens when a new homicide comes into our office, how investigators assemble in a briefing room and the flow of information begins, where decisions are made, and planning occurs. It is a bullpen, and the walls become increasingly covered with case-related information, including tasking. We're all looking at the same boards, the same information, building a timeline, connecting dots, and planning our next courses of action. As investigators, our investigations are guided through the nine principles of MCM, with management, ethical, and legal considerations being the most predominant when it comes to making decisions.

We need to look at all the angles and be able to justify our directions and focus later. Did we use discretion, and if so, why? How did we conclude the course of action we took was the best available? Did we employ a decision-making process that resisted investigative tunnel vision and other systemic risks? Both have the potential for disastrous results.

In our investigations, we assign a Devil's Advocate. That person challenges all of us to look at all sides of an issue, our course of action, theory, et cetera. It is an essential role to ensure we make the best possible decisions we must be able to defend later, including in a courtroom.

The first time I remember being challenged by a Devil's Advocate was while I was assigned to the Drug Unit. It was the mid-2000s, and my team and I had spent the summer buying copious amounts of crack cocaine from a variety of street dealers trafficking this insidious drug on different corners around the downtown area. Working the streets like this allowed us to view the underbelly of the city's core, and we learned that a large part of the street-level supply was coming from one man. Some, who described him as fiercely loyal to his "family," considered him god-like but ruthless toward anyone who went against his grain. He was never far from the action, and we often saw him sitting back in the shadows, watching. Although his presence was visible, he was never foolish enough to allow those not part of his organization to buy cocaine directly from him, and, as a result, he was insulated from prosecution—or so he thought.

As the summer went along, we slowly began to gather evidence against this individual through the infiltration of his "soldiers" used to traffic his product. This, in turn, led us to identify a half-dozen stash locations where we believed drugs were being stored. As these pieces fell into place, plans were drawn up to take down this drug supplier, including seizing his drug inventories. We wanted to execute all of the warrants simultaneously, knowing that as soon as the first warrant was conducted, evidence at any of the other locations would be in jeopardy of being tampered with or destroyed. The plan required collaboration and coordination with a significant number of resources.

I was the lead investigator; I had drawn up my plan and was ready to go. On takedown day, warrants in hand, I met with approximately eighty officers assigned to help. As I finished up my briefing, a very senior ranking officer in attendance asked, "So where will this all be coordinated?" I thought about it. "My vehicle."

"Not good enough." The high-ranking officer recognized that without a central command post or communication hub, things could go awry quickly and pull apart the plan at the seams. Reflecting on it, he was right. For this plan to be successful, we needed to be mindful of the principles of the Command Triangle, communication, and leadership, and in his view, these principles would be non-existent if I were going to coordinate it all from my vehicle. With his injection of wisdom, we updated the plans immediately. Several others and I stayed back and coordinated the entry teams and arrests from one central hub. The takedown and stash recoveries were a success, thanks in no small part to that astute officer and us making that subsequent tweak. This antithetical role is designed to question prevailing theories, assumptions, and plans to make the best decisions possible, and that's exactly what happened. When it's not there, things can go very, very wrong.

When I left the world of an undercover operator, I became an investigator with the Organized Crime Unit. One of my early assignments was to lead the task force assigned to deal with a violent street gang with a swift uptick in shootings, resulting in at least one homicide. The strategy at the time was to cool the violence by disrupting the group, targeting their cocaine racket, and putting as many of the players in jail as possible. We identified the highest-risk suspects to focus on first. A variety of strategies were implemented to gather evidence—including several surveillance techniques. I met with members of my investigative team and hatched a plan to conduct a specific strategy on one of the targets. The plan was to be executed under the cover of darkness in the wee hours of the following morning at the suspect's residence.

From the beginning, I was concerned that going to his home would increase the safety risk for our team, and it was decided that we would seek assistance from our Tactical and K9 Units for added cover and assurance that, although dangerous, all would work out okay. I should mention that I had never before considered using these specialized forces in an operation, and, in hindsight, I recognize this should have been a red flag.

The following morning, while I was still tucked safely in my bed (my tasks for the day didn't include this surveillance job), members of the operational team made their way out to the target's residence. It was 4:10 a.m. when I received a call from the supervisor in charge of the operation. In a calm, dead serious voice, he informed me that shortly after arriving at the suspect's residence, members of the team had been spotted by the target who opened fire, likely thinking the shadowy figures in the alley that night were rival gang members who had come to settle a score, not police officers in plain clothes.

Mission failed.

The second part of the sergeant's message was the most important: everyone was accounted for, and none of our members had been hit. They had checked each other for bullet holes and wondered how each had been able to get out of that alley unscathed. Luckily for the target, the whole incident unfolded in seconds, and the snipers did not get a chance to crack off a return shot to stop his threat.

This incident still troubles me. How did our planning go so terribly wrong? It came down to not having a Devil's Advocate in my corner; no one suggested the plan wasn't safe enough, that the end did not justify the means. If they had, they would have been right. In this case, my surveillance objectives did not outweigh the risk I placed our members in, and this taught me a valuable lesson:

Listen to your gut when it calls your mind to attention.

Risk Management

Risk Management is the process of defining and analyzing risks and then deciding the appropriate course of action to minimize or mitigate those risks while still achieving operational goals. Recently, I took a course that highlighted what I had already been practicing. This simple workflow process below succinctly captures basic but relevant questions we should all ask ourselves when deciding on a course of action:

(Information Review)
- What do we know?

- When did we know it, and from whom?
- What are we going to do about it?

(If/Then Process)
- Option identification.
- Pros and cons of each option.
- Prioritizing options.
- Selection of best option.

(Action Criteria)
- Necessary?
- Risk effective?
- Acceptable?

The first step in managing risk is to recognize where it is coming from.

There are human risks to consider, such as arrogance, careerism, noble-cause corruption, scope creep, bias, tunnel vision, and groupthink—all nasty little things that can thwart an investigation or a team's success. These risks can be mitigated when someone recognizes them and is brave enough to step up and say something.

There is a definite risk whenever someone over- or under-estimates a person or thing, and arrogance contributes to that miscalculation.

Careerism is when the impact on a person's career

is factored into the decision-making process. Our careers are important, but we must be cognizant that we may make choices to benefit our career over the best choices for the case or others. These aren't necessarily conscious actions, but that doesn't make their consequences any less negative. In the story above, there was what looks suspiciously like careerism and even a little arrogance involved. It was my first experience leading a major investigation, and it was a fairly big project in the city. I was also acting the part of a detective but technically did not have that ranking. I wanted to. I wanted to prove myself and do a great job. I just didn't understand that wisdom or my gut was not leading the way I was going about it that night.

Noble-cause corruption is when a person's good intentions steamroll process and, in the case of police, potential evidence. For example, if an officer suspects there is something in a car, peeks without a warrant, sees a weapon known to be missing, and then applies for a warrant to get the item he already knows is there. Or, more gripping, an officer feeling justified in torturing a known child killer or abductor to recover the body or still-living child. These are particularly uncomfortable because they stem from a place of noble intent, such as saving kids and stopping murderers from more killing.

Scope creep happens when new information pulls attention from the original goal to chase a shinier object. In an investigation, that could be finding a bigger "fish" to pursue, like I talked about in chapter four's *White Picket Fences*. This can derail the effectiveness and efficiency of investigations faster than you can say, "Police! Don't move."

Bias is human—we are programmed to have preferences. But, having preconceived preferences serves no one when trying to find the truth. Again, we are called to:

> *Be self-aware. Identify bias before it inhibits sound decision-making.*

This holds true in life or investigating. A good example of bias that resonates for me came after taking a course on drownings. During the course, the instructor spoke specifically about the bias that is built into cases like these and gave us illuminating examples. Imagine being the first responder to the drowning of a two-year-old child in a bathtub where there had been a frantic parent on the other end of the 9-1-1 call reporting she had just left the bathroom for a minute, and when she got back, the child was face down in a foot of water. She posed this question to the group, "What is on the mind of every paramedic, fireman, or police officer as they enter the residence to save the child?" Likely, it is, "Oh my god, what a tragic accident." The truth is, it could be. We have all heard stories such as these, and we know it doesn't take an ocean for someone to drown. However, what if it isn't what our bias wishes it to be? Our biases and naïveté may get in the way of seeing the clues that show it as something more sinister than a tragic accident.

Did anyone note if Mom or Dad's clothes were wet? Were there towels or water on the floor to help substantiate the child was pulled from the tub after being discovered? Does the story really make sense? Why did a child who can sit unassisted in a foot of water not just sit up? These are valid and uncomfortable questions that rock our bias. As parents, we have logged hundreds of hours of bath time. How many times in those hundreds of hours have you had to save your child from drowning once they could sit up on their own? Think of the statistical improbability that in those few minutes the child was unattended, in the hundreds of hours of baths taken, that it was at that moment the child drowned? The desire to show empathy and compassion toward the parent and not think the worst from the outset is the bias that may prevent some investigators from seeing things differently and overlooking crucial evidence early on.

When someone falls out of a boat and drowns, and only one other person witnesses it, who is to say that person is not also the offender who pushed the victim out? Not unlike the husband who wishes to take a picture of his wife at the cliff's edge and then asks her to take a few more steps back to get more of her into the frame. Tragic accident or murder? Biases can sometimes get in the way of determining what really happened without the advocacy of a dissenting opinion.

There is also context bias. For example, our editors and Sarah noticed that there are more examples of female murder victims than males in the book. This was not by design; my career has included more cases of female homicide victims—a reflection of workload assignment more than anything else because, statistically, the numbers actually go the other way. There are more men murdered than women. Men are more likely to be murdered in deadly confrontations like bar fights, disturbances on the street, or drug and gang violence; women by domestic violence (their partners). Were they simply more cognizant of the overall tally, or perhaps more sensitive to gender or the circumstances of violence? Am I insensitive (as a man) or more neutral (as an experienced officer)? Our biases can also come from our context, how we have been conditioned. Did you notice the same thing our editors and Sarah did? Would it surprise you to know up until this part of the book, there have been over twenty examples where a man was the victim of a violent death, but which stories do you remember more? Your answer is likely fueled by your context and what you have been conditioned to notice in life.

Tunnel vision is the bane of investigators everywhere. It is a common phenomenon seen in all aspects of life when normally diligent and attentive people don't recognize they are looking within a narrow scope, and the consequences can be astronomical. For investigators,

🦋 *Following facts, not theories is tunnel vision's only counterstrike.*

Combating it takes practice and consistent self-awareness. Looking at examples of tunnel vision can be confusing, perhaps especially so in the context of law enforcement. How do investigations narrow possibilities so precariously when evidence supports a wider scope? It doesn't make sense, but it happens. Clarity is compromised when someone or a group has tunnel vision and there is no Devil's Advocate to identify and point out the limiting mindset.

In 1981, Thomas Sophonow was convicted of murdering Barbara Stoppel, a sixteen-year-old girl from Winnipeg. Through three trials, he maintained his innocence. The police and prosecution held fast to their belief of his guilt. In 1998, the crime was re-investigated by the Winnipeg Police Service, and in 2000, they issued a statement stating that Sophonow was not responsible for the crime and they had identified another suspect. The formal inquiry that followed found several instances of what former Supreme Court Justice Peter Cory would describe in the inquiry as tunnel vision. The original investigation found what they thought was a possible, albeit weak, connection between Sophonow and the murder weapon, and the investigation then focused solely on him. Evidence to the contrary was either ignored or dismissed altogether. It was later discovered there had not, in fact, ever been a connection. This study is a classic example of the dangers of tunnel vision. Tunnel vision can hijack an investigation; the Devil's Advocate's role is to ensure that doesn't happen.

I have been on several investigations where we started out with a theory that the person responsible for the crime was "Weird Harold," only to learn later that it was not. In these cases, we kept throwing mud at the wall, and nothing stuck. That was because it wasn't who we thought it would be based on early evidence and circumstances.

One such case came after a young waitress was found murdered, her remains hidden in a laundry room hamper inside the home she shared with her five-year-old daughter, who was missing. Investigators were aware the woman had a tumultuous relationship with her ex, the father of her daughter. The couple had a bitter court fight over access to the child, and there were some very hard feelings as a result. The ex was on our radar as a person of interest in the murder and disappearance of the youngster. Our early suspect also had a history with police and owned a vehicle similar to the type of vehicle witnesses had seen around the time of the murder and kidnapping. Operating on the best evidence at the time, surveillance was immediately established.

Over the next seventy-two hours, plain-clothed police officers watched closely as the suspect went through grief, shock, and bewilderment—emotions anyone would go through if someone they once cared for and shared a child with had just been violently murdered and their daughter missing.

The lead investigator methodically sifted through the evidence—something did not feel right about the direction we were going. Never one to be swayed, he changed it up and became his own devil's advocate. He also put out into the media a few video stills from a CCTV camera in the area depicting the suspect's vehicle. A day later, our tip line received information that changed the course of this investigation completely when a woman known to the victims called the police to report that she believed her boyfriend was involved in the murder of the woman and the disappearance of the young girl. His cellphone records confirmed her suspicions after they were analyzed and used to locate the missing—deceased—youngster. Fingerprints and a confession later led to his conviction for this heinous crime.

Another case with similar parallels came after a grandfather had been found murdered in his home. An early victimology revealed eight years prior, he had witnessed his daughter be shot by a boyfriend with a shotgun. Thankfully, she survived. However, in the court case that followed, his testimony was used to help convict the offender of the near murder. Only weeks prior to the victim's homicide, the man he helped "put away" for the attempted murder of his daughter had been released from jail. Investigators scrambled to locate the recent parolee with a strong motive, tracking him down about eight hours north of the city in a work camp. The man had a solid alibi, and we had wasted a day. Finally, additional evidence pointed us in a new direction—a different man with a decade-old grudge against the victim.

The cases above demonstrate the real risk of following a theory versus following evidence and why having the Devil's Advocate role is so important in our briefing rooms.

Almost a decade ago, a jogger made a gruesome discovery just off the path: the dismembered body parts of a female littered the hillside of an inner-city park. At the time, I wasn't in homicide, but news spread quickly that investigators were worried the offender might not be done killing, and our city was about to experience a serial killer. Identifying the assailant was of the utmost priority. The media reported heavily on the case. The pressurized investigators looking for a break got one early on, as loose lips were about to sink someone's ship.

A bar patron came forward to police to report that the previous night, he had been drinking with a young man who told him he was the person responsible for murdering and dismembering the victim. Moving quickly, the confessor was identified and subsequently placed under twenty-four-hour surveillance. The police began to build a case for murder through the examination of evidence, beyond just his "confession," which they hoped would link him to the crime. In doing so, well-intentioned officers put to bed other lines of inquiry into the victim's life. This included a volatile common-law relationship with a partner who, while all this was going on, quietly packed up his things and left the city unnoticed by everyone—except the Devil's Advocate.

He stepped bravely forward and offered his insights into why everyone else may be wrong about the young drunk confessor and that he suspected it was the common law who had killed the victim. He made his case by following evidence, some of which had been unintentionally overlooked early on, in pursuit of a sexier theory. The Devil's Advocate broke up the groupthink serial-killer talk by identifying why he believed the spouse was responsible. It turned out he was right.

The antithesis or Devil's Advocate role in police investigations is so important. Well before the victim's case ever came in, all the investigators and managers involved created an office environment that allowed for everyone to be heard, where dissent from the popular viewpoint was recognized and respected. That attitude helped solve this case and spoke to the leadership at the time.

The Devil's Advocate wears a halo.

Theories can bog us down in tunnel vision and make things more complicated than they ever need to be. I believe most rumors start from a theory (without evidence), and we likely have all seen how damaging a bad rumor can be.

Systemic risks are also a danger. There are times when processes like policy and procedure, management, the media, poor training, and even the law can disrupt the flow and direction of investigations. There is a reason policies and procedures are updated. Their effectiveness can become obsolete, and they are arguably only as good as when they were last written. Inadequate training is a risk in investigations or any organization. Like policies and procedures, training is only as good as what is known to be possible. At some point, an officer will be put in a situation they are ill-equipped to handle. This is obviously not intentional, but there are many working parts on the job and too many we can't control.

The media also impacts investigations. Early reporting on crimes can modify investigational timelines and change the tempo; scrambling in an investigation is not a preferred place to be. Media may also report on information that disrupts the effectiveness of investigative strategies. Like inadequate training, this is not malicious. It simply happens. The law can also be a systemic risk because there are times when laws and precedent are still written in a way that impedes investigations or do not adequately protect victims. The law is heavier than policies and procedures. Laws also can be changed, but something has to trigger that change.

The Devil's Advocate asks the tough questions, identifies the human or systemic risks at play in effective decision-making, then takes the group's ideas and does their best to dismantle them. This is a crucial role because it is done when there is still time to adjust.

Simple Solutions

I believe the principle of Occam's razor is true. When it comes to finding the truth and making good decisions,

> *The simplest answer is likely the right one.*

In murder investigations, this wisdom often holds true, but we must be careful to always leave room for the exception. If we don't, the Devil's Advocate would remind us.

Sometimes, the decision to obtain a warrant is straightforward. Other times, case circumstances demand the decision be considered within a larger, more complex dialog, for example, if public safety is, or will be in jeopardy, or who exactly holds the expectation of privacy. In our office, if we have the luxury of debating whether we should obtain a warrant to search any location, thing, or receptacle, we always err on the side of caution when understanding a person's expectation of privacy. The Devil's Advocate reminds us to get the warrant. If we are debating this question in a briefing room, we know it will be debated in a courtroom, and, in these instances, getting the warrant is the simplest solution.

When the victim of a homicide is from the drug subculture or is a gang member, it is likely the suspect will also be from the drug subculture or the opposing gang—but not always. I remember a case where a high-ranking organized crime figure was murdered, not because of his gangster lifestyle but instead because of a lover's triangle that got way out of hand. Conversely, in suspicious missing persons cases, it has been my experience that *generally*, the last person who acknowledges seeing the victim alive is the person responsible for them going missing. I call this the *poof* phenomenon, as in *poof, they just disappeared.*

One example of this occurred after a young father seeking more access to his daughter decided one night to meet his ex's new husband and brother-in-law in an empty store parking lot to discuss his desire to be a larger part of his daughter's life. According to the brothers, who admitted to police that they had met with the victim and roughed him up a little that evening, he left the parking lot alive and must have just vanished (poof) from there. The father's remains were found in a burn barrel just outside city limits weeks later. The evidence that the brothers' account was dead wrong was overwhelming, and they were later convicted of his murder.

In another case, a husband stated that after coming home one night and arguing with his wife, he left to go sleep by himself, and when he woke up the next morning, poof, she was gone. Months later, her body was discovered buried in a plant bed at their home, and he confessed that he had put her there.

It makes sense the person who tells us the poof story is the likely suspect—but again, not always. A tragic example of this comes from a case I worked on several years ago. It was the start of the summer holidays, and families across the city were gearing up for their summer plans. Kids were out of school, and the fun and merriment of the season was in full swing. This time of year, routines can change, bedtimes get extended, and impromptu sleepovers can happen, as did in this case. The day before had been a busy time for the family in this story. Grandma and Grandpa were finally retiring and moving south. In preparation, they had hosted a large garage sale and invited their daughter and her children over to help. That night, as things were winding down, they decided one grandchild would stay the night with his grandparents while Mom and the younger child would return early the following day. The next morning, the mom arrived to a horrific, bloody crime scene, and her family members were missing.

What followed was the most intensive investigation of our service's history and a city gripped with grief for this nightmare. We worked around the clock and spared no resources to find the missing family members alive. That didn't happen. On an acreage outside the city, the investigative team discovered where this brutality had concluded. In this case, it had been the mother who first reported the disappearance and had been the last one to see them alive, but she had nothing to do with the atrocity. Instead, a twisted family acquaintance was responsible and convicted by a jury for his unimaginable crimes.

Bad guys try to use the simple solution adage to their own advantage. From my experience in child death investigations, when a child is of an age to walk, offenders will often state the injuries are from a fall down the stairs. Offenders use this argument as a simple, believable story to explain the multiple injuries discovered on the child. Stairs fit the bill. Few things inside the home could explain multiple impacts. When medical evidence disproves these claims, it becomes clear who the offender likely is because it's their story that becomes the issue.

A case in point was a homicide I was led on where a husband had, over the course of fourteen hours, restrained and beaten his wife to death after discovering she was having an affair. The husband wanted to leverage the beatings to force the victim to lure her lover back to the residence so the husband could do the same to him. She would not do it. Before she died, the suspect called police and stated he had found his wife on the road, an apparent victim of a hit-and-run. As in the case of the kid who *fell down the stairs*, once we figured out the story was bunk, identifying the husband as the culprit became relatively easy. Typically, when people make up a set of facts, it points to their own guilt.

Following Evidence

Evidence speaks for itself and should be front and center to why we form a basis for any belief. The Devil's Advocate should be there to always remind us, "You say that, but what is the evidence that forms that belief?"

David Simon sums it up well in his book a *Year on the Killing Streets* as he describes the examination of evidence:

> "A good detective looks at the scene and comprehends the pieces as a part of the greater whole. He somehow manages to isolate the important details to see those items which conform to the scene, those that conflict and those that are inexplicably absent."

In death investigations, we follow the principles behind what is referred to as the *Evidence Triangle* or *Golden Triangle* to help determine why someone died and, in cases of murder, who did it. Investigators committed to this course follow the trail of evidence, not a theory, in pursuit of the truth.

Facts find the truth.

This, of course, makes the Devil's Advocate happy.

The three points of the triangle comprise the body, the scene, and the history.

To establish the manner of death, all three pieces of the triangle must fit together like a puzzle before a final determination can be made on what happened. Puzzle pieces come from the evidence, not just a theory of what we think may have happened. Ignoring or overlooking any part of the triangle will distort the picture we are trying to build of what really happened.

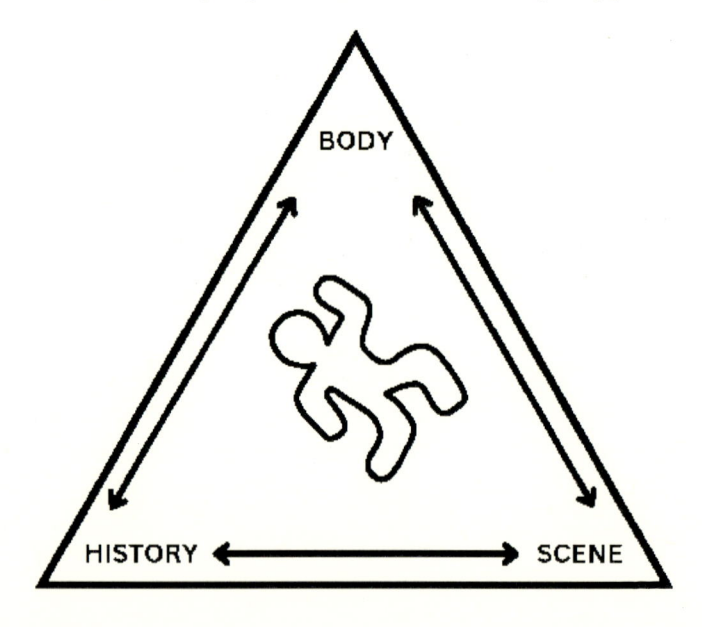

Mysteries are made when one side of the evidence triangle becomes ambiguous with another. A good tip for those aspiring mystery writers who are looking for a way to create the perfect plot twist in their next creative works.

As homicide detectives, we investigate not only murders but also collaborate with the Medical Examiner's Office on deaths their office deems suspicious. There are many reasons why the designation of suspicious is given, but it typically occurs when something in the triangle seems incongruent: a deceased person is found where it doesn't immediately make sense to find them, or the person is found in such a way that requires further explanation. A person found in a body of water, the side of the road, an alley, or a parkade are circumstances where more information is needed.

One day, each of us will die. When that happens, our death will be classified as one of four different manners of death: natural death, suicide, homicide, or accidental. When we begin a new suspicious death investigation, our end goal is to help the medical examiner (coroner in some jurisdictions) identify or classify the manner of death through the examination of evidence, with the assistance and competence of the Medical Examiner's Office. There are instances where a manner of death cannot be conclusively determined, and an undetermined classification is made. With undetermined deaths, what is really being said is there is not enough evidence or information to classify it into any of the other categories of death, or the circumstances don't conclusively add up to one of the other four designations.

An example of this is, as previously discussed, when we find bones or badly decomposed remains. It may be impossible for a medical examiner to determine the cause of death once the organs and tissues are gone, and all that remains is the skeleton.

Other instances where this can be a factor are with drug-related deaths. It is sometimes nearly impossible to know if the overdose was accidental, a suicide, or a lethal dose purposefully administered by a third party. We work hard to avoid undetermined designations so victim families are not left with unanswered questions.

How does this all fit together? How does it work to follow evidence (not theories) in tandem with the three corners of the Evidence Triangle to solve crimes or identify there was not a crime, with a Devil's Advocate keeping pace? Imagine you are the first responding officer to a sudden death complaint inside a residence. Upon arrival at the home, you enter the front door and note no signs of forced entry. As you make your way to the kitchen, you see the body of the victim lying face-up on the floor. In the victim's left hand is a large caliber handgun and there's a gunshot wound in the center of their chest. As you look around further, there is a calendar on the fridge with a crudely scrawled message, *very last day here*, scribbled on today's date.

Based on what the scene is telling us at this moment, you may theorize that the victim's manner of death is suicide. That conclusion, which makes sense, comes from an examination of the scene only. There are still two other corners of the triangle you need to investigate. You can't call it yet, and if you try, your Devil's Advocate should pound their fist against the table with a vehement *no*.

You delve deeper into this man's life; you examine his history and learn he was a gang member and prolific cocaine trafficker. In examining his phone, you find text messages from "Weird Harold" that suggest the victim owes money and messages that tell him he better pay up before something bad happens to him. You speak with several friends and family members and learn the victim was right-handed and had a history of depression.

Does any of this new information cloud your original assessment that the victim's death is a suicide? In this case, it may be the examination of the body that holds the final key to this puzzle. From it, we will learn if there was gunshot residue in his left hand, the distance of the handgun's muzzle when fired, and the trajectory of the bullet. These answers, along with the totality of evidence collected from his history and the scene, will hopefully allow us to determine the victim's manner of death to be either homicide with a staged scene or suicide. If it doesn't, his death will be ruled undetermined.

This scenario may seem a stretch because it lays out several possible twists and turns. From my experiences, I can confidently say it is not.

A perfect case in point comes from about a year ago on a cold January morning. A twelve-year-old girl was taking her elderly grandparents' recycling out to the garage when she opened the door and stumbled upon a horrific scene. Lying face down in a pool of blood was the body of a twenty-year-old man with no connection to the family.

When I arrived at the scene, the first thing I noticed

was no signs of forced entry into the detached garage. Inside, the medical examiner and I could see blood coming from a gaping wound on the top of the victim's head that appeared to be from a stabbing, which we suspected was likely the cause of death. He was fully clothed with the exception of one shoe, which had been removed and was lying near his body. No weapons were present at the scene. Several piles of feces were in the garage, and a "hideout" type shelter had been made with a few blankets over a workbench. It appeared he had been living or staying in the garage for some time—the family mentioned it had been about ten days since any of them had been in the garage. Both grandparents were in their nineties and explained that because of their age and health, they opted to use the carpark closer to the side of the house. The garage was mostly used as storage for things like cans and bottles and a few tools.

From my early analysis of the scene, I knew the victim had suffered a stab wound to his head, and there was no weapon present—hallmarks of a classic homicide. On-scene, I remember thinking whoever had been living in the garage with the victim was likely the culprit. The first break in the case came when the victim was identified from his fingerprints—the victim was well known to police and had an extensive history of violence and drug-type crimes. In fact, ten days prior to his discovery, the victim had been involved in an altercation at a residence a few blocks away from our scene. During that altercation, our victim had stabbed another man multiple times, and this individual had been rushed to hospital in life-threatening condition. During this incident, our deceased had also suffered a stab wound—to the top of his head—before he fled from the scene, presumably to the garage we had found him in. Based on this information—although still a homicide—thoughts turned to the possibility that it could be non-culpable if the victim taken to hospital with multiple stab wounds stabbed our deceased in self-defense.

The following day, I attended the autopsy of our deceased. The first surprise came when the doctor conducting the autopsy said, "*Det. Sweet, this man did not die as a result of a stab wound. Although the wound bled, it is superficial. It did not penetrate the skull.*" How did he die if it wasn't by homicide? The examination continued. "*Det. Sweet, do you see these ulcers on the stomach? These indicate the deceased was hypothermic at the time of his death. At this moment, his death appears natural.*"

Not what I expected at all.

Perhaps after fleeing the residence where the altercation occurred—and to get himself out of the bitterly cold January temperatures—the deceased sought refuge from the elements in the garage, only to ultimately succumb to the cold temperatures. It was minus thirty out, after all, and he wasn't dressed for such weather.

The examination continued.

"*Det. Sweet, I was wrong. Come have a look at his

stomach." Reluctantly, I did, and there it was, the final clue to how this individual died: two broken condoms and a third still tied with fentanyl inside. The deceased had ingested three condoms full of an opioid. Two of the three condoms had broken; this was an accidental drug overdose.

Now, it all made sense. Fearing the police were on their way after the altercation, the deceased ingested three condoms of fentanyl in case he was picked up by police responding to the initial incident. When he wasn't, he looked for a place to "lay low" and found an open garage. He made several attempts to void his system of the ingested drugs, leaving piles of feces on the garage floor. Before he could, two of the condoms broke, and the dangerous opioid entered his system, poisoning him.

When we investigate death, we inevitably find pieces of information and evidence at the scene, on the body, and within the victim's history that will surprise us or appear conflicting. The Devil's Advocate will always bring attention to these red herrings and the weaknesses in the case. It is essential to properly investigate each of these so that if the case goes to court, there are no issues. This is an accountability mechanism for effective and accurate decision-making; defending a position to the Devil's Advocate prepares us for the likely similar defense positions later.

To be clear, their opinion is not to be taken as gospel.

Their role is not to convince someone to agree with the opposite side of the argument. Rather, their role is to make sure it has been considered. The most effective Devil's Advocates understand the principles of management, as well as ethical and legal considerations, and make sure their arguments embody these principles.

If you are considering the use of the Devil's Advocate to assist in your decision-making process, I will leave you with a few thoughts. Ensure everyone on the project team understands what the role is and what its intent is, and if someone takes that role, make sure they identify themselves. If your advocate says, "I am going to PLAY the Devil's Advocate here," it should be enough of a heads-up to ensure they don't get a punch in the nose. Pick confident individuals to fill the role. They will require thick skin—their viewpoints will likely get smacked around by the others, even knowing this is an *essential* process. I would also recommend the role be shared around so no one in the room has the impression that *this person is an asshole*. Those turns can happen in the same meeting or briefing. In my work area, we don't formalize this role, but all step up to fill this position as required, and many of us are quite adept at it now. This brings me to my last point with the Devil's Advocate—be mindful that it stays productive and doesn't tip into limitless distraction. If every point gets debated for hours, it may be time to consider structuring the conversation differently: present the problem in an open dialog, have each in the group give their perspective only once, and then make a decision. This approach can be very effective in transforming an endless back-and-forth debate into something more fruitful—an informed decision.

How to Sell a Life Sentence

*"To the living, we owe the truth,
to the dead we owe respect."*
- homicide detective mantra

Until this point, I've shared experiences, lessons, philosophies, and strategies that have shaped the person and police officer I am. These lessons, from the responsibility I feel as a police officer to my ability to understand and listen to people to employing the right strategies for the situation, all come together when I sit in an interview room with a guy who has done unspeakable things, and I need to persuade him to tell me about them. In this room, we sell life sentences. How do we do that when the people walking in are certainly not interested in buying?

It has always fascinated me when people accused of crimes openly and candidly speak to the police; often, they have been told by their lawyer it is not in their best interest to do so. Despite the warning, many do, further implicating themselves, in great detail, in gruesome, heinous, and heartless crimes.

I once interviewed a suspect who was believed to have killed a woman he had just met and then disposed of her body in a city park. Several weeks later, a dog walker discovered her naked remains after noticing her white socks peeking out from under the brush. They dangled from her toes like she had been dragged by her ankles to that spot. Found at the end of summer with hot daytime temperatures and chilly nights, her body had degraded terribly. She was a single mother who had been holding down good jobs until her cocaine habit steered her off the safe route and led her to work on the street to feed her addiction. Her choices and circumstances required her to master different faces, which she managed for a while.

Everyone has a story.

Police had interviewed the suspect in this case on two previous occasions. In those interviews, he had always taken his lawyer's advice: *do not talk to the cops, don't say anything.* In fact, he took this advice so literally that in the second interview, he did not even want to provide his name to the interviewer—an experienced detective rarely shut down. So when I was asked to interview him for his third round of questioning, I knew I would be in deep. I focused on something I had learned over years of watching effective, sharp interviewers before me.

> *The key to selling anything is an effective presentation with a wee bit of influence sprinkled in.*

In my experience, few homicide suspects own up to their actions because it's the right thing to do. Rather, confessions are obtained once a suspect sees the overwhelming evidence against them and recognizes they are in an insurmountably tight spot. Then they buy what we are selling, a chance to tell their side of the story, sometimes to explain what happened, and sometimes to minimize the crime or their motive for committing it.

A famous case of a police interview made more famous once it was profiled on the CBC's Fifth Estate, was that of David Russell Williams, a decorated colonel in the Canadian military. Williams was taken into custody for questioning in the murder of a twenty-seven-year-old woman. In the interview, Williams was shown, along with other pieces of evidence, images of tire tracks and footwear patterns that had been taken from the crime scene and were demonstrated to match his own. Over the course of the ten-hour interview, Williams not only confessed to that murder but to another, as well as forcible confinement, two different sexual assaults during home invasions, and a number of break-and-enters in which women's underwear was stolen. He detailed his crimes, including where additional evidence could be found, and led investigators to the site where he had dumped his last murder victim's body.

In that interview, the investigators obviously gave a successful presentation of the evidence. It is what I would have to do if I wanted any chance for a third-time-is-a-charm interview with our silent suspect.

Selling life sentences requires a coordinated, thoughtful approach, with a lot of moving parts in the works long before a suspect is in the room or sometimes even before he is identified. Those moving parts range from who the presenter is and what experience they have, to what the evidence is and how it was collected, to the type of audio, video, or photo media collected or available to communicate evidence and any other applicable information, and so on.

Our interview process follows closely a traditional sales cycle, which you may already be familiar with.

At the top of the sales cycle is prospecting. When a new case comes into our office, we analyze case evidence, which we hope will lead to the identification of a suspect.

Next is research. We research our potential suspects. We may look at an individual's past criminal history or their past dealings with the police. We may search their social media or speak with their family or friends. We may also use surveillance to assist us in understanding more about our suspect.

Following research is an approach, that all-important first impression. For us, the approach starts with the arrest, and it is important that it is done legally and professionally. Once arrested, the suspect will then be brought back to our office, where they will be provided an opportunity to speak with counsel before ever stepping foot into our interview suite to meet the investigator, who will pitch them the evidence that has brought them onto our radar. During the presentation of the evidence, the interviewer will have to overcome objections by the suspect. An objection may be as simple as *"my lawyer said not to say anything"* to outright accusations that the evidence in the case is fraudulent. There are a number of strategies to help an interviewer overcome objections they face in the interview room. However, first and foremost, they must do so with a calm demeanor. More on this to come later in this chapter.

If an interviewer can successfully overcome whatever issue or fear the suspect has, then getting through to closing the deal (garnering a confession or admissions) becomes much easier. The delivery of the product we have just sold to an offender comes weeks later in a disclosure package to the prosecutor and then again, possibly years later, in a courtroom in front of a judge or jury. In the courtroom, the suspect will try to return what he bought—through arguments made by his counsel on the statement admissibility.

Asking for referrals ends the traditional sales cycle and begins a new one for businesses—difficult for us to do. However, our name and the way we have treated someone does have an impact and goes a long way. Often, in the strangest of ways, like discussed in chapter two with officers who were able to develop a rapport or even trust with difficult or wary families or professional counsel.

Interviewing is selling, which we will now get into the nuts and bolts of.

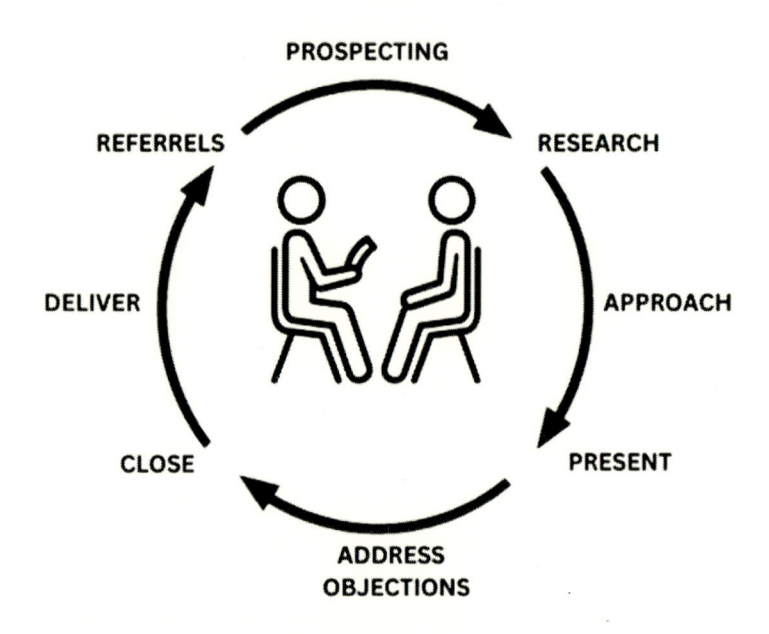

PROSPECTING
RESEARCH
APPROACH
PRESENT
ADDRESS OBJECTIONS
CLOSE
DELIVER
REFERRELS

The Presenter (Interviewer)

Who is doing the selling makes a huge difference in the successful outcome of any interview or client meeting. The best presenters are professional, charismatic, and charming. They are confident and knowledgeable about the subject matter (likability and authority influences). They are also effective in the use of self-deprecating humor and changes of inflection in their voice. They are animated with their hands and never hide behind the podium. They connect to their audience, bring energy to the room, and use relevant stories to keep the audience engaged.

Can you imagine buying a house from someone who was not confident or an authority on the property and community in which you were looking to buy? What are the chances someone would win a debate or argue a position while being aloof? These are not likely scenarios. It is the same in a police interview. A bad guy is unlikely to confess to the square-peg-in-a-square-hole personality.

You really do catch more flies with honey.

This means carrying out interviews in a respectful manner, free of judgment. Given the subject matter, this is a difficult thing; it's why changing paradigms and having the ability to compartmentalize can be such assets. Interviews conducted in this manner help eliminate any legal arguments about a statement's admissibility months or even years down the road. As you may recall, *if the court identifies threats, coercion, or inducements that came through in the bad cop's role, the statements may be dismissed.*

Great presentations combine various types of media to reinforce talking points. Audio, video, pictures, and props can be very persuasive to a person buying what you are selling, as was the case in the earlier example with Russell Williams being shown the tire tracks and footwear patterns. Simply being told something does not have nearly the same impact as also being shown or listening to it. There is a world of difference between reading the transcript of a 9-1-1 call and hearing it played during an interview or courtroom presentation. Videos of the offender in the area at the time of the crime or committing the crime make a difference and can be a chilly reminder of just how dark it can get. Crime scene photographs have a similar effect. All of these mediums are collected to tell the same story, the same case—but viscerally.

Suspects emotionally respond to evidence that triggers any of the five senses in an interview room, just as judges and juries do in a courtroom and customers do in a showroom. Those quirky facts, interesting details, and haunting truths plug people into what actually happened, moving from the distance of a theoretical discussion to the up-close-and-personal experience of the tangible, even if it's horrific. In murder investigations and trials, that which is horrific must be communicated to get through our natural naïveté.

Imagine if I told you a true story about a domestic assault where the offender dragged his wife around the kitchen by her hair, only to free her when the police arrived. This scenario likely conjures some sort of image in your brain. Would that image change if you were sitting in the courtroom and the talking head on the stand produces a large freezer bag collected at the scene stuffed with long blond hair stained red with blood in the places where it had been pulled from her scalp?

For many people, there is a reason why seeing is believing. Our minds often can't accept the true story; we cannot allow ourselves to go that far into the abyss. It is simply too dark, and our inherent naïveté and aversion does not allow us to get there. For the most part, people want to think the best of others, and sometimes, it is easier to avoid or downplay the violence committed around us every day. When we see the stash of bloodied hair in a freezer bag, we are no longer innocent of that darkness. We then understand it is real; people make choices to hurt others.

In another domestic-related case I worked, a husband had handwritten in black marker on the wall near the front door: *Don't come back here, Stacy, or this will be your head.* Beside the message was a fist-shaped hole in the drywall. Days later, his wife was dead. We had graphic evidence of intent, but a photograph of the threatening message and the hole in the wall didn't communicate the impact it had on us at the scene, so we cut out that part of the wall and were prepared to bring it into court to better capture how truly horrifying domestic violence can be.

In another case, a toddler died in the care of a babysitter. Statements by the caregiver indicated that the child had fallen down a flight of three stairs. *Go figure.* The injuries seen in the hospital and then later at autopsy made this story implausible to the doctors. An examination of the scene revealed other inconsistencies. The story was a lie.

Instead of spending the interview circling futilely around the plausibility of the babysitter's tale, we decided to build a replica of the stairs. On the day of her arrest, the caregiver was brought into the staged room and confronted with a flight of three stairs built with care by our fleet and facilities department. Over the course of the following five hours, we showed the caregiver statements of witnesses, first responders, medical documents, and scene photographs, and finally provided an opportunity to participate in a re-enactment using the stairs and a life-sized doll. She declined. Instead, she watched as I showed her how her story was not possible. I believe that 3D re-enactment solidified for her that everyone knew her story did not hold water. Months later, she pled guilty to the crime of manslaughter despite not making a statement to me that day.

Rapport Building

Rapport building is the warmup before you start pitching 100-mile-an-hour fastballs.

This will surprise no one, but a homicide interview room doesn't inherently inspire someone to open up and honestly say what happened, especially if the suspect is guilty. So, we must create that space. There are several ways we can do this. The ability to accurately read a person and use effective storytelling can create a space of equality and identify the right themes to find out what really happened. It makes sense we are apt to like people with whom we have common ground. The social influences of reciprocity, conformity, and likability are all used to achieve this. We speak candidly to those with whom we are comfortable.

The ability of an interviewer to read a person is crucial to develop a rapport and identify themes that will motivate them to buy what you are selling. Take Sarah and me. Based on just our pictures and the way we present ourselves, you likely see two very different people. Which one of us would you guess to be the more conservative, and which one is more liberal? What kinds of things made you arrive at those conclusions? What are you basing your assessment on? We are, in fact, exactly how we have been stereotyped. I am certainly the more conservative of the pair, Sarah the free spirit. So, what does this mean?

If you were to ingratiate yourself to either one of us, searching for clues of commonality is a good place to start. For example, discussing sustainable energy practices will pique Sarah's interest quickly, and she'll likely follow your conversation more readily than if you talked about your love of big business tax loopholes. In my case, commonality may be found in conversations around fancy restaurants you've attended or where you bought your last suit. I would also be more receptive to ideas about current economic security than any environmental legacies.

Sometimes, as the seller (investigator), you may have to make up the commonality, which is permitted under the law. For example, if, in the rapport-building phase, you learn the suspect likes to spend time in the mountains hiking, guess what? Now, so do you. If a suspect wants a Big Mac, guess what you're eating for lunch? I once interviewed a female offender who had a known disdain and distrust for the case's primary investigator. It was decided that early in the interview, I would throw the lead detective under the proverbial bus, stating I was not influenced by his rush judgments and recognized they came from his inexperience as an investigator. This individual was all smiles and couldn't have agreed more. Over the next hours, we talked at great length, and, in the end, she made several critical mistakes in her statements that ultimately assisted in her conviction.

Introducing equality can help close the gap between two people who are on different sides of an important table.

In the Williams example, the interviewer decided not to refer to the ex-colonel by his title, but instead only by his first name, Russell. This strategy worked to create the equality he required to ingratiate himself to a man who probably believed he was of a higher social standing than the mere cop in front of him. Our minds can close when we perceive a power imbalance, either in our favor or not.

That's why balance in relationships is so important, and when in an interview, I work hard to build that balanced space so the real story has a greater opportunity of coming out.

Storytelling helps us build rapport with a suspect. When I tell him a story from my life that relates to his predicament, making it clear I understand the gray because how could I not when my story has such applicable parallels too, the suspect knows I'm listening. The story can be complete crap, but that's not the point. The point is, *I'm listening.* This style of presentation facilitates theme development, connection, commonality, and cooperation (keys to the likability influence) that help create the space for the accused to buy the opportunity to tell their side of the story.

Hitting on the right theme is equivalent to hitting a home run. If you work in an appliance store and a customer walks in to buy a new washing machine and dryer because they are tired of having the repair person out every second week, what they are actually saying is they are looking for appliances with a proven track record and good warranty. Recognizing this, you have identified a solid theme to help you sell the product. In an interview, suspects actually say what they want to hear, and it is the interviewer's role to regurgitate that information later. This is how I identify themes and adjust my questioning accordingly. I can ask questions like, "What do you think should happen to a person who commits a serious crime?" If the accused replies that serious crimes demand counseling and apologies, the theme narrows to apologies. Perhaps the interviewer tells the suspect that in cases like these, an apology to the victim helps the healing process, and the suspect sits forward, maybe even asking me questions—or not. Maybe he smirks, expresses disdain for counseling, and likens apologies to excrement. Obviously, I wouldn't pursue that theme; I'd go fishing again until the theme for that suspect was revealed. We all have buttons. In a homicide interview, it is about finding the applicable button to open up the dialog.

Reminding people they are not alone and that others have faced similar dilemmas helps when the suspect understands they are being recognized for a human flaw instead of a personal one. This is another powerful theme and creates an empathetic connection. An example of this could be individuals who have shaken babies to death, which is a deplorable crime that brings loads of disgust and contempt from the community. In a crime such as this, what do you think would happen if the offender were introduced to the theme that almost all new parents with a colicky baby become frustrated and that they just need to put the baby down and walk away before they make the same mistake? Or reminding the suspect that many parents have support systems in place they can lean on, or that others don't necessarily suffer from alcohol or drug addictions? How do you think offenders respond when a police interviewer expresses an understanding of the circumstances? Changing the *monster* argument to a *bad mistake* will inevitably lead some people to choose their "out" and buy into the themes you created as you listened. Of course, this is not always an easy task in an interview with a suspect who has done something deplorable. This is why understanding shades of gray and the ability to shift paradigms are essential tools in the interviewer's toolbox.

Why is all of this important? Understanding what a person likes and what their interests are before a pitch will guide you toward what themes to build on. What if you were tasked with selling the same car to both Sarah and me? How would you take what you know about each of us to sell that same vehicle? For Sarah, you would likely focus on the vehicle's practicality, its robustness in off-road terrain, its high eco-ratings, and the ease of add-ons like a bike rack or ski carrier. For me, you would focus on selling the vehicle's sleek look and leather seats, how easy it is to keep clean, and its status symbol and rank. It's the same vehicle, but to be successful, you would utilize very different selling points to make each sale.

This awareness is crucial during undercover work but also very much in the interview room. How do you know if your first impressions of a person are correct? Asking test questions can confirm or correct assumptions you have made and may also provide more fine-tuned information. "Correct me if I'm wrong, but I imagine you are a person who loves to get out into the mountains on a weekend?" Or, "You seem to be a guy that likes nice things. What are you looking for in (insert product detail here)?" The answers to these questions will help guide your responses later. Just like we size up suspects, they are sizing us up, too. This is why it is so important that you are an authority on the product you're selling and the case you are presenting, and why it is vital to be prepared.

When I was still pretty green in the interview room, and before I had developed any semblance of a poker face, I interviewed a suspect who we believed had been involved in a gangland shooting. All was going fine and, as he started to talk about what had happened, I thought, *I got him!* My eyes lit up, my voice quivered, and then—*BAM!* The suspect's eyes actually bulged when he realized how close he had come to telling me what he had done. Needless to say, he clammed up tight, and I learned a valuable lesson.

Sometimes, it is prudent to hold your cards close to your chest.

The Pitch (Presenting the Evidence)

The pitch is presenting the totality of evidence collected through the police investigation. During the pitch, good interviewers weave in themes identified during rapport building and may also introduce new ones. The evidence is shown and explained to the suspect. None of the facts can be misrepresented; an interviewer cannot say they have the suspect's fingerprints or DNA at the scene if they don't. If they do anyway, and the suspect buys into what the interviewer is selling, precedent states the confession will be deemed inadmissible later. Essentially, the product sold will be returned. When delivering the pitch, the interviewer must be mindful of the keys to effective presentation and deliver the evidence in a meaningful and confident way. At their disposal should be pictures, crime lab reports, quirky facts, or interesting details.

I have also found it useful at times to encourage the suspect to correct any evidence they believe is wrong or has been misunderstood, and have even got them up and out of their chair to tape pictures to the wall or examine more closely the evidence already presented. When I do this, I am having the suspect participate in the process, but I am careful to only ask someone I feel will acquiesce. Otherwise, I risk upsetting the balance of equality in the room I have worked so hard to get.

Don't pick a fight you can't win.

That only creates ripples you don't want to be swamped by. This sounds like an easy rule to follow, but I have seen time and again good interviewers get into pissing matches with suspects over situations that didn't matter and situations they couldn't win. A common example of this is when a suspect is placed in an interview room and takes the interviewer's chair. When the interviewer enters the room to begin his interrogation, he asks the suspect to change chairs, and the suspect refuses. Now what? The interviewer cannot force him out of his chair, so he picks a fight that he can't win, and the bad guy scores a point before the game has even begun.

Let's return to the suspect who didn't even want to give his name to the police, the one I was assigned by the Command Triangle to interview next. I was given the necessary information I would need to conduct the interview and give a solid presentation. When you are in the interview room, you are the franchise, and the decisions or calls you make are live. There is no time delay or chance to see the replay, but there are breaks. Obviously, you're not going to take the break when the guy is in the middle of a confession; you pause when you know you're hitting walls. These well-placed timeouts are a chance to collect your thoughts or collaborate with the investigative team watching the interview via the camera feed (not one-way glass). They are that sober second thought which identifies the theme to work harder on and the ones to shy away from.

When I entered the room that day, the first thing that struck me was the angry energy rolling off him. He had pushed his chair into the corner of the room. He sat with his right leg crossed over his left knee with his right foot vibrating a fierce staccato. His arms were folded across his chest, and when he did answer a question, it was with a single word in a belligerent tone. Maybe he believed that by being angry, he could intimidate me. I called him on it early, and my phone promptly pinged. It was a message from the team watching: *easy, easy, easy*. They thought my snapback was counterproductive. There was a risk it might not have worked, but I created an atmosphere of equality in the room.

Straight off, the accused made it clear all he would do was sit, keep his mouth shut, and listen to whatever I had to say. As I continued to build themes and rapport, I could tell that one of the biggest fears he had, what he was so angry about, was how his actions would impact his family. His family was a topic he wanted to avoid. So, I did—for the time being, and floated other themes past him. It is the listening and watching, the testing to get the one that really resonates. Themes about guilt, violence, and his role didn't resonate with him. The victim's flaws, though, were the themes that did. His responses suggested he thought he'd *only* made a bad decision. That he was not a monster.

For the next couple of hours, I presented evidence, which included statements from witnesses, crime lab reports linking the victim DNA to his vehicle, crime scene photographs, entomology reports, computer forensic reports, and, most damning, a taped confession he made to a friend. As the minutes ticked by, I watched the suspect become more aware of how strong the case against him was. His foot had stopped vibrating long ago; his arms were no longer crossed. He leaned forward in his chair, both feet firmly planted on the ground, and looked at the evidence while I explained its significance. When I finished the presentation, I simply asked, "Would you agree that most people sitting in your chair would say this doesn't look good?"

Closing the Deal

The key to closing the deal is empowering a person to make their own decision.

If you push, the suspect retreats, and you lose all the ground you had gained. Most people don't respond well to being hammered. The social influences of commitment, scarcity, and conformity are powerful but are not so pervasive and persuasive that everyone buys into them all the time. It is a person's choice what they do or don't buy or say.

When you've got a solid case and provide the suspect time and space to look at all their options to see the big picture, it encourages them to come to you to find out what exactly you're selling. In an interview, there is a fine line between the point at which a suspect shuts down and the point at which they make a truthful incriminating statement. I have seen that, *Oh, shit! That was close!* look on suspects' faces when they realize a conversation with you is dangerous. That comes from applying too much pressure and asking too many invasive questions. Don't push. Encourage a person to tell their side of the story instead. To be effective, an investigator must make the accused understand what's in it for them. How will talking and explaining their version help and not hurt them? What do they stand to lose if they don't? What would happen if the police evidence spoke for them instead of being able to explain their actions themselves? People have their reasons for doing what they do, the need to be understood, and for their gray to be recognized.

Asking a suspect to put themselves in the shoes of another is one way to talk about morality and guilt without getting too personal, and the influence of conformity puts the weight of ethics on the suspect's shoulders.

If you were a juror, what would you be thinking?

Who do people respect more? A guy who runs from his mistakes or one who faces them?

Do people feel better after they apologize, or do they feel worse?

Most suspects want to tell their side of the story; they want to be heard, but because their crimes can be heinous, some have a hard time. They don't want to lose face. As the interviewer, it's my job to show them compassion (even if I'm not feeling any) and to harness the themes that resonated with them through the course of the interview:

I understand the concept of being incarcerated is scary to you, but there is a life to be had in jail and opportunities to help you and others. Alcohol and drugs can change people and make them act in pretty bad ways. Society understands this now. Is this what happened to you? If this was more like an error in judgment rather than a premeditated attack, that is really important information to know.

In the case of the murdered woman whose story started out this chapter, the accused's anxiety about his family and unwillingness to talk about them gave me an understanding of what this suspect needed.

"You are going to be perceived as either a monster or a guy who made a big mistake. Right now, most people would think you were a monster."

That was the moment the interview changed. The accused, overwhelmed with the thought he could be perceived in such a way, admitted to "consensual rough sex" that had gotten "out of hand" and gave a very detailed confession in which he blamed the victim as much as himself for her murder.

This is when I shut up, leaned back in the chair, put my hands behind my head, and listened while he stood and went through the process of re-enacting the crime, giving specific details of both holdback and new information that were later used to corroborate his story. Sweat beaded on his head while he spoke. They had negotiated a price for sex so she could get her next eighty-dollar fix of cocaine. He said, during sex she had asked to be choked—highly unlikely, as women in these scenarios don't typically prioritize their own orgasms—and that was how she had then died. He grew so comfortable with me that he talked in depth, with the finest of details, on what had occurred in the back seat of his vehicle.

If the suspect had said nothing, the overwhelming evidence would have spoken for him, and he would indeed be seen as a monster. In the end, he told his version of events. He was angry, not because he had killed a woman, but because he had created a situation that humiliated and embarrassed his family. Was it cold-blood murder or rough sex that went too far? The only other person who knows that truth, for sure, is dead. Sometimes, there is no final answer, not one you trust, anyway.

The stakes are high when selling a life sentence, and there is a reason homicide detectives have years of service under our belts. We need that accumulation of experience. I remember how impatient I was as a rookie, like when I was waiting for my partner as he calmed that homeowner. Would I have learned something valuable on the other call with the fleeing suspect? Of course. But I learned *to leave people better than we found them* so acutely that night because of my impatience to get on the seemingly more memorable hot call. Even my humility when I eventually learned what LNU meant was a good lesson for me; my confidence is a blessing that only gets wiser when it is occasionally tempered. This all comes with hindsight.

Experience takes time. Let it.

Conclusion: Gavel Drop

"Be the change you want to see in the world."
- Mahatma Gandhi

I share these lessons I learned on the job so you might benefit from the roads I took in life. Some lessons came easy. Some were unbelievably hard. All made me who I am today. I am no longer the fresh-faced recruit, as eager to help as to prove myself. I'm older, I hope wiser, I know harder. It has indeed been a long road full of triumphs and tragedies, the cost higher than I want to tally. For better or worse, this is me. The job has shaped me, but I know I've left my mark, too. Just like we all do. We all impact those around us, and no one lives in a bubble, immune to the decisions of others.

Sharing these stories has helped me re-live happier moments and process darker ones through the clearer lens of hindsight. When we started, I was eager to write, to get it done. I wasn't sure exactly what to expect from the experience. It would probably be cathartic, maybe enlightening, and no doubt it would make me feel vulnerable. This journey has been all of those and then some. It is an interesting thing, taking inventory of your life, what you've learned, how you've lived, and then writing it down for others to digest, hopefully with more positive take-aways than not.

I can't explain why some of us are called into service. I know the compulsion to help is real. Maybe there is no explanation needed. Maybe it just is. So, we do it and own our path the best we know and learn how. Our life really is a reflection of our choices. Every day, with the choices we make, we either affirm or forsake the path we want. The more I experience, the more I understand how gray the world we live in is. There is deep value in having perspective and an open mind and knowing just how much of an asset understanding discretion is.

That's not wishy-washy. It is with this attitude that I am able to see people more clearly and with fewer blinders. Our circumstance, address (or lack thereof), or choices don't negate our humanity. We need others. Our interactions help us pinpoint our place in space, a triangulation, if you will. It is our relationships that give us our bearings, where we are in our life, so we can figure out if that's where we want to be. That's why those unwritten social rules have so much power, because somewhere deep down, we know we are in this together, that there are rules of order, even when people dismiss them. We set so many things in motion—that *butterfly effect* is real, although sometimes it feels like a hurricane instead of a wing flutter.

Having processes to make great decisions, with mechanisms for deeper understanding, as well as checks and balances, helps us navigate our world with a greater chance of success. We all matter, and we all make a difference. The choice of what path we tread is ours.

It is my sincere intention that sharing what I've learned over a twenty-five-year career can have a positive impact on your life and help you make decisions that support the happiest possible you. Because, for some reason, against serious odds, I still give a damn.

🦋 *Love people.*

101 Lessons

1. Our history does not define who we are, but it can influence who we become in unpredictable ways.
2. It is up to each of us to choose to believe in ourselves.
3. It is not the years of service, but the volume of decisions, experiences, and mistakes made that build a person's expertise.
4. Leave people in a better place than you found them.
5. Mentors can be as unexpected as their lessons are wise.
6. Why jump over fences when you can look for gates?
7. Books never resolved a barroom brawl unless they were used as a weapon or shield.
8. Under the provisions of the Ways and Means Act, there is always a way and always a means to solve problems and dilemmas.
9. Opportunities to make a positive difference are all around us.
10. Every day, by our actions and words, we affect the quality of life for others, and for ourselves.
11. By helping others, we create a life of meaning for ourselves.
12. You are never too small to make a difference.
13. Courage is placing ourselves in vulnerable situations, including opening ourselves to be hurt or judged, but trusting the outcome is worth it.

14. A life of service is so much more than an occupation or calling. It is a philosophy of living.
15. Owning your path is taking responsibility for not only the direction of your life but also for the choices and people you include in it every day.
16. Our best compass comes from trusting our instincts, following our hearts, and staying true to our core values.
17. By owning our path, we are better able to help someone else own theirs.
18. Real life doesn't have a template.
19. Our relationship with success, not unlike happiness, is really up to us.
20. A lucky break has to have someplace to land.
21. The differences between success and failure are the words "try" and "do."
22. Failure is part of the evolution toward success.
23. Surround yourself with successful people.
24. It is not hard to be a bit better than average.
25. Define what success actually means to you.
26. Just because we can do something doesn't mean we should.
27. Discretion is making decisions in the gray.
28. Consideration creates a positive presence.
29. When discretion is either ignored or applied at the wrong moment, its wisdom is missed.
30. We get into trouble when we assume we know what is best for another.
31. When we only think in black and white, we become narrow-minded to the greater game playing out before us.
32. Absolutes can be dangerously limiting.

33. Never fear other possibilities could exist.
34. People will say extraordinary things when given the space to be heard.
35. Just because something has always been done one way doesn't mean it is the right way.
36. Not everyone lives behind white picket fences.
37. Often, those who are not the easiest to love are the ones who need it the most.
38. We should resist comparing our life to others, we really have no idea what their path is.
39. If we want to influence how others view us, we must match our actions to our intentions.
40. Respect is a currency.
41. Grudges have room to grow when we are not free to speak openly.
42. Staying adaptable gives us the agility to see our choices.
43. Being willfully ignorant of dangerous behavior is bad secret-keeping.
44. Do better. Be better.
45. Staying out of dark places keeps us safe.
46. Only lend to others what you can afford to lose.
47. Our mindsets and attitudes can either support or undermine us.
48. Naïveté is a beautiful and pure part of the human condition, something to be admired, not despaired.
49. Experience and time can make difficult things easier to deal with.
50. We don't need to rehash the harsh details of a traumatizing event to allow ourselves to come to a place of peace or healing.
51. Changing paradigms is like turning a coin to see the

other side.
52. Perspective is a powerful antidote to worry.
53. Cultivate a habit of appreciation.
54. The easiest way to enjoy memories, honor legacy, or feel a presence is with a clear mind, absent of anger or other emotions.
55. Only look when you need to, and avoid peeking when it isn't prudent to do so.
56. Remembering that things can always be worse somehow helps when we are trying to overcome our own challenges and pain.
57. People we help today are more likely to want to help us tomorrow.
58. Sometimes, the easiest person to lie to is yourself.
59. If you wish to keep your relationships in proper balance, remain true to your word.
60. Don't take yourself too seriously.
61. Find your passion and master it.
62. Free choice is not forfeited by an influencer.
63. When we feel pressured, we hasten our decision-making process, and that can lead to errors in judgment.
64. Take a moment and think, "Whose best interest does this really serve?"
65. When a person acts like they don't care, believe them.
66. Love requires freedom to trust a person will stay, and if they don't, freedom to trust a relationship has run its course.
67. Our actions create ripples (or tsunamis) in the world around us.
68. Challenges create opportunities for wisdom.
69. Be mindful of your curiosity. It informs our actions and

can lead us to great discoveries or dark places.
70. Embrace life today.
71. Be mindful of what we are setting into motion—and mitigate the risks—before they become problems we can't easily fix.
72. Sometimes, the absence of information is a clue in itself.
73. Play to the long game.
74. Positive messages are the engines that inspire people, build confidence, and create positive action.
75. Nothing significant can be built on shaky ground.
76. Collaboration with the right partner is key to making decisions that move us forward.
77. When we hold ourselves and others to account, we are practicing maturity and demonstrating responsibility.
78. Often, it's the quiet guy in the corner who usually has the best ideas.
79. Informed action is required to resolve a problem.
80. When we have things in our life that require a task force, assemble one.
81. All partnerships need to be nurtured if we are to have any expectation of keeping them.
82. Inspire people to rise above that tenacious grip of mediocrity.
83. Life is full of karmic decisions.
84. Listen to your gut when it calls your mind to attention.
85. The first step in managing risk is to recognize where it is coming from.
86. There is definite risk whenever someone over or underestimates a person or thing, and arrogance

contributes to that miscalculation.
87. Be self-aware. Identify bias before it inhibits sound decision-making.
88. Following facts, not theories, is tunnel vision's only counterstrike.
89. The Devil's Advocate wears a halo.
90. The simplest answer is likely the right one.
91. Facts find the truth.
92. Everyone has a story.
93. The key to selling anything is an effective presentation with a wee bit of influence sprinkled in.
94. You really do catch more flies with honey.
95. Rapport building is the warm-up before you start pitching 100-mile-an-hour fastballs.
96. Introducing equality can help close the gap between two people who are on different sides of an important table.
97. Sometimes, it is prudent to hold your cards close to your chest.
98. Don't pick a fight you can't win.
99. The key to closing the deal is empowering a person to make their own decision.
100. Experience takes time. Let it.
101. Love people.

PEEL'S PRINCIPALS

1. The basic mission for which the police exist is to prevent crime and disorder.
2. The ability of the police to perform their duties is dependent upon public approval of police actions.
3. Police must secure the willing cooperation of the public in voluntary observance of the law to be able to secure and maintain the respect of the public.
4. The degree of cooperation of the public that can be secured diminishes proportionately to the necessity of the use of physical force.
5. Police seek and preserve public favor not by catering to public opinion but by constantly demonstrating absolute impartial service to the law.
6. Police use physical force to the extent necessary to secure observance of the law or to restore order only when the exercise of persuasion, advice and warning is found to be insufficient.
7. Police, at all times, should maintain a relationship with the public that gives reality to the historic tradition that the police are the public and the public are the police, the police being only members of the public who are paid to give full-time attention to

duties which are incumbent on every citizen in the interests of community welfare and existence.
8. Police should always direct their action strictly toward their functions and never appear to usurp the powers of the judiciary.
9. The test of police efficiency is the absence of crime and disorder, not the visible evidence of police action in dealing with it.

(Sir Robert Peel's Principles of Law Enforcement, 1829)

Patrolman David M. Young

My grandfather David M. Young, born on August 7, 1880, in Dundas, Ontario, became naturalized as a US citizen in January 1904 when he entered into his first marriage.

In 1905, he joined the rank and file of the New York Police Department (NYPD), where, according to some records, he received three medals for bravery over his career.

When my grandfather joined the NYPD, the department was under transition in a number of ways. According to historians Joshua Ruff and Michael Cronin, who wrote the book *New York City Police* (that my cousin gave me) about my grandfather's time of service, much was changing in the bustling Big Apple's police department, some of it impacting history:

- The boroughs of New York City had just consolidated, and the NYPD became responsible for policing three hundred square miles of the diverse communities in Manhattan, Queens, Staten Island, Brooklyn, and parts of the Bronx.

- With the innovation of the automobile in the early 1900s, traffic in the boroughs and particularly Manhattan—the city's financial district—caused streets and avenues to become packed with cars, making crossing difficult and burdening policing resources to help control the flow. According to Ruff and Cronin, it was not until the 1930s, when traffic signals came into existence, that the responsibilities of traffic control began to lift from the shoulders of the NYPD's Traffic Squad.

- By 1909, there were over a hundred officers on bicycles patrolling for speeders. At that time, the fine for speeding was ten dollars. In 1912, when speed limits increased to fifteen miles per hour, the police department began to change tactics to catch speeders and rolled out a motorcycle squad to compete with faster-traveling automobiles.

- The force also began to diversify from a predominantly Italian and Irish membership. In 1911, the NYPD hired Samuel Battle, their first African-American patrol officer. Throughout his career, he fought discrimination and earned the respect of his peers to move up the ranks of the organization, becoming a lieutenant and parole commissioner. No less significant, the NYPD appointed the first six women to the force in 1918, including Ellen O'Grady, who would become the first woman to serve as a deputy police commissioner for the NYPD.

- By 1911, police stationary posts were being used to guard the city. Under this model, constables on patrol (COPs) were deployed like sentries into the middle of intersections to stand stationary as a visible presence while other patrolmen walked the block. This practice ended when they realized deploying resources in this manner handicapped the strength of resources by half, as those stationary officers were never permitted to leave their posts.

- By 1912, the use of Bertillon cards to identify criminals was replaced by the more exact science of fingerprinting. Bertillon cards looked like mugshots but recorded physical measurements of a person as a key to identification.

- Organized crime groups began their occupation of the city, including the notorious Black Hand Italian mafia. Sophisticated organized crime groups rose higher in prominence around 1919 when liquor prohibition laws came into effect. By then, my grandfather had left the department to pursue other possibilities, perhaps a good thing because, according to Ruff and Cronin, 168 police officers died in the line of duty during the prohibition era.

Following his tenure with the NYPD around 1918, my grandfather returned to Canada and settled in the province of Alberta, where he became a Justice of the Peace. During this time, his first marriage dissolved. He met my grandmother, who, legend has it, was his housekeeper, and went on to have two more children with her.

In February 1967, six years before I was born, my grandfather passed away, but despite never knowing him personally, I can't help but feel a connection to him and his path. For those who know me well, you will understand this sentiment. For those who knew both of us, I am told you would agree with the echo of my mom's voice: "You are a lot like your grandfather."

Included in this material are some of those lasting legacy pieces that I hope you will enjoy perusing as much as I did growing up. Special thanks to my cousin Capri Rasmussen, who, being the custodian of this part of my family's history, helped pull this section of the book together in the eleventh hour and supplied some of the material for inclusion into the manuscript.

Dave Sweet

Section 263 of my grandfather's 1923 Canadian Criminal Code where the penalty for homicide conviction in those days was death.

> **Bull Dogs Protect Bartender.**
> When Roundsman Boyle and Patrolman Young, of the Fifth avenue station, Brooklyn, Sunday attempted to make an arrest for violation of the excise law at No. 204 Union street, two bull dogs were sicked at them by the bartender. The dogs had to be subdued before Boyle and Young could make arrests. The bartender was held for trial.

More memorabilia from my grandfather's era.

SKELETONS IN MY CLOSET

Lifesaving medals and memorabilia from the era.

PLUCKY "COP" ARRESTS TWO TOUGHS WHO BEAT HIM

FEB. 6

Policeman David M. F___ is very thankful to-day that he is in no worse condition than he is after a desperate encounter with two belligerent men early this morning while patrolling his post.

He came across the two men on Union street near Hamilton avenue. They were raising high jinks and the policeman told them that they were obstructing the sidewalk. He ordered them to move on, whereupon they turned upon him and one grabbed his nightstick away from him and the other held his arms. The man with the nightstick rained a shower of blows with both club and fists upon the officer, smashing his helmet and beating him about the body.

Young finally broke away and pulled out his pocket stick. Then it was his turn, and he certainly made good if the condition of one man's face is conclusive evidence.

Alone, he landed his men in the station house and there they gave their names as Vigo Hanson, of St. George, Staten Island, and Paul Abrahamson, of 139 Hamilton avenue. To-day Magistrate Tighe, in the Butler Street Court, held them in $100 bail each for further examination and complimented the officer on his pluck.

On his way home just before one o'clock on Tuesday morning, Mr. Young heard a cry for help coming from under Pier 35, Brooklyn. Right ahead of him as he reached the end of the pier, was the dim figure of a man fighting desperately with the tide. In an instant Mr. Young had plunged in, reached the man, and brought him to shore. The rescued man, William Garrity, a laborer, forty years old, was taken unconscious to Long Island College Hospital and there revived.

Mr. Young, who now lives at No. 58 Columbia Place, Brooklyn, saved, while a policeman, the life of a man who was drowning in the East River, receiving after his retirement, the Congressional Medal; while the Medal of the Volunteer Life Saving Corps was also awarded to him.

SAILOR'S HARD LUCK.

Made Chance Acquaintance and Was Robbed.

John Sandell, a sailor, struck up a chance acquaintance, about 3 o'clock this morning, with Andrew Anderson, 25 years old, of No. 26 Hicks street. The two were walking on Union street, between Hamilton avenue and Van Brunt street, when Sandell was suddenly struck on the head, choked and thrown down. His watch was taken from his pocket.

Policeman Daniel Young saw Anderson running away and followed him. As the policeman gained on the man, he threw the watch into the street. Anderson was placed under arrest and in the Butler Street Court this morning was held for examination.

Footnotes

1. Cialdini, Robert. "Secrets from the Science of Persuasion." Video, 11:50. Posted November 2012. https://www.youtube.com/watch?v=cFdCzN7RYbw&feat ure=youtu.be.

2. Daily Mail Reporter. "I don't! Quarter of Women Have Turned down a Marriage Proposal with Most Fearing Man Popping the Question Wasn't 'the One' or that it 'Didn't Feel Right.'" (Commissioned study by travel firm SuperBreak.) *Daily Mail*, February 9, 2015. https://www.dailymail.co.uk/news/article-2946638/I-don- t-Quarter-women-turned-marriage-proposal-fearing-man- popping-question-wasn-t-one-didn-t-feel-right.html.

3. Sohn, Amy. "You've Canceled the Wedding, Now the Aftermath." *New York Times*. May 19, 2016. https://www.nytimes.com/2016/05/22/fashion/weddings/canceled-weddings-what-to-do.html.

4. Bradsher, Keith. "Left at the Altar: Modern Tale of Woe." The New York Times, (month and day unknown) 1990.

https://www.nytimes.com/1990/03/07/garden/left-at-the- altar-modern-tale-of-woe.html.

5. Brown, Brené. "Empathy." RSA Shorts. Video, 2:53. Posted December 2013. https://www.youtube.com/watch?v=1Evwgu369Jw&feature=youtu.be.

6. Ottawa Police Service. "Sir Robert Peel's Principles of Law Enforcement 1829." Copyright 2018. https://www.ottawapolice.ca/en/about-us/Peel-s- Principles-.asp.

7. Ruff, Joshua, and Michael Cronin. *New York City Police*. The New York City Police Museum. With Foreword by Police Commissioner Raymond W. Kelly. New York: Arcadia Publishing, 2012.

Reflections From the Closet: Behind the Scenes

STARK PUBLISHING — PUBLISHER

What follows on the next few pages are behind-the-scenes notes from both Dave Sweet and Sarah Kades as they reveal in-depth and insightful personal reflections about various aspects of working on this project together.

DAVE SWEET

Sarah and I are happy to bring you the first book in my *Unconventional Classroom* series. It has been my vision to highlight positive, universal lessons my career in law enforcement has taught me, often through the lens of tragedy. Through our books and my presentations, we'll share that wisdom to a larger audience. Completing *Skeletons in My Closet* with Sarah was the first step along this journey. I think it is safe to say we are both pleased with how this book has come together and even evolved in the past five years.

We have framed the stories and lessons mindfully, and with the same sense of social responsibility that a career in policing demands. I believe Sir Robert Peel was right when he said,

> "Police are the public and the public are the police; the police being only members of the public who are paid to give full-time attention to duties which are incumbent on every citizen in the interests of community welfare and existence."
> (Sir Robert Peel's Principles of Law Enforcement, 1829)

We all have a responsibility to each other, including ourselves, to pay attention, to care, to avoid apathy or expect that someone else will notice something that needs noticing. It is important we do our part to keep our communities, and each other, strong, safe, vibrant and healthy. I wish we didn't have tragedy as our teacher. Sometimes we do, and when that happens we must quiet our minds enough to find the lessons in its message.

I hope we have written a book that our peers, our families and my Service, can be proud of. The opinions, views and philosophies reflected in this book are mine and may not represent those of the organization I work for. Every effort has been made to respect the privacy of citizens and the delicacy of the situations described in the book. Identifying descriptors, such as names, dates, and specific details, have in many cases been changed.

"Have you learned the lessons only of those who admired you, and were tender with you, and stood aside for you? Have you not learned great lessons from those who braced themselves against you, and disputed passage with you?"
 - Walt Whitman

SARAH KADES

Several years ago, Detective Dave Sweet approached me to write a book of universal lessons from a homicide investigator's perspective. It was not a typical angle, but Dave's like that. *Skeletons in My Closet* is an unconventional police memoir that takes readers on a ride-along to the darkest corners of society, but also reveals poignant truths about life, death, and how we can all coexist together.

We hope it is as gripping a read as it is inspiring, and that you found the danger and grit tempered with compassion and humor. That was our aim, anyway. Dave is a pretty good mix of sharp corners, raw honesty, and empathy.

We are about to take you behind the scenes. What's it like working with a homicide detective? I'll tell you. What's this particular one really like? Read on. How did we roll with each other's very different writing processes? Good question.

Dave could tell you what he's like to work with, but he'd probably omit stuff like his complete disregard for punctuation. It was beyond frustrating until I realized it was the perfect chance to practice my Zen mind- reading skills. And that, dear reader, is just one example of putting these lessons into practice, in this case, reframing and perspective. There is so much more.

It doesn't have to be difficult finding common ground with someone holding a different world view or point of reference. Dave and I had our own challenges and successes working together. We butted heads and both feel the book is stronger for it.

Skeletons in My Closet is Dave's distilled wisdom from a distinguished career in a large western Canadian police service, a career that has taken him from the Drug Unit to the Organized Crime Section to Homicide. Now he's sharing his hard-earned life lessons with those on the other side of the crime scene tape. He shares the traumas, triumphs and tragedies of his twenty-year career in law enforcement, from going undercover to infiltrate drug rings, to piecing together criminal hierarchies, to investigating gruesome murder scenes. He also reveals the human side of policing: meeting people on the worst day of their lives, helping them pick up the pieces, bringing resolution to victims and their families, and the toll all of it takes on an officer. *Skeletons in My Closet* is a frank look at how one homicide detective faces the unimaginable every day.

OUR EVOLUTION TO SUCCESS

DAVE SWEET

The book's evolution surprised me. It was never a question of *if* we would finish it. Both Sarah and I were committed to the project from the get-go. How we would take decades of memories and experiences in my head and translate them in a meaningful and engaging way was another matter entirely. We started building with those first ideas. As the book came into focus, we developed and included additional themes and content. The relationships of the experiences and lessons were not linear, and we wanted the reader to have effective take-aways. We grouped the lessons into ten themes, each a chapter. The first nine build on concepts that culminate in the tenth chapter, *Selling Life Sentences*.

Our writing process also evolved. In the beginning, Sarah and I decided to work to our strengths and previous experience. I give approximately thirty presentations each year and am comfortable communicating information in that format. For years, Sarah interviewed Elders for Traditional Knowledge studies. It made sense to start our project in our respective wheelhouses. I'd give a presentation and Sarah would write the chapter from the presentation.

We quickly realized that didn't work for us for a few reasons. I wanted to be more hands-on in the actual writing. It's hard to co-author a book without actually writing. We also realized that when Sarah wrote from a presentation instead of an interview, the context was different and my voice that works so well in a presentation format didn't translate the same for the book. Without the dialogue of an interview, too many of the nuances that we wanted were being lost.

We switched it up. I wrote raw content, Sarah crafted and made me make sense and not sound like an asshole. That might seem harsh, but I know this job has adjusted my normal. I don't know how many times I told Sarah it is impossible to offend me anymore. I've simply seen too much.

It was a balancing act to find time to complete the

project, my work schedule can get hectic. I had my expectations and Sarah had hers. We e the world incredibly differently, and that's before any dead bodies or crime scenes come into play. There were moments of frustration. Don't ask me about water sound therapy or Sarah about scotch.

I am grateful for her help; her hand was required to temper the realities of writing real life. Through this process I have found myself cathartically reflecting on my career and have come to realize that *damn, I have learned a lot*. When we are in the thick of our lives we don't often step back to get that perspective, to take that inventory of where we are, where we've been, and which direction we're heading. Writing the book gave me that opportunity. The more I wrote, the more I remembered. It wasn't a floodgate opening, but a few vaults long- closed were pried open during this process.

As our original outline continued to expand, there was minimal chapter shuffling. Rather, it was more the question of where to weave in the additional content within the chapter framework. We went back and forth, discussing where the stories made the most sense. Sometimes a single memory held numerous lessons. Where would the best impact for the reader be?

I felt bad, but just a little, when I remembered more to include. We thought we had a section done and then, wouldn't you know it, more memories or lessons came up. There was a story and lesson so new and raw it had yet to be added to the *Skeletons in My Closet* manuscript.

That's what it was like when new stories came in. Sarah, being Sarah, always said that was part of the process, but a few times I wondered when we would just have to cut ourselves off so we could finish.

LEAVE PEOPLE BETTER THAN YOU FOUND THEM

SARAH KADES

Some of my favorite early feedback on the project has been how unorthodox our approach was. As you can imagine, this project has had some heavy material and I needed to find ways to process. At one point prior to working on this book together I mentioned to Dave I was researching Buddhism to help with my sense of peace and overall tranquility. The look he gave me was priceless, in his world I am the poster child of relaxed. In mine, I knew I needed to re-discover my center. Perspective is a fascinating beast.

Lessons from a homicide detective is a unique approach, as is Dave calling himself out, sharing stories of when he was wrong or realizing he had not made the best decisions. Not everyone would open up like that.

PERSPECTIVE IS AN ANTIDOTE TO WORRY

DAVE SWEET

While writing *Skeletons in my Closet*, I realized just how much of a lifestyle policing has been. It has given me the opportunity to work with great people, and to meet inspiring families and victims. It has also given me opportunities for my own personal growth and the ability to change my thinking, to alter perspectives and face challenging circumstances with a *glass half-full* approach.

LISTENING TO THE SILENCES

SARAH KADES

Throughout this project, I have listened to what Dave hasn't said as much as what he has. When we all listen to each other, when we notice the voice of the pauses, as much as we do the words, we hear that much more. As Dave recounted his time with an undercover street team, I couldn't help but wonder about those moments of pause, as he replayed past experiences in his head, making sense of memories before sharing. We all have stories, and Dave racked up quite a few during his three-year tenure with the Drug Unit. He gained unique perspectives, one of which was just how different the public's perception and attitudes toward various people within a community can be. It was a lesson he learned first-hand.

JUST BECAUSE YOU CAN DOESN'T MEAN YOU SHOULD

DAVE SWEET

This project has provided the opportunity to articulate concepts I lived with but didn't consciously focus on. One of my guiding principles was, *how would I want to be handled in any given situation if roles were reversed?*

B.B.D.S (BIG BOY DEBRIEFS)

SARAH KADES

Much of the tension we experience in life can be traced back to a breakdown in communication. Our relationships are strained every time we muzzle our own voice or don't listen when someone really needs us to hear. Miscommunication further muddies the waters when we think we understand what's going on, but actually don't. Sometimes we can find this out in painfully humbling ways.

Bottom line, effective communication is one of those key building blocks of solid, healthy relationships. This includes more than just individuals; families, workplaces, and communities can all benefit from honest, respectful dialogue. When our ears are open, we're also better able to articulate our thoughts, points and ideas. As fabulous a tool as tension is in a novel (says the writer), in real life it blows. We can make a positive difference in our relationships when we say what we mean and listen like we actually care.

SARAH KADES

Our project has unwittingly given plenty of opportunity for our own misunderstandings. I once texted Dave regarding edits and word choices with no idea that what I had perceived as a simple two-sentence reply he took as implied grump. I got an immediate call for clarity. We could laugh about it then and I'm still l a u g h i n g   n o w because I know h o w sideways life can get when misunderstandings occur.

Another time, we were in a cafe working, Dave was sitting across from me, and I was having a rare moment of nearly losing my shit, albeit silently. I tend to be pretty chill, and I can't even remember what I was frustrated about, but I remember internally I was red-lining. (Fear not, dear reader, I know I've inspired the same in Dave.) He responded by reading aloud to me the *Support Systems* section from the chapter **White Picket Fences**, reminding me that these support systems are our parachute and a sanity-check.

WRITING REAL LIFE

DAVE SWEET

From the beginning Sarah embraced an important concept. *When you're collaborating with someone writing a memoir, you need to let him tell his story.* She crafted and wove the stories in the book with a deft and conscientious hand. She understood what I was trying to accomplish, and that understanding informed her writing. In my view, this was critical.

Throughout this project, Sarah received an indoctrination of sorts into some very shadowy places, she would have to, if she were to tell my story. That increased when, after receiving feedback suggesting more grit, we began to layer in more edge where originally we had chosen not to. This had a Pandora's box effect for both of us. Sarah had to burrow deeper into writing about homicide and pain, and I had to venture further into my memory to flush out some of the visceral details. I did my best to explain what I had witnessed through my five senses.

DAVE SWEET

Sarah was not used to processing that level of dark emotion in the same way I was not used to working with someone who would ask, "Yes, but how did that make you feel?" In the end, Sarah allowed me to write my story, and shared the same vision. We made it through this process smiling, still speaking to each other, and with no knives in the back. I truly can't thank her enough.

WORKING WITH A HOMICIDE DETECTIVE

SARAH KADES

Before this book, I knew Dave in a peripheral sort of way. He was that homicide detective who gave presentations to writing groups, pleasant enough, with a sense of humor, and surprisingly patient. Dave's schedule is no less crammed than everyone else's, arguably more so with the time sensitivity of murder investigations, yet he always answered writer questions long after the allotted presentation time was up. He also used his own brand of humor to offset the topic's heaviness. For years he was just that guy who graciously answered law enforcement questions from writers wanting to more accurately depict characters or hammer out plot points.

The past couple of years that random peripheral shifted into first person narrative. He's still pleasant enough if there is an energy drink at hand. His sense of humor is dark but entertaining the few times I've seen it off-leash. His patience extended to my bottle-necked edits and I knew to bring in humor when needed, as there are indeed heavy parts to the book. I had to adapt to working with someone in the I-work-with-death club. My brain tripped on his texts.

Me: Want me to take a crack at that next chapter lead-in?
Dave: Would you? I'm on a fresh one and going to autopsy this afternoon.
Me: *(long pause while I shift brain gears)* No prob. Stay safe.

A simple "yes" would have sufficed. Still, it helped me get into Dave's head so I could better craft the book. When he went radio-silent I plugged more into his world and knew a case had come in. Dave's resting state is intense. He was tenacious to the point of pestering when we worked on this project. I say that with a bit of awe. He hammered out raw content and then did his best to give me space while I crafted it. I got used to the constant background hum of Dave's energy, except when a case came in. Then he went silent, the hum gone.

After a few days I actually checked in to make sure he was okay. He was fine. He just had that intensity focused on the new case. It was unsettling when I stopped to think about how different each of our days was. When I was finessing a particularly tricky paragraph, Dave could be exercising a warrant, attending an autopsy or in court on the witness stand. I remember once when I was making a French press of coffee he was on a stake-out. Different worlds.

I've been asked, "What is Dave really like?" When I was trying to figure out our myriad differences, I realized that he's a child of the 80s, whereas I'm a product of the 90s. What difference does that make? Let's turn to music to explain. The sound track to his impressionable years included Bon Jovi, Duran Duran, The Cult and Metallica. Mine was the likes of Ani Difranco, Indigo Girls, Sarah McLachlan, and Melissa Etheridge. Okay, I totally listened to Bon Jovi, too. Who didn't?

He's all-inclusive resort, I'm road trip camping.
He's action movies, I'm books.
He's fancy suits, I'm yoga pants.
He's Birkenstocks . . . wait, so am I.

Okay, that last one is an anomaly, but you get my point. All joking aside, I didn't know what it would be like working with a homicide investigator. Turns out, pretty interesting—and distressing too. Dave has had such a distinguished career because people hurt each other. That reality snags, repeatedly. However, everyday people throughout our communities make a positive difference, from a smile or a stranger's kind word to something more dramatic. Working with a police officer has reminded me there is overwhelming darkness but also incredible light in this world.

LIVING THE LESSONS

SARAH KADES

There is an alchemy to translating real-life experience to real words on a page. Perhaps the greatest transformation, though, was within ourselves. I know I am different. I had open exposure to others' scars. That brought a context I had never been privy to before, but also healing lessons.

I had the chance to test those lessons on a cold Friday after a long snowy winter. I drove through an alley with a maze of compacted snow, built-up ice, and pools of frozen slush. The nearly impassable route had prompted me to detour my access that particular day. Besides being the lesser of two evils for navigating, that detour kept me from crossing gunfire.

It was around noon, and I was driving slowly, nearly at my destination. I heard weird popping noises, like firecrackers, but different. Could that be ice? I rolled to a stop. The noises stopped, too. I remember thinking the ice must be in a crazy condition to mimic firecrackers when you drive over them. How quaint the first things I thought of were innocuous. Writing a nonfiction book with a homicide investigator hasn't completely scrubbed my naiveté and it never crossed my mind that it could be gunfire, or that a police officer had been shot.

Earlier, my husband had called to tell me about an attempted carjacking in the area, but as I neared, I saw a police truck driving away. I figured if they were leaving, all must be okay. I now see how over-simplified that assumption was.

Once there, I attempted to continue my day, but heard sirens and saw a line of police vehicles streaming into a back street. Then I noticed I had missed four calls and a frantic text from my husband. Police were alerting people to hide in basements, lest a stray bullet fly too close.

It hadn't been firecrackers or ice I'd heard. A police officer had been gunned down. That messed with my head, knowing I had heard the gunshots that went into a person's body.

For nearly two hours I stayed huddled in that basement, listening to what sounded suspiciously like occasional gunfire. I had my phone, I could text and call my husband, assuring him I was okay. Dave was busy doing police things but checked in to make sure I was hunkered down. A writer friend reached out too and kept me company when I needed to give voice to what I was hearing without alarming my already-worried husband. I felt reasonably safe underground. I just had to stay put, however long that would be.

New sounds, like someone outside the door, did a painfully exquisite job of terrifying me. Stories from the book flooded my mind. How different it is to live through, versus simply write about, fear. Before that moment, I was theoretically scared. I knew there was danger but I knew how to mitigate my access to it. That moment I knew fear.

I looked around the basement trying to form a plan. Where was the best place to hide that still had escape options? What could I use as a weapon if necessary? I don't know how much time lapsed before I realized whoever was outside had gone, but I remember realizing my terror had eased. From what I've heard since, it was likely emergency services. At that time, the bad guy was holed up in a garage burning to the ground.

For several days, I processed the event in different stages: looking for gunmen everywhere, nausea, restless pacing, shaking hands, way too much adrenaline, lack of appetite, no sleep, too much sleep, bursting into tears in front of random police officers, and an epic migraine. I didn't want to be dramatic or useless. Part of me wanted to shake it off, but a louder part of me knew it wiser to process so I could let it go. Suppressing lingering emotions would surely backfire.

My body's physical symptoms confused me. I had not been hurt, but was responding to the stimuli. That threw me. I even asked Dave if I was overreacting. Now I see how silly that question was. Fear is a normal response to what happened that day. It also gave a healthy dose of perspective and was a potent reset button to slow down—I had been letting things beyond my control bother me way too much.

INVESTIGATOR'S COMMENTS

DAVE SWEET

In police work, Investigator's Comments often accompany written affidavits. They give added context or information to provide clarity, and highlight certain concepts and linkages in our applications to the court.

Early on in our process it dawned on me that we could include a parallel to an investigator comment in our book. I thought Sarah could provide her own commentary on how the lessons and stories resonated with her. I asked her if she would write her version of an Investigator's Comments, a *Sarah's Comments* for additional perspective.

She wrote several, and although we liked what they contributed, we thought they interrupted the flow of the narrative and ultimately decided not to include them in the final main text of the manuscript. I want to include some of them here, as they really highlight what I hope readers experience, their take-aways and reflections on the lessons.

Comments from Chapter 1, A Life of Service

SARAH KADES

Sarah's Comments: I can't help but reflect on the word sacrifice. In the past, it has always implied a one-way street, but now feels like more. Sacrifice is not synonymous with martyrdom, rather it is plugging into a greater good and working to achieve a higher collective positive. There is a trade-off. In my experience it is the currency of time and attention more than anything else, but it is for something that matters. There is a reciprocity in sacrifice. When we make sacrifices for something that matters deeply to us, even at a cost, the sacrifice is allowing us to be true to ourselves.

Comments From Chapter 2, Owning Your Path

SARAH KADES

Sarah's Comments: We get out of life what we put

into it. Work, relationships, heck even dinner, all have the same equation. The quality of our experience is directly proportional to our effort and energy. Want epic experiences? Put in epic effort. Sometimes it is our attitude that is the effort made. I let my previous career slip away because it stopped satisfying me. It couldn't and wouldn't again because I had changed. I was channeling my attention and energy elsewhere. We thrive under care and attention and our life is a reflection of where we are directing our energy.

COMMENTS FROM CHAPTER 4, WHITE PICKET FENCES

SARAH KADES

Sarah's Comments: As I was writing, I was thinking about lessons. This project has a way of doing that. It feels like there are always opportunities to learn, improve, realize or understand something. Then I wondered, when does learning stop and a lesson actually sink in? I think when we let a lesson sink deep enough within that it becomes part of our wisdom, we have learned it. Maybe that's the link between lesson and wisdom. If we're just repeating lessons, it's like simply practicing math equations with no real-world applications. When we utilize what we have learned, it goes from theoretical to relative applicability. Each of us decides which lessons we choose to learn, and which we allow to sink deep enough to become part of our own wisdom.

COMMENTS FROM CHAPTER 5, THINKING FROM A DIFFERENT BOX

Sarah's Comments: When we were working on this chapter I couldn't help thinking about the inherent burden of particular jobs. Back in Chapter One, we discussed the reciprocity of sacrifice as doing what matters, even when the cost is high. I wondered if those who shoulder these burdens realize they carry what would be difficult, or impossible for others, and if this was another component of a life of service.

Dave didn't bite when I asked him about it, but a personal experience makes me at least consider the possibility. A couple of years ago I was walking my dog off-leash in a well-used urban green space when he stopped and refused to go further. This was highly uncharacteristic and no amount of coaxing got him moving, except in retreat. I cut the walk short, curious and a bit concerned about his odd behavior. The next day, neighbors said that, where I was headed, a body had been reported found by a former military man. I was grateful for this stranger who was better equipped to handle finding a dead body, and for my dog who refused to allow me to walk into an unfamiliar situation. Even if those in emergency service fields don't consider that part of the role, I do. Thank you.

Author Dave Sweet

Dave Sweet is a retired veteran homicide detective who has investigated some of Canada's most gruesome and tragic cases.

Over his 25-year career, Dave worked as a patrol officer, an undercover police officer and led several task forces targeting gangs and organized crime groups. In 2009, Dave joined the ranks of the homicide unit where he spent over 14 years specializing in homicide, missing person, and suspicious death investigations.

Dave earned the Chief's Award for Investigative Excellence in 2017, the Governor General's Exemplary Service Medal in 2021 and the Queens Platinum Jubilee Medal in 2022.

Dave lives by the mantra "love people" and his inner strength and mindfulness is rooted from that perspective.

You can connect with Dave at:
http://unconventionalclassroom.ca

Author Sarah Kades

Sarah Kades writes narrative non-fiction and eco-thrillers. Her writing is largely inspired by her previous careers as an archaeologist and Indigenous Knowledge engagement lead, where she routinely lived in tents, caught rides in helicopters and gaped at the incredible landscapes around her.

Sarah is a two-time Energy Futures Lab Banff Summit storyteller, Canada Council for the Arts grant recipient, and has presented at the British Society of Criminology conference on the application of using arts-based approaches. When she's not writing you can find her teaching Remotely Piloted Aircraft Systems at a Western Canadian polytechnic, bumping into her next adventure, or trying to figure out where in the garden to put the makeshift wood fired pizza oven.

You can connect with Sarah at:
http://unconventionalclassroom.ca

The Unconventional Classroom

Skeletons in my Closet is the first of a series of books co-authored by Dave Sweet and based upon his decades of experience in law enforcement and his resulting reflections, learnings and philosophies.

Look for the other titles in *The Unconventional Classroom* series starting in 2024.

- **Skeletons in my Closet** — 101 Life Lessons From a Homicide Detective (with Sarah Kades)

FORTHCOMING

- **Undaunted** — An Exploration of Courage and the Virtues of Uncommon People (with Susan Forest)

- **Whispers** — What Happens When We Die (with Mark Leslie)